D0936511

THE STATUS OF
BIRDS IN BRITAIN
AND IRELAND

THE STATUS OF
BIRDS IN BRITAIN
AND IRELAND

Prepared by the
Records Committee of the
British Ornithologists' Union . Records Committee

and edited by
D. W. Snow

Blackwell Scientific Publications
Oxford, London and Edinburgh

ISBN 0 632 08140 6

First published 1971

Distributed in the U.S.A. by
F. A. Davis Company, 1915 Arch Street, Philadelphia, Pennsylvania

Printed in Great Britain by Western Printing Services Ltd, Bristol
and bound by Webb & Co Ltd, Glamorgan and London

CONTENTS

CONTENTS

FOREWORD

The need for a new check-list of British and Irish birds has long been apparent. It is appropriate that this should again be produced by the British Ornithologists' Union, as the senior authority. While no list of this nature can ever be completely up to date, it should present the latest reliable information and a consensus of opinion on matters of judgment by leading experts of the day. For this reason the Council of the Union encouraged those entrusted with the task to consult widely, and it will be apparent from the Introduction how many people have been involved, at one stage or another, in the preparation of the finished work. The part played by J. L. F. Parslow in the compilation of the main text deserves special mention. It is an indication of the complexity and thoroughness of the work of the Union's Records Committee, who were primarily responsible, that the analysis of the raw material and the preparation of the new list has taken more than eight years.

A work involving so many matters of opinion cannot hope to achieve universal approval in all its aspects. Arguments for and against the acceptance of 'assisted passage', or of the 'Hastings rarities', will continue for many years. So also will opinions differ concerning the thorny problems of taxonomy and sequence. To await international agreement on these last two subjects would have postponed publication of the new list indefinitely. Certain compromises have therefore been adopted which, while they may attract criticism in some quarters, will appeal to the majority as realistic in the absence of universally accepted decisions. In this respect, taxonomy and the order in which species are classified are largely man-made conveniences, the importance of which can easily be over-estimated.

To most ornithologists the chief value of the new list will be its accurate descriptions of the present status and distribution of species, and their categorisation by means of simple codes for easy reference. These categories should be regarded not as static but as dynamic.

Amendments will be issued by the Records Committee in the light of new information which is constantly accumulating. In this manner it is hoped to avoid the long hiatus which followed publication of the last check-list, in 1952.

The Council records its gratitude to the members of the Records Committee, especially J. L. F. Parslow, and to all those who contributed to this important publication.

Guy Mountfort
President

INTRODUCTION

In October 1962 the Council of the British Ornithologists' Union decided to put in hand the preparation of a new check-list. The last one had been published in 1952, and was already badly out of date. A number of new species had been added to the British and Irish lists, and a steady flow of additional immigrants was virtually assured by the Union's acceptance in 1956 of the principle that birds were entitled to the benefits of assisted passage when on transatlantic flights (see *Ibis* 98: 156–7). Furthermore, in August 1962 a recommendation had been made to delete from the British and Irish list six species and a dozen subspecies, as a result of critical examination of the circumstances surrounding the recording of the so-called 'Hastings rarities', and the status of a larger number of scarce species was also affected.

The council decided that a special List Committee should not be formed, but that the task should be laid on the shoulders of an existing committee, the Union's Records Committee.

In the past the production of a new check-list has provided the opportunity to bring the taxonomy and nomenclature of our birds up to date; indeed, these features have on occasion formed one of the main contributions and purposes of the list. A conspicuous feature, however, of the Records Committee has been the lack of specialists in taxonomy among its members, owing to the fact that it was formed simultaneously with the Taxonomic Committee. The Records Committee accordingly felt able to undertake the compilation of the new list only if the problems of sequence, taxonomy and nomenclature were resolved by adopting the published work of one or more recognised authorities, to be decided on by the Council and thereafter followed in such a manner that the Records Committee should not be called on to assess the merits of subsequent differing taxonomic proposals.

This position was accepted by Council. It was decided to follow the nomenclature used by Vaurie, in his two-volume work *The Birds of the Palearctic Fauna*. At that time (1963) the second volume, dealing with the non-passerines, had not appeared, but Dr Vaurie most generously supplied the Committee with a typescript of the essential parts and offered his services in any other way that might be required. The problem of deciding what sequence to adopt was much more difficult to resolve. Discussions went on in and out of Council, decisions were made and reversed. It was a matter on which many conflicting opinions were held with equal tenacity; and not from mere stubbornness, for there are, as all who have been concerned with sequences will realise, great difficulties in reconciling the claims of conservatism with the need to progress, and there are different interpretations of what constitutes progress. Furthermore, there is the need to look to the future and adopt a sequence that will not hinder international agreement at a later stage. It would be tedious to recount the various stages of the controversy, the final outcome of which was the decision to adopt the sequence used in Peters' *Check-list of Birds of the World*, except in a few cases where more recent work has shown very strong grounds for modifying it. At the same time, it was agreed that minor modifications might be made to Vaurie's nomenclature in the light of subsequent published work.

To recommend such modifications to the sequence and nomenclature, a small *ad hoc* sub-committee, consisting of D.W.Snow, C.J.O. Harrison and D.Lack, was set up in March 1970, when the main text of the check-list was nearing completion. A small number of recommendations were made, which are listed in Appendix 1.

There is a major difficulty in using orthodox trinomial nomenclature in a work such as this, which deals with a region where much of the geographical variation in bird populations is clinal. It is often misleading to state the ranges of subspecies as though they had well-defined boundaries, while an adequate description of the clines, as they are understood, would run to far too great a length. It may be that in the next edition of this work some radically different method of indicating geographical variation will be adopted. For lack of a new method the conventional treatment has been followed here and mention is made, under the species concerned, of major cases of clinal variation. The reader should be aware of the fact that the boundaries between subspecies, as given here, should not be interpreted too rigidly, and that many of them are necessarily arbitrary. Neverthelesss, the conventional treatment provides the only convenient way that is available of labelling the different populations of many of the migratory species which visit or pass through this country.

It was felt that the check-list should try to provide much fuller information on the status and particularly on the distribution of British and Irish birds than had been included in its predecessors, and at the same time that it should show our avifauna against the backcloth of the world distribution of the genera concerned. The original format on which the new list is now based was devised and drawn up by I.J.Ferguson-Lees. It was soon realized, however, that the requisite information was unobtainable from existing literature or collected records, as far as our breeding birds and regular passage migrants and winter visitors were concerned. Accordingly a special enquiry was launched in the autumn of 1964. It received whole-hearted support from local ornithological bodies throughout England and Wales, while the surveys in Scotland and Ireland were organised by D.G. Andrew and Major R.F.Ruttledge respectively. In this way information was obtained for every county, and the major islands, in Great Britain and Ireland. In view of the much wider scope of the work, it was subsequently decided to drop the time-honoured but perhaps somewhat meaningless word 'check-list' from the title, in favour of something that better indicated the subject matter.

In an effort to hasten completion of the work, Council now decided to retain for some months the services of J.L.F.Parslow, who was co-opted to the Records Committee in 1967. Before Mr. Parslow joined the Committee, he had spent a year, under a grant from the Nature Conservancy, studying changes in the status of British and Irish breeding birds, during which time he had analysed the results of the distribution survey already referred to. The raw material of this survey, which was published in a series of papers in *British Birds* in 1967 and 1968, is now deposited at the Edward Grey Institute of Field Ornithology at Oxford, where the Committee hopes that it will be of use to anyone with a serious interest in it.

The other members of the Records Committee are deeply appreciative of Mr Parslow's unsparing efforts and notable achievements, both when working full-time on the list and in his spare time during many subsequent months. The major part of the credit for this book must go to him. Indeed he compiled almost the whole of the text apart from about 80 species (in the families Pandionidae, Accipitridae, Falconidae, Tetraonidae, Phasianidae, Gruidae, Rallidae, Otididae and Turdidae) which were written by I.J.Ferguson-Lees. Earlier, brief summaries (many of which had to be re-written to achieve uniformity) mainly of foreign distributions of each species, based on Dr. Vaurie's work, had been prepared by the following people, each of whom covered about 40–50 species: H.G.Alexander, J.S.Ash, W.R.P.Bourne, the late R.K. Cornwallis, D.T.Lees-Smith and the Wildfowl Trust per H.Boyd and M.A.Ogilvie. When undertaking participation in this task, W.R.P. Bourne accepted an invitation to join the Committee as a co-opted member for the period of preparation of the list. The help given by D.T.Lees-Smith and the Wildfowl Trust is gratefully acknowledged. In addition, J.L.F.Parslow wishes to express his gratitude to Robert Hudson for his critical appraisal of an earlier draft and particularly for additional information relating to ringing recoveries, and to Dr David Lack for accommodation and library facilities at the Edward Grey Institute, Oxford.

Some members of the Union's Records Committee have long been worried by the impracticability of maintaining a single 'British and Irish list', which separates the sheep from the goats on evidence that is not always adequate, and on which all the admitted species have the same formal status. As a result of the deliberations of a newly consti-tuted Records Committee in 1970 (when the text of this work was already virtually complete and the Committee which compiled it had been disbanded), it was recommended to Council that a system of categories should be adopted and should be used in the present work, and this recommendation was accepted by Council. The following four categories are recognised:

A. Species which have been recorded in an apparently wild state in Britain or Ireland at least once within the last 50 years. (Transatlantic visitors, for which the possibility of assisted passage cannot be ruled out, are included in this category.)

B. Species which have been recorded in an apparently wild state in Britain or Ireland at least once, but not within the last 50 years.

C. Species which, although originally introduced by man, have now established a regular feral breeding stock which apparently maintains itself without necessary recourse to further introduction.

D. Species which have been recorded within the last 50 years and would otherwise appear in category A except that (1) there is a reason-able doubt that they have ever occurred in a wild state, or (2) they have certainly arrived with ship-assistance, or (3) they have only ever been found dead on the tide-line; also species which would otherwise appear in category C, except that their feral breeding populations may or may not be self-supporting.

It is envisaged that this tiered system of categories should be dynamic and not static; a species may move to either a higher or a lower category as a result of further knowledge, new records, or the passage of time. Species in category D should, moreover, not have the same formal status as species in categories A–C, and in particular should not form part of the main text of any published list. They are accordingly listed here in Appendix 3.

In these islands, where new records accumulate at bewildering speed from an army of ornithologists, it is impossible to publish a text that is completely up to date. It has been necessary to draw a line at 31 December 1968 and include in the main text only the records obtained up to that date. For most species this matters very little, as two more years' records do not alter the general pattern. But there have been some records since the end of 1968 which significantly alter the status of a few species, for instance the successful breeding of the Golden Eagle in England in 1970, for the first time since the 18th century. These additional records are listed in Appendix 2, which has been compiled by I.J.Ferguson-Lees and J.T.R.Sharrock.

THE TREATMENT ADOPTED

In the systematic list as now presented, the following points and conventions have been observed. For convenience, the points discussed in the preceding paragraphs are included.

Nomenclature. Vauries' *Birds of the Palearctic Fauna* is followed for all Palaearctic species, except as mentioned in Appendix 1. For American species, the nomenclature follows that of the 1957 *A.O.U. Check-list.* The findings of the International Commission for Zoological Nomenclature have been followed, and errors in original orthography corrected.

Sequence. As in Peters' *Check-list of Birds of the World*, with modifications listed in Appendix 1. The sequence for the warblers, the only Palaearctic family not dealt with in Peters, follows Vaurie.

Accepted species. Those listed in the 1952 check-list, as modified by subsequent reports of the British Records Committee:

First Report *Ibis* 98 (1956): 154–7
Second Report *Ibis* 100 (1958): 299–300
Third Report *Ibis* 102 (1960): 629–30
Fourth Report *Ibis* 105 (1963): 289–91
Fifth Report *Ibis* 113 (1971): 142–5
Sixth Report *Ibis* 113 (1971): 420–3.

The 'Hastings rarities' recommended for rejection by E.M.Nicholson and I.J.Ferguson-Lees (*Brit. Birds* 55 (1962): 299–384) have been omitted from this book. Similarly, in the case of vagrant petrels, the recommendations of W.R.P.Bourne (*Ibis* 109 (1967): 141–67) have been followed.

Categorisation. Each species has been assigned to one of the four categories A–D, as explained above. The majority are in category A, but in the cases of those which are not, the appropriate letter is placed at the right-hand margin level with the species name. Species placed in category D are not included in the main list, but are listed separately in Appendix 3.

Status and distribution. This has been taken in the main (a) for birds of regular occurrence, from the Committee's distribution survey of 1964–5; (b) for rare visitors to Great Britain (i) during 1958–68, from the reports of the *British Birds* Rarities Committee, and (ii) before 1958 from the literature generally; (c) for scarce visitors to Ireland, from *Ireland's Birds* (1966) and the *Irish Bird Reports*.

General lay-out for each species. After the name, the information is presented in the following order:
(a) World distribution
(b) Distribution of subspecies relevant to Britain and Ireland (or 'Monotypic', if no subspecies have been described)
(c) Status and distribution in Britain and Ireland, each paragraph being preceded by one or more of the following abbreviations:

RB	Resident breeder	FB	Former breeder
MB	Migrant breeder	WV	Winter visitor
IB	Introduced breeder	PV	Passage visitor
CB	Casual breeder	SV	Scarce visitor

RB and MB are frequently used in combination—for 'resident' breeding species in which a substantial part of the population leaves Britain and Ireland in the winter. For those species, e.g. House Sparrow, in which it is known or suspected that only a small or minute proportion of the population winters overseas, only RB is used. Similarly, in the case of migrant breeders where individuals occasionally remain here in winter (e.g. Yellow Wagtail, Turtle Dove) only MB is used. Winter visitors (WV) and passage visitors (PV) are frequently combined into a single paragraph to save repetition; 'PV' implies the occurrence in Britain and Ireland of transient populations of birds which breed and winter overseas, while 'WV' relates to those populations which 'winter' (in the case of some species, e.g. Turnstone, 'wintering' may relate to year-round, but non-breeding occurrence).

Indications of the relative abundance of each species have not been given except in the case of breeding birds. For each of these, immediately following RB, MB etc., one of the following terms is used, each of which refers to an estimate of the probable number of breeding pairs in Britain and Ireland (see Parslow, *British Birds* 60 (1967): 2–6):

extremely rare 1–10	not scarce 1000–10,000
very scarce 11–100	fairly numerous 10,000–100,000
scarce 101–1000	numerous 100,000–1 million
	abundant over 1 million

To simplify the summaries of British and Irish distribution, the Outer Hebrides and Inner Hebrides are treated as if they were counties, Rutland is combined with Leicestershire, London is included in Middlesex, and Monmouth is covered by England rather than Wales.

MEMBERSHIP OF THE RECORDS COMMITTEE

The membership of the Records Committee during the period of preparation of this list was as follows: H.G.Alexander (Chairman), D.G.Andrew, J.S.Ash, W.R.P.Bourne, the late R.K.Cornwallis, J.H.Elgood, I.J.Ferguson-Lees, P.A.D.Hollom (Secretary) and J.L.F. Parslow.

The present committee (as at the end of 1970), who alone were responsible for the initiation of the 'A–D' system of categorisation, consists of: I.J.Ferguson-Lees (Chairman), I.C.T.Nisbet, R.F.Ruttledge, J.T.R.Sharrock (Secretary), F.R.Smith and K.Williamson.

ACKNOWLEDGEMENTS

In addition to the persons already mentioned, the Committee expresses its grateful appreciation to all of the following, who went to much trouble to provide the detailed information requested by the Distribution Survey, and thus made possible what many will think the most valuable section of this work:

D.G.Andrew
R.H.Appleby
Brother P.Aspin
K.Atkin

R.H.Baillie
A.C.Baird
L.Baker
E.Balfour
D.K.Ballance
J.Ballentyne
A.Baptie
Mrs R.G.Barnes
F.Barrington
J.E.Beckerlegge
D.G.Bell
T.Hedley Bell
W.K.Bigger
O.Blyth
T.Boyd
W.Brotherston
W.F.A.Buck
H.O.Bunce
P.J.Chadwick

S.J.Clarke
E.Cohen
W.M.Condry
J.Cudworth
W.A.J.Cunningham

H.H.Davis
R.H.Dennis
G. des Forges
G.Dick
H.Dickinson
A.Dobbs
J.Donaldson
J.W.Donovan
Sir Arthur B.Duncan
Dr G.M.Dunnet

G.M.S.Easy
Dr W.J.Eggeling
T.Ennis

E.C.Fellowes
J.Field
Miss W.U.Flower

P.R.Foulkes-Roberts

Dr J.A.Gibson
M.Goodman
A.G.Gordon
F.C.Gribble
D.Griffin
J.Griffiths

D.D.Harber
J.M.Harrop
N.Harwood
Mrs A.Heathcote
R.Hewson
R.A.O.Hickling
G.Holohan
P.Hope Jones
P.N.Humphreys
E.N.Hunter

Dr D.Jenkins
W.E.Jones
K.A.Kennedy
F.King

Sir John Langham
Rev. J.Lees
Miss R.F.Levy
J.Lord

J.MacGeoch
J.A.McGeoch
K.S.MacGregor
I.Maclean
D.W.Makepeace
J.R.Mather
W.Matheson
W.S.Medlicott
Prof M.F.M.Meiklejohn

O.J.Merne
T.D.H.Merrie
D.H.Mills
Rev. G.W.H.Moule
Dr R.K.Murton

J.P.Newell

J.E.O'Donovan
W.J.O'Flynn
B.O'Regen
C.Oakes

C.E.Palmar
Miss E.M.Palmer
P.J.Panting
J.L.F.Parslow
W.H.Payn
Dr I.D.Pennie
G.A.Pyman

Dr M.C.Radford
G.A.Richards
Dr R.Richter
E.L.Roberts
P.J.Roche
Major R.F.Ruttledge

B.L.Sage
Col H.Morrey Salmon
P.W.Sandeman
Lt Col C.F.Scroope
M.J.Seago
J.R.Sheppard
A.J.Smith
F.R.Smith
R.T.Smith
R.W.J.Smith
K.G.Spencer

J.Stafford

D.M.Stark

P.J.Stead

G.Stephenson

R.Stokoe

K.E.Stott

Lord David Stuart

C.M.Swaine

C.F.Tebbutt

Miss V.M.Thom

A.D.Townsend

R.J.Tulloch

L.A.Urquhart

L.S.V.Venables

Dr T.R.Waddell

Dr C.W.Walker

A.J.Wallis

Dr A.Watson

A.D.Watson

P.S.Watson

Hon. D.M.Weir

B.Weld

N.J.Westwood

A.W.Williams

T.L.Wood

J.G.Young

Order GAVIIFORMES

Family GAVIIDAE

Genus GAVIA Forster

Holarctic genus of five species, all (but two only marginally) in Palaearctic, four breeding in Europe and two in the British Isles, where the other two occur as visitors, one regularly, the other as a vagrant.

Red-throated Diver   A
Gavia stellata (Pontoppidan)

Holarctic. Breeding distribution circumpolar, from high arctic latitudes south to southern Greenland, Iceland, northwest Ireland, Scotland, southern Scandinavia, 58°N across Eurasia to Kamchatka, Sakhalin and the Kuriles, British Columbia, Quebec and Newfoundland (known in North America as Red-throated Loon); between 83°N and 47°N. Winters at sea from southern edge of breeding range south to the Mediterranean, Japan and southern United States.

    G.s.stellata (Pontoppidan) breeds entire range except southern Franz Josef Land, Spitsbergen and Bear Island.

    MB (or **RB**). Scarce. Distributed rather locally in Scotland from Arran, south Argyll and north Perth northwards, including all large islands of the Western and Northern Isles; commonest in extreme northwest and north; absent from northeast Scotland. Occasional breeding recorded Ayr and suspected Kirkcudbright. Also breeds very locally in Donegal, Ireland. Breeding grounds are occupied only in summer. Movements in winter largely unknown, but two Shetland-ringed birds were found in winter off northwest France.

    WV and **PV**. Widely distributed off all coasts in winter, but scarce off those of the Northern Isles and extreme north of Scotland. Occasionally wanders inland (almost annually to reservoirs around London), most often during cold weather. Present on coasts outside breeding range from September to May, with well-marked spring and autumn passage on some coasts, especially those of the North Sea and eastern English Channel. These winter visitors and migrants presumably originate mainly from northern Europe.

Black-throated Diver   A
Gavia arctica (Linnaeus)

Northern Palaearctic and marginally Nearctic. Breeds from Scotland, Fenno-Scandia and Baltic States east across northernmost Eurasia to Anadyrland and Kamchatka, including southern Novaya Zemlya, south to northern Poland, central Russia, Kazakhstan, Mongolia and Sakhalin; also western Alaska (known as Arctic Loon in North America); between 74°N and 50°N. Winters in coastal waters and at sea south from the southern edge of breeding range to the Mediterranean, Black Sea and Japan.

G.a.arctica (Linnaeus) breeds entire range except eastern Siberia and Alaska.

MB (or **RB**). Scarce. Distributed locally in Scotland north from Arran, south Argyll and north Perth, including some larger islands in the Hebrides, but not Orkney and Shetland, nor northeast Scotland. Has bred occasionally in southwest Scotland (Ayr) since 1956. Breeding grounds are occupied only in summer and whereabouts of population in winter are not known.

WV. Occurs regularly off all Scottish coasts (except extreme north) and the east and southeast coasts of England in winter, mainly September to May; occasionally offshore elsewhere and inland (including not infrequently on large reservoirs around London in cold weather), but only very rarely anywhere in Ireland. These winter visitors presumably originate mainly from northern Europe.

Great Northern Diver   A
Gavia immer (Brünnich)

Northern Nearctic and marginally Palaearctic. Breeds from Alaska east along arctic coasts of North America to Greenland, south to Washington and New England; also Iceland, probably Bear Island, and possibly Jan

Mayen, occurring also in summer in extreme northern Norway (known as Common Loon in North America); between 76°N and 43°N. Winters mainly south of breeding range in coastal waters of North Atlantic and Pacific, south to Morocco and the Gulfs of Mexico and California.

Monotypic.

WV. Mainly October to May, less often in other months although some non-breeding birds remain through the summer in northern Scotland, and may occasionally be seen in summer farther south in the British Isles. Winters regularly and most commonly off coasts of Scotland, Ireland and southwest England, and occurs regularly in small numbers off most other coasts, though it is infrequent or irregular along the coasts of several counties of eastern England. Occasionally found inland, usually sick birds or in cold weather. The origin of these winter visitors is not known, but presumably they include birds from Iceland.

White-billed Diver   A
Gavia adamsii (Gray)

Northern Holarctic. Breeds from the Kola Peninsula, northern Russia and Novaya Zemlya, east across northern Siberia and Alaska to the Boothia Peninsula, south to about 67°N in Siberia and the Great Slave Lake in Canada (known as Yellow-billed Loon in America); between 76°N and 63°N. Winters at sea south of the breeding range, south to northern Norway, northern Japan and British Columbia.

Monotypic.

SV. At least 21 recorded, all but three since 1946. Recorded in every month from November to June, all on the northeast coast between Yorkshire and Shetland, except one Cornwall and one, found dead, inland in Northumberland.

Order PODICIPEDIFORMES

Family PODICIPEDIDAE

Genus PODILYMBUS Lesson

Nearctic and Neotropical genus of two species, one of which has wandered to the British Isles.

Pied-billed Grebe   A
Podilymbus podiceps (Linnaeus)

Nearctic and Neotropical. Breeds throughout most of the New World from central British Columbia, south Mackenzie and Nova Scotia south to Argentina; between 60°N and 45°S. Mainly sedentary but inland North American populations are migratory.

(*P.p.podiceps* (Linnaeus) breeds North America south to central Mexico.)

SV. Seven records, concerning perhaps only three individual birds: Somerset (December 1963, August–October 1965, May and July–November 1966, May–October 1967, and May–July 1968), Yorkshire (June–November 1965) and Norfolk (November 1968). Subspecies not determined, but probably nominate *podiceps* since this is the partly migratory race.

Genus TACHYBAPTUS Reichenbach

Palaearctic, Oriental, Australasian and Ethiopian genus of five species, one in Palaearctic, breeding in Europe and the British Isles.

4

Little Grebe A
Tachybaptus ruficollis (Pallas)

Palaearctic, Ethiopan and Oriental. Breeds across Europe and southern Asia, north to the British Isles, southernmost Sweden, central Russia, Russian Turkestan, Manchuria and Japan, south to Malaysia and India; also throughout most of Africa, and in the Philippines, and Indonesia east to New Guinea and the Solomons; between 59°N and 35°S. Mainly sedentary but northernmost birds move south in winter within the breeding range.

T.r.ruficollis (Pallas) breeds Europe and north Africa east to the Ukraine, Turkey and the Near East.

RB. Fairly numerous. Widely distributed; absent from Shetland and Pembroke, irregular in Inner Hebrides, but otherwise breeding in every county, though rather locally in some in southwest England, central Wales and northwest Scotland. Mainly sedentary.

WV. Widely distributed (but absent from Shetland and some inland areas of Scotland) mainly on fresh water but also in small flocks on tidal estuaries and occasionally offshore. Wintering population includes some immigrants from the Continent, mainly October to April.

Genus PODICEPS Latham

Cosmopolitan genus of 12 species, four in Palaearctic, all breeding in Europe and three in the British Isles, where the fourth occurs as a winter visitor.

Black-necked Grebe A
Podiceps nigricollis Brehm

Holarctic and Ethiopian. Breeds discontinuously, locally and often somewhat erratically across southern and central Europe (from south Sweden south to Spain, Sicily and the Black Sea) east through Asia Minor to central Asia; again in Ussuriland; also in northwest, eastern and southern Africa, and in western North America (where known as Eared Grebe); between 62°N and 35°S. Sedentary and migratory; winters mainly within breeding range and in south and east Asia.

P.n.nigricollis Brehm breeds throughout Palaearctic range.

MB (or **RB**). Very scarce. Regular nesting at present confined to two or three sites in the central Scottish lowlands. No established populations now known elsewhere, but has bred sporadically in many counties of England and some of Wales and south Scotland. Formerly bred in four or five counties in Ireland (in force in Roscommon). Winter range of breeding birds not known.

WV and **PV**. Mainly August to May, with evidence of passage, especially in late summer and early autumn. Occurs regularly in winter on south and east coasts north to Norfolk, in the Firth of Forth, Wigtown, Anglesey and Glamorgan, and in winter or on passage on larger inland waters in several counties of central and southern England. Irregular elsewhere, and rare in north and west Scotland and Ireland.

Slavonian Grebe   A
Podiceps auritus (Linnaeus)

Holarctic. Breeds from Iceland, Scotland, Scandinavia and the Baltic States east across Siberia to Kamchatka and Amurland, mainly between latitudes 63°N and 50°N; also Alaska, Canada and the northern United States (where known as Horned Grebe); between 69°N and 45°N. Winters mainly in coastal waters to the south of the breeding range, and sometimes reaches as far south as the Mediterranean, southeast China and southern United States.

P.a.auritus (Linnaeus) breeds Palaearctic part of range.

RB. Very scarce. Restricted to northern Scotland, where breeds locally in Inverness, Sutherland and Caithness, and at least occasionally in Moray and Aberdeen.

WV. Regular in winter, September to May (mainly November to February), on parts of all coasts, also occasionally inland especially on large reservoirs in London area, where almost annual. Some evidence of passage in spring and autumn.

Red-necked Grebe   A
Podiceps griseigena (Boddaert)

Holarctic. Breeds from Sweden, Finland and north Russia south to Germany, the Balkans and the Ukraine, east to the Kirghiz Steppes; again from east Siberia south to Manchuria, and in Alaska, Canada and the northern United States; between 69°N and 40°N. Winters south to the Mediterranean, southeast China and the southern United States.

P.g.griseigena (Boddaert) breeds Europe and western Asia.
P.g.holbollii Reinhardt breeds North America and eastern Asia.

WV. Regular in very small numbers to a few parts of the east coast from East Lothian southwards, August to April (mainly October to March). Recorded occasionally on other coasts (but only rarely in northern Scotland and Ireland) and inland on reservoirs, annually on those around London. *P.g.griseigena*.
SV. One *P.g.holbollii*, Ross (September 1925).

Great Crested Grebe   A
Podiceps cristatus (Linnaeus)

Palaearctic, Oriental, Ethiopian and Australasian. Breeds locally over most of the Old World from Britain, southern Fenno-Scandia and 60°N in Russia south to north Africa and Turkey, east to Tibet and China; also in eastern and southern Africa, Australia and New Zealand; between 66°N and 46°S. Sedentary and migratory, in northern hemisphere wintering south to the Mediterranean, north India and southeast China.

P.c.cristatus (Linnaeus) breeds in Palaearctic and Oriental regions.

RB. Not scarce. Breeds very locally in Aberdeen and perhaps Moray, and widely over most of Britain south from Angus, north Perth and Dunbarton, becomes increasingly more numerous in central and southern England (breeding in every county except Cornwall, Devon and Monmouth) but much less so in Wales (where scarce or irregular in most counties, and absent from Pembroke and Glamorgan, though one pair bred in the latter county in 1968). Absent Isle of Man. Breeds fairly widely in Ireland (not western coastal districts) south to Limerick, north Tipperary, Offaly and Dublin; also Wexford and occasionally in other southern counties. Most smaller breeding waters are abandoned in winter but there is no evidence of emigration to the Continent.

WV. Widely distributed on all coasts and many larger inland waters from Firths of Clyde and Forth southwards, most numerous on large reservoirs and coasts in southeast England, least so in southwest Ireland, where rare. Extent of immigration from the Continent is not known.

Order PROCELLARIIFORMES

Family DIOMEDEIDAE

Genus DIOMEDEA Linnaeus

Oceanic (southern hemisphere and North Pacific) genus of eleven species, three of which have wandered to the North Atlantic and at least one to the British Isles.

Black-browed Albatross   A
Diomedea melanophrys Temminck

Oceanic in southern hemisphere. Breeds on islands off southernmost South America, on South Georgia, the Falklands, Kerguelen, Heard, Macquarie, Campbell, the Auckland and Antipodes, and probably others; between 50°S and 55°S. Disperses north towards the tropics outside the breeding season.

Monotypic.

SV. Thirteen recorded, all but two of these during 1963–68. Two found inland: Cambridge (July 1897), Derby (August 1952); one frequented the gannetry on the Bass Rock, East Lothian, during May to September 1967 and April to July 1968, and was also seen off Berwick in February 1968; the remainder were seen offshore: Cork (September 1963, June, September, October 1967, and August 1968), Kerry (August 1944), Devon (April 1965), Yorkshire (November 1965, October 1967, October 1968). In addition, albatrosses, not identified specifically, have been recorded on a further 14 occasions: Lincoln (November 1836), Orkney (July 1894), Northumberland (February 1895), Fair Isle (May 1949), Donegal (September 1963, September 1966), Yorkshire (September 1954, November 1963, September 1966),

Cornwall (August 1964), Cork (September 1967, and July, August (two together) and September 1968).

Family PROCELLARIIDAE

Genus FULMARUS Stephens

Oceanic, bipolar genus with a single superspecies having representative species in the higher latitudes of both hemispheres.

Fulmar A
Fulmarus glacialis (Linnaeus)

Oceanic. Breeds in the Atlantic area on Baffin and Devon Islands, Greenland, Jan Mayen, Iceland, Bear Island, Spitsbergen, Novaya Zemlya, Faeroes, west Norway, British Isles, and northwest France, and in the Pacific in the Kuriles and on islands in the Bering Sea; between 81°N and 47°N. Winters at sea, reaching as far south as Iberia, Japan, Baja California and New England.

F.g.glacialis (Linnaeus) breeds Atlantic area.

RB and **MB**. Fairly numerous—probably rather over 100,000 occupied nest sites in Britain and Ireland. Originally confined to St. Kilda, colonized Shetland (Foula) in 1878, and has since spread progressively southwards to almost every suitable part of the British and Irish coastline except southeast England (birds prospecting, but no certain nesting between the Isle of Wight and east Norfolk). Disperses at sea outside breeding season, and British-ringed birds commonly reach Greenland, Newfoundland and northwest Europe. May be seen in British waters throughout the year and nesting cliffs are visited by some birds in most months. Rarely wanders inland.

Genus PTERODROMA Bonaparte

Oceanic (in the Southern, Pacific, Atlantic and Indian Oceans) genus of

20 or more species, three or more in the central North Atlantic, one of which has strayed once to the British Isles while three from other oceans have wandered to other parts of Europe.

Capped Petrel   B
Pterodroma hasitata (Kuhl)

Oceanic. Breeds Hispaniola and formerly at least in Jamaica and the Lesser Antilles. Disperses at sea, and prone to occur in eastern North America after late summer hurricanes.

    P.h.hasitata (Kuhl) breeds Hispaniola (and Lesser Antilles).

    SV. One, Norfolk (March or April 1850).

Genus BULWERIA Bonaparte

Oceanic, one superspecies with representative species in the Arabian Sea and in the other northern oceans.

Bulwer's Petrel   A
Bulweria bulwerii (Jardine and Selby)

Oceanic. Breeds in the central North Atlantic and Pacific archipelagos, including the Cape Verde Islands, Canaries, Salvages, Madeira group, Azores, Marquesas, Hawaiian Leeward islands, Bonins, Volcanoes, and off the coast of China; between 40°N and 10°S.

    Monotypic.

    SV. Three: Yorkshire (May 1837, February 1908), Cork (August 1965).

Genus CALONECTRIS Mathews and Iredale

Oceanic genus of two species, one breeding in the southern North Atlantic and Mediterranean, and wandering north to the British Isles.

Cory's Shearwater   A
Calonectris diomedea (Scopoli)

Oceanic. Breeds Mediterranean islands, Canaries, Salvages, Madeira group, Azores, and Cape Verde Islands; between 43°N and 15°N.

Disperses at sea west to the American coast, north to the mouth of the English Channel, and winters off South Africa.

C.d.borealis (Cory) breeds North Atlantic islands, except the Cape Verdes.

PV. Recorded April to November, mainly July to September when annual in recent years; also rarely in winter. Sometimes in some numbers off southwest Ireland (as in August 1962, July 1963 and June 1968), with small numbers nearly annually off southwest Cornwall and the Isles of Scilly, and less frequently or erratically off other coasts north to Fair Isle. *C.d.borealis* collected once (Norfolk, January 1966), subspecies not determined for the remainder.

Genus PUFFINUS Brisson

Oceanic, cosmopolitan genus of 11–14 species, two breeding and two wintering in the North Atlantic, one breeding in and the other three visiting the British Isles, one of them infrequently.

Great Shearwater   A
Puffinus gravis (O'Reilly)

Oceanic. Breeds Tristan da Cunha group, Gough Island and (regularly?) the Falklands. In non-breeding season occurs mainly on the Grand Banks of Newfoundland and in Greenland waters, but is also widely dispersed in the North Atlantic east to Rockall.

Monotypic.

PV. Occasionally March and April, more commonly May and June, regularly July to September (sometimes in numbers, for example in 1965 when a marked general influx, including over 5,000 on two separate days in September off Cape Clear, Cork), rare after November. Mainly off western Ireland, the Hebrides, south Cornwall and the Isles of Scilly, less frequent off other coasts from Shetland southwards.

Sooty Shearwater   A
Puffinus griseus (Gmelin)

Oceanic. Breeds New Zealand region, around southern South America, the Falkland Islands, and in small numbers off southeast Australia and Tasmania; between about 40°S and 55°S. Disperses throughout the

Southern Oceans, and migrates north in the Atlantic and Pacific, reaching northern parts of both oceans.

Monotypic.

PV. Earliest in April and May, most August to September, exceptional after November. Occurs off most coasts, regularly and most numerously in northern and western offshore waters, also less frequently and numerously off North Sea coasts, but only infrequently and in small numbers off southeast England.

Manx Shearwater   **A**
Puffinus puffinus (Brünnich)

Oceanic. Breeds (this species or close allies) in the Westmanns, Faeroes, British Isles, northwest France, Madeira, Azores, Mediterranean islands, islands off California and Mexico, Hawaii, and in New Zealand area; between 64°N and 45°S. Migrations complex; North Atlantic population winters off eastern coasts of South America.

P.p.puffinus (Brünnich) breeds North Atlantic.

P.p.mauretanicus Lowe (Balearic Shearwater) breeds Balearic Islands, disperses north up the west coast of Europe.

MB. Numerous. Large colonies on islands in the Isles of Scilly, off Pembroke and Caernarvon, Kerry, in the Inner Hebrides, and on St. Kilda; smaller colonies on Lundy, Isle of Man and possibly south Argyll, various parts of the Irish coast and its islands (Cork, Galway, Mayo, Donegal, Antrim, Down, Dublin, Wicklow, Wexford), Outer Hebrides, Orkney and Shetland. Resident from about February to October, rare in other months. Offshore movements (in east in summer perhaps involving mainly non-breeders) may occur in all months, April to September on east coast south to Norfolk, as well as off western coasts. Scarce off southeast England. Exceptional inland, where most records concern recently fledged young picked up exhausted in September. *P.p.puffinus*.

PV. *P.p.mauretanicus* is recorded in rather variable numbers, June to November (most July to October), exceptionally from March and in December and January. Chiefly off Cornwall and along the English Channel coast east to Dorset, smaller numbers on other coasts north to the Hebrides and southeast Scotland.

Little Shearwater A
Puffinus assimilis (Bonaparte)

Oceanic. Breeds Atlantic islands from Madeira and the Caribbean region south to Gough Island, also widely on islands in the Pacific and Indian Oceans; between 32°N and 40°S. Disperses at sea outside the breeding season.

P.a.*baroli* (Bonaparte) breeds Madeira, Canaries and Azores.

SV. About 34 recorded, three-quarters of these since 1964. Six P.a.*baroli* (at wide intervals, 1853–1960), one April, four May, one August, from Kent, Norfolk (three), Cheshire and Cork. The remainder refer to sight records, probably of this race: one Caernarvon (May 1951), one Cornwall (October 1967), the rest from Cork, Kerry and Donegal, all during 1964–68, and all August to October apart from one each in April and June.

Family HYDROBATIDAE

Genus OCEANITES Keyserling and Blasius

Oceanic (Southern Ocean) genus of two species, one migrating north of the equator and straying to the British Isles.

Wilson's Petrel A
Oceanites oceanicus (Kuhl)

Oceanic. Breeds from Antarctica north to islands near the subantarctic convergence; between 49°S and 70°S. Migrates north to about 45°N in the Atlantic and less far north in other oceans.

O.o.*exasperatus* Mathews breeds Antarctica north to South Georgia.

SV. At least five recorded, with other possible reports in 19th century but only one acceptable in this: Cornwall (August 1838, and perhaps others at that time; October 1967), Inner Hebrides, Fermanagh

and Down (all October 1891). One of the Irish specimens identified as
O.o.exasperatus.

Genus PELAGODROMA Reichenbach

Southern Ocean and central North Atlantic monospecific genus,
recorded once in the British Isles.

Frigate Petrel   **B**
Pelagodroma marina (Latham)

Oceanic. Breeds in the subtropical North Atlantic and Southern Ocean;
between 30°N and 50°S. Winters mainly in the tropics.

P.m.hypoleuca (Webb, Berthelot and Moquin-Tandon) breeds in the
Salvages.

SV. One, Inner Hebrides (January 1897).

Genus HYDROBATES Boie

Oceanic (Atlantic and Mediterranean) monospecific genus, breeding in
the British Isles.

Storm Petrel   **A**
Hydrobates pelagicus (Linnaeus)

Oceanic. Breeds Westmanns, Faeroes, British Isles, northwest France,
north Spain, Canaries, and at least in western Mediterranean; between
64°N and 32°N. Winters off western and southern Africa.

Monotypic.

MB. Numerous. Breeds regularly and numerously on certain islands
off western and northern coasts: Isles of Scilly, Pembroke, Outer
Hebrides (including St. Kilda), Orkney, Shetland, and on many islands
off western Ireland from Cork north to Donegal. Formerly bred
Antrim and west Ross (and may still do so in the latter); a few pairs
breed at least occasionally off Cornwall, Caernarvon, Anglesey, perhaps elsewhere, especially off west Scotland; has bred exceptionally in
south Devon, East Lothian and Wexford. Resident April to November;
casual in winter. Recorded irregularly on east and south coasts, and
seldom strays inland.

Genus OCEANODROMA Reichenbach

Oceanic (North Atlantic and North Pacific) genus of 12 species, two in North Atlantic, one breeding in the British Isles, the other occurring as a rare straggler.

Madeiran Petrel A
Oceanodroma castro (Harcourt)

Oceanic. Breeds St. Helena, Ascension, possibly the Gulf of Guinea, Cape Verde Islands, Salvages, Madeira group, Azores, Galapagos, Hawaii, Japan, and probably elsewhere; between 40°N and 16°S. Disperses at sea in those regions outside the breeding season.

Monotypic.

SV. Two: Hampshire (November 1911), Mayo (October 1931).

Leach's Petrel A
Oceanodroma leucorrhoa (Vieillot)

Oceanic. Breeds in North Atlantic from New England to Labrador and in the Westmanns, Faeroes and Outer Hebrides; also around the North Pacific from Japan to Baja California; between 64°N and 30°N; also (this species or close ally) in the western Pacific and Indian Ocean. Winters throughout the tropical Atlantic and eastern tropical Pacific, and (this species or ally) in the Indian Ocean.

O.l.leucorrhoa (Vieillot) breeds entire range except the southern periphery in the Pacific.

MB. Not scarce but extremely local. Breeds St. Kilda and outlying Hebrides (Flannans, North Rona, Sula Sgeir), and, in the past, occasionally on islands off western Ireland; occurs on the latter occasionally, and regularly on Foula and elsewhere in Shetland in the breeding season and may breed on Foula at least. Present April to November, rarely December.

PV. Mainly September to November, in very variable numbers. Chiefly on western coasts, irregular elsewhere and inland, but large wrecks occur in some years, as in 1881, 1891 (most birds in the northwest), 1899, 1908, 1917, 1952 (most birds in the south).

B

Order PELECANIFORMES

Family SULIDAE

Genus SULA Brisson

Coastal and oceanic (throughout temperate and tropical parts of all oceans) genus of seven to nine species, four in the North Atlantic, one in European seas with its headquarters in the British Isles.

Gannet A
Sula bassana (Linnaeus)

Oceanic in temperate zone. Breeds on both sides of the North Atlantic, with races or close allies in South Africa, and southwest Australia with New Zealand; between 66°N and 47°S. Partial migrant to lower latitudes.

   S.b.bassana (Linnaeus) breeds locally Newfoundland, Gulf of St. Lawrence, Iceland, Faeroes, Norway, British Isles, Channel Islands and northwest France.

   MB and **RB**. Fairly numerous, with a total breeding population in Britain and Ireland of about 100,000 pairs. Breeds colonially Grassholm (Pembroke), Scar Rocks (Wigtown), Ailsa Craig (Ayr), St. Kilda, Sula Sgeir (Outer Hebrides), Sule Stack (Orkney), Hermaness and Noss (Shetland), Bass Rock (East Lothian), Bempton (Yorkshire), Bull Rock (Cork), Little Skellig (Kerry), Great Saltee (Wexford); and formerly on four other islands. First-year birds migrate farther south than adults (some of which may remain in British waters throughout the year) and reach the western Mediterranean and the Gulf of Guinea, with most wintering off West Africa.

   PV. Mainly March–April and September–October, but passage

16

and/or feeding movements occur in most months of the year. All coasts, though most numerous off western Britain and Ireland. Vagrant inland. Extent of involvement of birds from colonies outside the British Isles is not known, but several ringed in the Channel Islands have been recovered here, and Iceland-Faeroes birds must pass along western coasts at least at times.

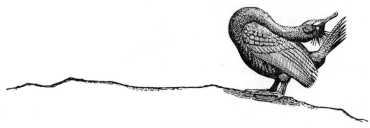

Family PHALACROCORACIDAE

Genus PHALACROCORAX Brisson

Cosmopolitan and mainly coastal genus of 24 species, nine in Palaearctic, three breeding in Europe and two in the British Isles.

Cormorant   A
Phalacrocorax carbo (Linnaeus)

Nearly cosmopolitan (not South America). Breeds from Iceland, Faeroes, British Isles, northwest France and Scandinavia, discontinuously eastwards on coasts and inland waters throughout most of the southern Palaearctic region, east to Sakhalin and Japan, south to Turkey and into southern India and southern China; also in northeastern North America and west Greenland, and in the Ethiopian and Australasian regions, but rarely on oceanic islands; between 72°N and 47°S. Partial migrant over much of its range, the Atlantic population reaching as far south in winter as New York and Portugal.

P.c.carbo (Linnaeus) breeds Nova Scotia, Labrador, west Greenland, Iceland, Faeroes, British Isles, and west Norway east to the Kola Peninsula.

P.c.sinensis (Shaw and Nodder) breeds locally over most of central and southern Eurasia from southern Sweden and the Low Countries eastwards.

RB and **MB**. Not scarce. Breeding colonies scattered widely on rocky southwest, west and north coasts of Britain and Ireland, and much more locally on east and southeast coasts, with none between the Isle of Wight and north Yorkshire. Single inland colonies are situated a few miles inland in Wales (Merioneth) and Scotland (Wigtown), and there are also a very few well inland in Ireland. Disperses to all coasts and, more locally, to inland waters outside the breeding season, some birds migrating south as far as Portugal. *P.c.carbo.*

PV and **WV**. *P.c.sinensis* probably occurs regularly in southern England, where ringed birds (from Denmark, Germany and the Low Countries) have been recovered in winter and occasionally in other months, but it is indistinguishable in the field from *P.c.carbo.*

Shag　　　　　　　　　　　　　　　　　　　　A
Phalacrocorax aristotelis (Linnaeus)

Western Palaearctic. Breeds on coasts of Iceland, Faeroes, British Isles, Kola Peninsula to southern Norway, northwest France, west Iberia and Morocco, Mediterranean and Black Sea; between 71°N and 30°N. Mainly sedentary, though first-year birds are partial migrants.

P.a.aristotelis (Linnaeus) breeds in northern part of the range south to west Iberia.

RB. Fairly numerous. Breeds widely and colonially on rocky southwest, west and north coasts of Britain and Ireland (but none on coast of northwest England), and locally on east and south coasts. Mainly sedentary, with some dispersal after the breeding season to other coasts of the British Isles, some (mainly first-year) birds reaching Continental coasts from Norway south to Biscay. Accidental inland, though occurs quite widely and in some numbers during periodic winter wrecks.

WV. Ringing shows that birds from the Channel Islands reach the English south coast, probably regularly, as may individuals from colonies in northwest France.

Family FREGATIDAE

Genus FREGATA Lacépède

Oceanic (throughout tropics) genus of five species, one in the tropical Atlantic, wandering at least once to the British Isles.

Magnificent Frigate-bird   **A**
Fregata magnificens Mathews

Oceanic in the tropical Atlantic and east Pacific. Breeds Cape Verde Islands, West Indies, along both coasts of the Americas from Baja California and British Honduras to southern Brazil and Ecuador, and in the Galapagos; non-breeders are regular on Atlantic coast of the southern United States. Strays fairly widely along coasts and occasionally occurs well out to sea.

Monotypic.

SV. One, Inner Hebrides (July 1953). In addition an unidentified frigate-bird was seen off Aberdeen in August 1960.

Order CICONIIFORMES

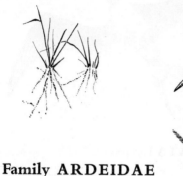

Family ARDEIDAE

Genus ARDEA Linnaeus

Cosmopolitan genus of about ten species, three in Palaearctic, two breeding in Europe, one breeding in and one visiting the British Isles.

Heron   A
Ardea cinerea Linnaeus

Palaearctic, Oriental and Ethiopian. Breeds from the British Isles, central Scandinavia and about 60°N in central Asia east to Japan, south to Africa, Madagascar, India, Malaysia and the East Indies; between 64°N and 35°S. Sedentary and migratory; some northern populations winter south to tropical Africa and north India.

A.c.cinerea Linnaeus breeds over most of the Palaearctic and Oriental regions except in the extreme east, and Africa.

RB. Not scarce. Widely distributed, breeding locally (mainly colonially) in every county of Britain and Ireland except Flint and Denbigh, five small counties in southeast Scotland, and Shetland; most numerous in southeast England. Outside the breeding season disperses widely within the British Isles, some (mainly immature) birds reaching the continent of western Europe, south to Iberia.

WV. Immigrants from the Continent (chiefly Scandinavia and the Low Countries) reach all parts of Britain and Ireland, mainly August to April. Occasionally also in other months, and probably some passage in spring and autumn, especially in southeast England.

Purple Heron A
Ardea purpurea Linnaeus

Palaearctic, Oriental and Ethiopian. Breeds northwest Africa, Iberia, France and the Netherlands, and from Sicily, north Italy and Poland east through Russia, southeast Europe and Asia Minor to the Kirghiz Steppes, again from Manchuria south to India and the East Indies, also in southern Africa with Madagascar; between 53°N and 35°S. Migratory and sedentary; some European birds reach as far south as tropical Africa in winter.

A.p.purpurea Linnaeus breeds east to the Kirghiz Steppes, south to Africa (not Madagascar).

SV. Over 160 records; one to 20 birds annually in recent years, usually singly though occasionally up to five together. Chiefly April to October (especially late April–May), rarely in winter. The great majority have been recorded in England (especially in the east and south from Norfolk to the Isles of Scilly), only a few in Wales and Scotland (eastern counties north to Shetland), and just two in Ireland.

Genus ARDEOLA Boie

Palaearctic, Oriental and Ethiopian genus of four species, three in Palaearctic, one breeding in Europe and straggling to the British Isles.

Squacco Heron A
Ardeola ralloides (Scopoli)

Palaearctic and Ethiopian. Breeds from southern Spain and locally in southern France through the Balkans, southern Russia and Asia Minor to Turkestan, south to Iraq and Africa with Madagascar; between 48°N and 33°S. Northern populations winter in Africa.

Monotypic.

SV. About 100, the great majority before about 1914 and only at intervals of years since, for example only six or seven since 1954. Chiefly May and June, on to October, with one to two in most other months. Records mainly from England (especially in the southwest and East Anglia), also twelve Ireland (especially in the southwest, but none since 1919 except for one, Dublin, October 1967), and about four each in Wales and Scotland.

Genus BUBULCUS Bonaparte

Now nearly cosmopolitan genus of one species, breeding in Europe and straying to the British Isles.

Cattle Egret
Bubulcus ibis (Linnaeus)

A

Originally southern Palaearctic, Oriental and Ethiopian, now nearly cosmopolitan, after colonizing the Americas and being introduced to Australia. Breeds northwest Africa, southern Spain, Portugal, Transcaucasia to Transcaspia, south to the orient, Arabia, and Africa south of the Sahara; recently in Australia and America; between 40°N and 35°S. Chiefly sedentary, but erratic and migratory also.

B.i.ibis (Linnaeus) breeds Palaearctic and Ethiopian regions.

SV. Four records involving seven individuals: Devon (October 1805), Norfolk (October 1917), Sussex (April 1962: four together and a fifth singly). Others recorded, for example Derby, July 1966 and September 1968, but these may refer to birds that had escaped from captivity.

Genus EGRETTA T. Forster

Cosmopolitan genus of about seven species, six in Palaearctic, two breeding in Europe both of which wander to the British Isles.

Great White Egret
Egretta alba (Linnaeus)

A

Nearly cosmopolitan. Breeds from central Europe, Turkey, central Asia and Japan south to New Zealand, Australia and southern Africa; also widely in North and South America; between 50°N and 44°S. Northern populations migratory; Palaearctic birds winter south to northern Africa, northern India and eastern China.

E.a.alba (Linnaeus) breeds from Austria and Czechoslovakia east to Japan.

SV. Ten: Yorkshire (about 1825; 1834), Nottingham (before 1838), East Lothian (June 1840), Cambridge (May or June 1849), Yorkshire (summer 1868), Perth (May 1881), Cornwall (September–October 1948, May 1951), Dorset (August 1951).

Little Egret   A
Egretta garzetta (Linnaeus)

Southern Palaearctic, Oriental, Australasian and, locally, Ethiopian. Breeds northwest Africa, Iberia, southern France and locally elsewhere in southern Europe, east through the Balkans and southern Russia and across southern Asia to central China and Japan, south to Australia and eastern and southern Africa; between 50°N and 35°S. Migratory and sedentary, the European population wintering from the Mediterranean southwards.

E.g.garzetta (Linnaeus) breeds entire range except Philippines to New Guinea and Australia.

SV. Almost 100 recorded, nearly all since about 1940, with up to twelve annually in recent years. All months, March to October (mainly May–June), occasionally remaining into or even through the winter; individuals often stay for some weeks. Chiefly on the English south coast (especially in the southwest), but also fairly frequently in recent years in southwest Ireland; less often elsewhere in England, Wales and Ireland, and only rarely inland and in Scotland, where four records, north to Orkney and Shetland. Sight records (the majority above) do not exclude *E.thula* (Molina), Snowy Egret of the Americas.

Genus NYCTICORAX T. Forster

Nearly cosmopolitan genus of two species, one widespread, including Palaearctic, breeding in Europe and wandering to the British Isles.

Night Heron   A
Nycticorax nycticorax (Linnaeus)

Nearly cosmopolitan (not Australasia), mainly between latitudes 50°N and 50°S. Breeds throughout most of this region excluding much of Africa, while it is local in Europe, where colonies are thinly scattered from the Mediterranean and Black Seas north to the Netherlands and Czechoslovakia. Sedentary and migratory; the European population winters in tropical Africa.

N.n.nycticorax (Linnaeus) breeds France, Netherlands and Czechoslovakia south to the Mediterranean and east to Japan and the East Indies.

SV. Probably over 200 recorded; one to six in most recent years, the majority wild vagrants, but probably not all, since some recent records may refer to wanderers from a free-living colony at Edinburgh Zoo. Chiefly in spring, March to June (especially April), but has been found in every month. The records, especially recent ones, have been most frequent in southwest England (Isles of Scilly to Hampshire), with fewer in East Anglia, and the rest scattered mainly in eastern counties north to Aberdeen and Orkney, west to Wales, Ireland (especially Cork), and the Outer Hebrides.

Genus IXOBRYCHUS Billberg

Cosmopolitan genus of eight species, one in Palaearctic, breeding in Europe and perhaps sporadically in the British Isles, where it otherwise occurs as an annual vagrant.

Little Bittern   A
Ixobrychus minutus (Linnaeus)

Palaearctic, Ethiopian and Australasian. Breeds from Iberia, France, the Netherlands and the Baltic States across Europe and west Asia east to Sinkiang, south to the Mediterranean basin, Iran and northwestern India; also in tropical and southern Africa, Madagascar and Australia; between 60°N and 40°S. The Palaearctic population winters mainly in tropical Africa.

I.m.minutus (Linnaeus) breeds Palaearctic region.

(**CB**.) No published proof, but occasional breeding strongly suspected in East Anglia in 19th century and also in southern England in 1947, while apparent pairs have summered in Surrey (1956), Somerset (1958), Huntingdon (1960), and perhaps elsewhere.

SV. Over 200 recorded, almost annually in recent years, usually one to three, but as many as 13 in one year. Apart from one in January, all recent records are for the period April to September, with the great majority in spring; the species has been noted occasionally in other months in the past. Recorded chiefly in the southern half of England and Wales, occasionally north to Shetland and west to Ireland.

Genus BOTAURUS Stephens

Cosmopolitan genus of four species, one in the Palaearctic, breeding also in Europe and the British Isles, where one other has occurred as a vagrant.

Bittern A
Botaurus stellaris (Linnaeus)

Palaearctic and Ethiopian. Breeds across Eurasia from southern Fenno-Scandia, mid-Russia and mid-Siberia, south to northwest Africa, Iran, Mongolia, north China and Japan; between 61°N and 34°N; also in southeast Africa. Migratory and sedentary; winters south to northern tropical Africa, northern India and southeast China.

B.s.stellaris (Linnaeus) breeds over the whole of the range except southeast Africa.

RB. Very scarce, probably rather under 100 breeding pairs. Extinct at end of 19th century; re-established itself in East Anglia in early 20th century. Norfolk and Suffolk remain its headquarters, but a few pairs also breed very locally in Kent, Anglesey and Lancashire, and it has bred at least once in a total of eleven counties since 1940.

WV. Small numbers from the Continent, August to April, but most November to February. Chiefly in the southern half of England and southwest Wales, but recorded at least occasionally in all English and most Welsh and southern Scottish counties, though only rarely in north Scotland and Ireland.

American Bittern A
Botaurus lentiginosus (Montagu)

Nearctic. Breeds from British Columbia, Hudson Bay and Newfoundland south to California, Texas and Florida; between 55°N and 25°N. Winters south to Mexico and the West Indies.

Monotypic.

SV. About 52—three-quarters of this total before about 1914, and recorded only infrequently since; the only records during 1958–68 were Caernarvon (September 1962) and Galway (December 1964). Mainly October–November, but also in all months September to March. About 20 from England (nearly all in south coast counties), five Wales, eight Scotland (widely scattered, Dumfries to Caithness), and 19 Ireland (also widely scattered).

Family CICONIIDAE

Genus CICONIA Brisson

Palaearctic, also Ethiopian, genus of three species, two breeding in Europe and wandering to the British Isles, where one bred at least once in the 15th century.

White Stork   A
Ciconia ciconia (Linnaeus)

Palaearctic, sporadically Ethiopian. Breeds northwest Africa and Iberia, and from northeast France, the Netherlands, Denmark, Germany and the Baltic States south to the Balkans, Asia Minor and northern Iran; also Turkestan to western Sinkiang; between 60°N and 30°N; has bred in small numbers in South Africa. Winters in tropical and southern Africa, and in smaller numbers from Iraq to northern India.

    C.c.ciconia (Linnaeus) breeds east to western Russia and northern Iran.

    FB. One old breeding record, Edinburgh 1416.

    SV. Over 100 recorded, nearly all before 1900 and only a few since at intervals of years, apart from a remarkable influx of at least 13 birds (including a party of four) in East Anglia and southeast England in April 1967, resulting in a series of records that summer north to Aberdeen and west to Wiltshire, including prolonged stays of eight and twelve months by two birds in Norfolk. Most previous records are March to May, but in recent years also in September, December, January and February (some of these may refer to escaped birds). Like those in 1967, individuals may remain in one place for some time or wander from county to county. Past records are mainly from East Anglia, but the recent ones are widely scattered, north to Scotland. Only four recorded Ireland, none since 1909.

Black Stork A
Ciconia nigra (Linnaeus)

Palaearctic, locally Ethiopian. Breeds Iberia, and in central Europe from northern Germany north to the Baltic States, to about 60°N in central Asia, east Manchuria, south Korea and China, south to the Balkans, Turkey and Iran; between 61°N and 30°N; also in southern Africa. Winters in tropical Africa, northern India and eastern Asia.
Monotypic.

SV. About 28 (most in last century and only four in the last 20 years), chiefly May–June but also in all months, March to November. One Scotland (East Lothian, May 1946), the rest England: Isles of Scilly (two), Devon, Dorset (two), Somerset, Sussex, Kent (four), Middlesex, Oxford, Suffolk (five), Norfolk (three), Worcester, Yorkshire (three), Durham, Northumberland.

Family THRESKIORNITHIDAE

Genus PLEGADIS Kaup

Cosmopolitan (but very local) genus of one or two species, breeding in Europe and wandering to the British Isles.

Glossy Ibis A
Plegadis falcinellus (Linnaeus)

Cosmopolitan, but very discontinuous. Breeds from northeast Italy through the Balkans and Turkey to Turkestan, south to India and Malaysia, and locally in Africa; also east Australia and southeast North America and the Caribbean; between 50°N and 35°S. Sedentary and migratory; European birds winter mainly in tropical Africa.

P. f. falcinellus (Linnaeus) breeds almost entire range, but is replaced by close ally or race elsewhere in the Americas.

SV. Irregular, becoming increasingly so, with a recent average of fewer than one record a year, and none during 1966–68; formerly not infrequently in small parties. Chiefly September to November, occasionally in winter, less often in other months. Records are widely scattered through Britain and Ireland with most in southern coastal counties.

Genus PLATALEA Linnaeus

Palaearctic, Oriental, Ethiopian and Australasian genus of five species, one in Palaearctic, breeding in Europe, formerly breeding in and now visiting the British Isles.

Spoonbill   **A**
Platalea leucorodia Linnaeus

Palaearctic, Oriental and Ethiopian. Breeds locally in south Spain, the Netherlands, and from central Europe discontinuously across central Asia to Manchuria, south to the Red Sea, India and Ceylon; also Mauritania; between 53°N and 10°N. Northern populations migratory, wintering south to the Mediterranean, Kenya and southeast China.

P.l.leucorodia Linnaeus breeds entire range except southern Red Sea islands.

FB. Bred in England and Wales till 17th century.

SV. Small numbers recorded annually in East Anglia and southwest England, not infrequently on other coasts of England and Ireland (but mainly in the south), occasionally inland and in Wales and Scotland. Occurs singly and in small parties, and often lingers for long periods. Recorded regularly in all months, with a tendency in East Anglia for most to occur from May to July (rarely overwinters), and elsewhere for most to occur from September to March (individuals overwinter fairly regularly in southwest England and in Cork).

Order ANSERIFORMES

Family ANATIDAE

Genus CYGNUS Bechstein

Holarctic, Neotropical and Australasian genus of five to seven species, three in Palaearctic, all breeding in Europe and one in the British Isles, where the other two occur chiefly as winter visitors though one has bred.

Mute Swan
AC
Cygnus olor (Gmelin)

Palaearctic. Breeds British Isles and from southern Sweden, Denmark and the Netherlands discontinuously east across Europe and Siberia to Baikalia; between 60°N and 40°N. Partially migratory, wintering within the breeding range and beyond it south to the Mediterranean, south Iraq, northwest India, east China and Korea. Introduced in the eastern United States, Australia, New Zealand, and elsewhere.

Monotypic.

RB. Not scarce. Widely distributed, breeding throughout Britain and Ireland except Shetland and parts of northwest Scotland, most numerously in southern England; semi-domesticated in many places. Immigration and emigration probably mainly accidental or due to hard weather, but much local movement, particularly short-distance moult-migrations to form sizeable flocks on estuaries, in harbours or on large shallow inland waters.

Whooper Swan
A
Cygnus cygnus (Linnaeus)

Palaearctic. Breeds Iceland, northern Fenno-Scandia and across northern

Russia and Siberia to Anadyrland, Kamchatka and Sakhalin, north to the Arctic Circle or just beyond, south to about 60°N in Russia, 55°N in central Siberia, and 50°N in the far east; between 71°N and 47°N. Replaced by a close ally (perhaps race) in North America. Mainly migratory, wintering south to the Mediterranean and Caspian Seas, northwest India and southeast China.

Monotypic.

CB. Small numbers (some of which may be injured birds) remain in summer in northern Scotland and Ireland, occasionally breeding in Scotland, though rarely successfully; the most recent breeding records are 1939 and 1968.

WV. Immigrants, mostly from Iceland but probably also from northern Eurasia, arrive October–November and leave March or April, and winter throughout Scotland, northern England, north Wales and Ireland; recorded annually in English east coast counties south to Kent and in southwest England, but only erratically and in small numbers in central and southern England, most often in hard weather. No evidence of regular onward passage to the Continent.

Bewick's Swan   A
Cygnus bewickii Yarrell

Northern Palaearctic. Breeds southern Novaya Zemlya, Kolguev and Vaigach Islands, tundra of north Russia and Siberia from the Kanin Peninsula to the Kolyma, and in the far east also in the taiga zone; between 74°N and 61°N. Represented by a close ally (perhaps race) in North America. Winters in the British Isles, France, Netherlands and southern Scandinavia, and in eastern China and Japan.

Monotypic.

WV. Immigrants, probably from the western end of the breeding range, usually arrive in November, are most numerous January–February, and depart late March or early April. Regular in eastern (notably Yorkshire) and parts of southern England (notably on the Ouse Washes, Huntingdon/Cambridge/Norfolk, and at Slimbridge, Gloucester, with marked increases at both localities in recent years), Wales and, formerly most abundantly, Ireland, with numbers varying considerably from winter to winter; has greatly decreased in Scotland where now irregular except for very small numbers annually in Aberdeen.

Genus ANSER Brisson

Holarctic genus of nine species, eight in Palaearctic, four breeding in Europe, but only one in the British Isles, where four other species occur, two commonly, in winter.

Pink-footed Goose; Bean Goose   A
Anser fabalis (Latham)

Northern Palaearctic. Breeds east Greenland, Spitsbergen, Iceland; Scandinavia east to western Siberia, north to arctic coasts and southern Novaya Zemlya, south to 60–62°N; Siberia from the Yenisei to Anadyrland south to the Russian Altai; between 80°N and 49°N. Winters south to the British Isles, Mediterranean, Iran, south China and Japan.

A.f.brachyrhynchus Baillon (Pink-footed Goose) breeds east Greenland, Spitsbergen, Iceland; winters British Isles and north France to Germany.

A.f.fabalis (Latham) (Bean Goose) breeds forested tundras of northern Fenno-Scandia and Russia east to the Urals; winters northwest Europe (notably the Netherlands) south to the Mediterranean and Black Seas.

A.f.rossicus Buturlin (Bean Goose) breeds open tundras of south Novaya Zemlya, and the Yamal, Gydan and Taimyr Peninsulas; winters Netherlands, north Germany, and southeast to Russian Turkestan and central China.

WV. The whole population of *A.f.brachyrhynchus* from Greenland and Iceland winters in eastern, central and southern Scotland, south into Lancashire and Denbigh in the west, and to Yorkshire, Lincoln and Norfolk in the east, arriving mid-September to mid-October, leaving April to mid-May, and occurring on passage in the Hebrides and northwest Scotland at these times; occasional elsewhere (regular in Gloucester till very recently), accidental in southern England (usually during cold weather), and rare in Ireland. Birds from Spitsbergen occur only as stragglers. *A.f.fabalis* was formerly a common visitor to eastern and southern Scotland and eastern England, but now occurs regularly, in small numbers, only in Kirkcudbright, Northumberland and Norfolk, less regularly and in very small groups in Dunbarton, Cumberland, Lancashire, Lincoln and Gloucester, and occasionally elsewhere; rare in Ireland; regular flocks occur from late December to February, but stragglers accompanying flocks of *A.a.albifrons* may be found from

October to March; some stragglers in southern England resemble
A.f.rossicus.

White-fronted Goose A
Anser albifrons (Scopoli)

Northern Holarctic. Breeds tundras of northern Eurasia eastwards from
the Kanin Peninsula to the Bering Strait, into Alaska and northwest
Canada, and in west Greenland; between 76°N and 64°N. Winters in
the British Isles, continental Europe, and east in Asia to Iran, northern
India, China and Japan, and in the eastern United States and Mexico.

A.a.flavirostris Dalgety and Scott breeds Greenland; winters principally in the British Isles, also in eastern North America.

A.a.albifrons (Scopoli) breeds north Russia and Siberia east to the
Kolyma; winters Europe east to northern India.

WV. Winter visitors of nominate race *A.a.albifrons* arrive late
September–early October, main numbers not till December, and depart
March, occurring annually in about 30 localities in England and Wales
south from Lancashire and the Wash, their main strongholds being in
Gloucester, Hampshire, north Kent, Carmarthen and Montgomery/
Shropshire, in that order; in Scotland and Ireland this form is a scarce
vagrant, though it may formerly have occurred regularly in Fife and
elsewhere in east Scotland. Almost the entire stock of *A.a.flavirostris*,
arriving mid-September to October and remaining till April (occasionally a few into May), winters in the British Isles, principally in Ireland
but also in the Inner Hebrides, north and west Scotland and, in small
numbers, in Cumberland, Lancashire and Cardigan.

Lesser White-fronted Goose A
Anser erythropus (Linnaeus)

Northern Palaearctic. Breeds from northern Scandinavia across nor-
thern Russia and Siberia to Anadyrland, north to about 74°N on the
Taimyr Peninsula, south to the northern limit of the taiga (about 65°N
in east Siberia). Winters in southeast Europe, on the Black and Caspian
Seas, and in Turkestan, northwest India, China, and (now rarely) Japan.
Monotypic.

SV. About 79 identified, the great majority since 1945; almost
certainly overlooked before this. Nearly all December to March, a few
September–November, one (an injured bird) April–May: 49 at Slim-

bridge, Gloucester (all 1945–68), 16 Norfolk (1949–67), nine Kirkcudbright (1954–59); also Northumberland (September 1886), Lincoln
(January 1943), Cardigan (February 1955), Clackmannan (January 1960)
and Wigtown (March 1960).

Greylag Goose   AC
Anser anser (Linnaeus)

Palaearctic. Breeds Iceland, and from Scotland and Scandinavia across
mid-Eurasia to the Pacific, south to Germany, southeast Europe, Iran
and Turkestan; between 71°N and 30°N. Mainly migratory, wintering
within the breeding range and south to the Mediterranean basin,
northwest India and south China.

    A.a.anser (Linnaeus) breeds Europe, perhaps also in Asia Minor.

    RB and **IB**. Scarce native population is restricted to the Outer
Hebrides and the extreme north of the Scottish mainland and is reinforced by feral stocks in Sutherland, the Inner Hebrides and southwest
Scotland, also in Norfolk and Essex. Artificial redistribution of birds
from southwest Scotland to various parts of Britain, notably the
English Lake District, Yorkshire, Kent and Anglesey, has been carried
out successfully in recent years.

    WV. Immigrants from Iceland arrive mainly from mid-October
onwards and depart by mid-April, and winter chiefly in central and
southern Scotland. Although total numbers have greatly increased, the
winter range is shrinking northwards and few Greylag geese now come
south to northern England, Wales and Ireland, where they were formerly numerous in some localities. Continental populations do not
regularly visit Britain, but four ringed here in winter have reached
Norway and Denmark, and some stragglers recorded in southern England resemble east European rather than Icelandic or native breeding
birds. The whole Iceland population winters within the British Isles.

Snow Goose   A
Anser caerulescens (Linnaeus)

Northern Nearctic, marginally Palaearctic (extreme northeast). Breeds
Wrangel Island (formerly also on the continental tundra of east
Siberia), arctic coasts and islands of North America, and northwest
Greenland; between 76°N and 66°N. Winters in North America south
to California, Louisiana and North Carolina, rarely in China and Japan.

A.c.caerulescens (Linnaeus) (Lesser Snow Goose) breeds Wrangel Island east to southern Baffin Island.

A.c.atlanticus (Kennard) (Greater Snow Goose) breeds Ellesmere, north Baffin and Somerset Islands and Greenland.

SV. Ones, twos and very small groups occur almost annually in Scotland and Ireland, less often England, but it is impossible to determine the true status because the species is kept in many British and European collections of waterfowl and escapes are quite frequent; full-winged birds often join flocks of other species of wild geese, as do genuine vagrants. Recorded in all months August to May, most often in October and December; *A.c.caerulescens* and *A.c.atlanticus* both identified, the former probably most frequently (including a high and increasing proportion of blue-phase individuals), though many sight records of white geese are insufficiently detailed for the race (or sometimes even the species) to be decided.

Genus BRANTA Scopoli

Holarctic (also Hawaiian) genus of five species, four in Palaearctic, three breeding in Europe, one of these—an introduced species—breeding also in the British Isles, where three other species occur in winter, two of them regularly.

Canada Goose   AC
Branta canadensis (Linnaeus)

Northern Nearctic (formerly also northeastern Palaearctic). Breeds Alaska, Canada, western and north-central United States, and in western Greenland; between 70°N and 37°N. Mostly migratory, northern populations wintering within the United States. Introduced in several parts of Europe (notably Britain and Sweden) and in New Zealand.

B.c.canadensis (Linnaeus) breeds eastern Canada; introduced British stocks most closely resemble this race.

IB. Not scarce. First introduced to England in 17th century, now widespread in England, chiefly in private parks, with main strongholds in Norfolk, Yorkshire, Derby, Lancashire, Cheshire and Berkshire; recently introduced or artificially reinforced in south Wales, Anglesey and many English counties, west to Devon and north to Cumberland and Yorkshire; few in Scotland (north to Perth), where breeding population quite considerable in 1939 (2,000+ birds) but virtually eliminated 1939–45, and no very general recovery since then; some in Antrim and Down, but no other colonies now known in Ireland. Mostly sedentary, but a moult migration from Yorkshire to the Beauly Firth, Scotland, has developed in the last 20 years, and some other breeding groups disperse in winter. No regular emigration, though Yorkshire-ringed birds have reached France in hard weather.

SV. A few individuals resembling the smaller, northern races have been seen since 1958 in the Hebrides and Ireland (mostly Wexford, also Sligo, Longford, Offaly, Down) and seem more likely to be vagrants than escapes from captivity; but racial assignment is impossible.

Barnacle Goose   **A**
Branta leucopsis (Bechstein)

Extreme northwestern Palaearctic. Three separate stocks, breeding in (a) eastern Greenland, (b) Spitsbergen, (c) south Novaya Zemlya, and possibly Kolguev Island and other islands around the Kara Sea; between 80°N and 70°N. Winters in the British Isles and northwest Europe.
Monotypic.

WV. Greenland birds are widely distributed, late October to May, on islands off west and north coasts of Ireland, on mainland of Sligo and Wexford, on the Outer and Inner Hebrides and along coasts of west Ross and Sutherland. Spitsbergen birds winter from late September to April or early May on the Solway Firth (Kirkcudbright, Dumfries, Cumberland); small numbers also occur frequently in Northumberland and eastern Scotland on autumn passage, less often in winter and spring. Siberian birds have very recently become regular visitors in small numbers to Gloucester and Kent but previously were only stragglers to England. Some occurrences in unusual haunts are undoubtedly due to escapes from captivity.

Brent Goose   **A**
Branta bernicla (Linnaeus)

Northern Holarctic. Breeding distribution circumpolar on arctic islands and coasts of Siberia and North America (where known as Brant); between 83°N and 63°N. Winters British Isles, northwest Europe (France to Denmark), and on both coasts of North America south to Baja California and Virginia.

B.b.hrota (Müller)—the pale-bellied form—breeds arctic Canada from Prince Patrick Island east to north Greenland, Spitsbergen, Franz Josef Land; winters mainly on the Atlantic coast of North America, also in northwest Europe.

B.b.bernicla (Linnaeus)—the dark-bellied form—breeds Kolguev Island, southern Novaya Zemlya, Siberia east to about 110°E; winters northwest Europe.

B.b.nigricans (Lawrence)—which may be a distinct species—breeds eastern Siberia, Alaska, northwest Canada (overlapping there with *hrota*); winters chiefly on the Pacific coast of North America, also in east Asia.

WV. *B.b.bernicla* is a regular visitor, September to April, mainly November to March with the largest numbers (10–15,000 in recent years) in January, to the east and south coasts of England, from Northumberland to Devon, particularly in Essex and Norfolk. *B.b.hrota* now occurs regularly in England only in Northumberland, January to March: these birds are probably of the Spitsbergen-Franz Josef Land stock, which formerly also occurred in Scotland but has ceased to do so regularly; up to 12,000 *B.b.hrota* (probably from northern Greenland) winter around the Irish coast, from early September to April. Odd individuals or small groups of both these races have occurred erratically in many parts of Britain and Ireland.

SV. At least one individual of the race *B.b.nigricans* was observed in Essex in February 1957 and February 1958.

Red-breasted Goose A
Branta ruficollis (Pallas)

North central Palaearctic. Breeds tundras of west Siberia from the east side of the Yamal Peninsula eastwards to the Khatanga basin; between 73°N and 67°N. Winters around the southern part of the Caspian and Aral Seas, also in southeast Europe.

Monotypic.

SV. About 22 records of apparently wild birds (two 18th century, five 19th century, three 1909–41, twelve 1950–67), November to March where dates known. Eight (all this century) from Gloucester, the rest mainly in southern England from Devon to Norfolk, also in Yorkshire, Northumberland, Pembroke and Shropshire/Montgomery. Vagrants are usually associated with Eurasian White-fronted Geese *Anser albifrons albifrons*. (A few other recent records in various parts of

England and Scotland are due to escaped captive birds, as indeed may be some of those noted above.)

Genus ALOPOCHEN Stejneger

Ethiopian and Palaearctic monospecific genus, formerly breeding in Europe; introduced to the British Isles, where it breeds in a feral state.

Egyptian Goose   C
Alopochen aegyptiacus (Linnaeus)

Ethiopian and southwestern Palaearctic. Breeds Syria, Israel, Egypt south to Africa south of Sahara; between 35°N and 10°N; formerly bred in central Europe in the Danube valley, and in northwest Africa. Mainly sedentary.
Monotypic.
IB. Scarce. Introduced England in the 18th century and has long been found in a feral state in several parts of this country, in numbers only in East Anglia, and there mainly in Norfolk (Holkham Park and the Broads).

Genus TADORNA von Oken

Palaearctic, Ethiopian, Australasian and Oriental genus of seven species, three (one perhaps extinct) in Palaearctic, two breeding in Europe and one in the British Isles, where the other occurs as an irregular visitor.

Ruddy Shelduck   A
Tadorna ferruginea (Pallas)

Southern Palaearctic. Breeds (in small and decreasing numbers in Europe), northwest Africa, south Spain, Greece, Bulgaria, Rumania, Moldavia and Turkey, and across central Asia to Amurland and Manchuria south to Israel, Iraq, Iran, Afghanistan and south China; between 53°N and 25°N. Probably mainly migratory, wintering south to northern Sudan, Arabia, southern India, Indo-China and Korea.
Monotypic.
SV. Influx June–July 1886 (parties up to six), a more notable influx June–September 1892 (flocks of up to 20) in many places, especially Ireland. Otherwise in ones and twos, mostly in autumn and winter, in

at least 30 widely scattered counties in Britain and Ireland. Escapes from captivity undoubtedly distort the true picture, but probably very few wild birds have occurred in recent years.

Shelduck A
Tadorna tadorna (Linnaeus)

Southern and western Palaearctic. Breeds British Isles, Scandinavia and Baltic States south to northern France, and discontinuously from the Balkans across central Asia to Transbaicalia, south to Georgia, Iran, Iraq, Afghanistan and west China; between 59°N and 27°N. Sedentary and migratory, wintering south to northern Africa, northern India and Burma.

Monotypic.

MB and **RB**. Fairly numerous. Widely distributed, breeding in flat coastal areas and estuaries in virtually every maritime county in Britain and Ireland (not certainly in Denbigh, Berwick, Banff and Leitrim); also very locally (but increasingly) inland in several parts, including Cambridge, Huntingdon and Nottingham in England, and on a few inland waters in Scotland and Ireland. Except in their first year, nearly all British birds migrate to northwest Germany or to Bridgwater Bay, Somerset, to moult; most juveniles also leave the breeding places in autumn. Small numbers occur regularly on passage on waters in most inland counties, though the bulk of the migrant population passes over inland areas without stopping.

WV. Extent of immigration not known, but birds ringed as young in Sweden, Norway, Denmark, Netherlands and Belgium have been found in Britain.

Genus AIX Boie

Holarctic genus of two species, one in the eastern Palaearctic; introduced to the British Isles, where it breeds in a feral state.

Mandarin Duck C
Aix galericulata (Linnaeus)

Eastern Palaearctic. Breeds from the Amur valley south through Ussuriland and Manchuria to northeast (perhaps also southeast) China and Japan. Mainly sedentary.

Monotypic.

IB. Scarce. As the result of escapes from captivity and deliberate releases in several parts of the country during this century, it has established itself as a breeding resident in southeast England, notably in Surrey and Berkshire, and also very locally elsewhere in England and in Perth.

Genus ANAS Linnaeus

Cosmopolitan genus of 39 species, eleven in Palaearctic, nine breeding in Europe and seven in the British Isles, where three others (from the Nearctic) have occurred as vagrants.

Wigeon   A
Anas penelope Linnaeus

Northern Palaearctic. Breeds Iceland, British Isles, and from northern Germany and Scandinavia east across northern Eurasia to Anadyrland and Kamchatka, south to central Russia, the southern Altai and Lake Baikal, also erratically farther south; between 73°N and 48°N. Winters in western and southern Europe, in Africa from Nigeria in the west to the level of the equator in the east, Arabia, India, Indo-China, southern China and the Philippines; a few reach North America.

Monotypic.

RB. Scarce. Breeds locally in the Northern Isles, more widely on the Scottish mainland south to Kincardine, Kinross, Stirling and Argyll, and very locally in southern Scotland (mainly Selkirk) and northern England south to northwest Yorkshire; breeds occasionally elsewhere, most often in East Anglia (due possibly to escaped birds) and north Wales, and only twice in Ireland. Most, if not all, migrate short distances, Scottish birds going to Ireland, but there is no certain evidence that any reach the Continent.

WV and **PV**. Immigrants greatly outnumber natives from September to March and winter regularly in all counties in Britain and Ireland, but especially on the coast. Immigrants from Iceland winter in Ireland, Scotland and northern England; few come here from Scandinavia; many in southern England are from northern Russia and west Siberia. Little indication of onward passage to France, but there are several recoveries of British-ringed birds from Italy in late winter.

American Wigeon A
Anas americana Gmelin

Nearctic. Breeds in North America from Alaska east to Hudson Bay and Manitoba, south to northeast California and Indiana; between 67°N and 40°N. Winters on both coasts of the United States, from British Columbia and Long Island south to the Gulf coast and to Costa Rica and the West Indies.
Monotypic.

SV. About 50 recorded (plus others regarded as probably having escaped from captivity), including four records of two together and one of a party of 13 in Kerry in October 1968 (with one still at the same locality in December 1968). These last birds apart, the records are for May (a pair), June (one), and September to March, with most in February; chiefly in Scotland (about 20) and England (about 11), also five (plus the 13 above) in Ireland and one in Wales. Most records are of males, or in some cases females accompanied by males. First-year birds recovered in Shetland (female, October 1966) and Kerry (male, October 1968) had been ringed in New Brunswick, Canada.

Gadwall A
Anas strepera Linnaeus

Holarctic. Breeds Iceland, British Isles, and from the Netherlands and southern Sweden across eastern Europe and Asia to Transbaicalia (and probably locally to Kamchatka), north to about 55°N, south to the Balkans, Iran, Afghanistan and Turkestan; also in North America, principally in the western Prairies; between 66°N and 30°N. Mostly migratory; winters in the south of the breeding range and south to north Africa, Iraq, Arabia, India, south China, Mexico and Florida.
Monotypic.

IB, RB and **MB.** Scarce. Distributed very locally (due in part to introductions), with strongholds in Norfolk (introduced 1850), Suffolk, Kinross (and adjacent parts of Perth and Fife), with smaller groups established especially in the last 40 years in the Isles of Scilly, Somerset, Surrey, Kent, Essex, Gloucester, Yorkshire and the Inner Hebrides; sporadically elsewhere in England, Scotland and northern and south-west Ireland, perhaps increasing, assisted by further introductions. Native birds disperse widely for the winter, many going to Europe.

WV. Immigrants, from Iceland and north European range, present from August to April in small numbers. Winter distribution not adequately appraised, but regular wintering flocks in various maritime counties in Ireland and locally in west Scotland from the Outer Hebrides to Kirkcudbright are presumably composed mainly of Icelandic birds, while those in eastern and southern England, as well as small numbers in south Wales, are perhaps of European origin. There is no evidence of any substantial passage of transient visitors.

Teal A
Anas crecca Linnaeus

Holarctic. Breeds Iceland, British Isles, continental Europe from northern Fenno-Scandia south to France, Italy and the Balkans, across Asia to Anadyrland, Kamchatka and Japan, Aleutians, North America from Alaska to Newfoundland, south to California, and the central and northeast United States; between 73°N and 37°N. Winters south to tropical Africa, India, the Philippines, central America and Antilles.

A.c.crecca Linnaeus breeds Palaearctic part of range.

A.c.carolinensis Gmelin breeds North America except Aleutians.

RB. Not scarce. Breeds throughout Scotland, northern England, Ireland and very thinly over most of Wales, most numerous in Scotland though nowhere abundant; also very locally in central and southern England, mainly in coastal counties, though odd pairs occasionally well inland. British birds believed not to migrate regularly, although moving to Ireland, France and Spain in cold weather. *A.c.crecca.*

WV and **PV.** Residents greatly outnumbered from September to April by winter visitors and passage migrants from Iceland, Scandinavia, the Baltic States and northwest Russia, those from Iceland wintering mainly in Scotland and Ireland, while those from the east predominate in the south and east of England. Onward movements to Ireland, France and Iberia (and exceptionally farther) vary greatly from year to year, and are most marked and extensive in hard weather. *A.c.crecca.*

SV. About 50 males (females not identifiable) of the American race *A.c.carolinensis* reported (three before 1880, five 1936–50, the rest since 1951, annually in recent years), October to May, most March, April and November; England 25 (in 15 counties), Ireland eleven, Scotland twelve, Wales two together (Cardigan).

Mallard   A
Anas platyrhynchos Linnaeus

Holarctic. Breeds southern Greenland, Iceland, Faeroes, British Isles, continental Eurasia, mainly between limits 70°N and 40°N (but south also to Iran), east to Kamchatka and the Commander Islands; also northwest Africa, and North America south to central Mexico; between 70°N and 20°N. Sedentary and migratory; winters south to north Africa, Iraq, central India, southeast China, Mexico and the Antilles. Introduced New Zealand.

A.p.platyrhynchos Linnaeus breeds in entire range except Greenland and southern North America.

RB. Fairly numerous. Very widely distributed, breeding in every county in Britain and Ireland, though scarce in some western districts, especially northwest Scotland. British breeders do not usually migrate, though some may move to France or Ireland in hard weather, while the population of southeast England is continuous with that of the Netherlands. Artificial rearing and re-stocking is widely practised.

WV. Immigrants, arriving September to December, departing February to April, come from Iceland (few), Scandinavia, the Low Countries, Baltic and Russia; few immigrants reach west Britain and Ireland, while those in the north are mostly Scandinavian. In harder winters late influxes may occur, some visitors moving to France or Ireland, but there can be little regular passage.

Black Duck   A
Anas rubripes Brewster

Eastern Nearctic. Breeds eastern North America from the west side of Hudson Bay and Labrador south to North Carolina, now spreading slowly westwards in the north of the Mississippi basin and south of the Prairie provinces of Canada; between 60°N and 35°N. Winters in southeast United States.

Monotypic.

SV. Four: Kilkenny (February 1954), Wexford (February 1961, November 1966), Kent (March 1967).

Pintail   A
Anas acuta Linnaeus

Holarctic, and islands in south Indian Ocean. Breeds Iceland, British

Isles, most of Eurasia north of 50°N to arctic coasts, most of North America south to California, the central United States and Pennsylvania, and west Greenland; between 73°N and 35°N; also Kerguelen and neighbouring islands in the Indian Ocean. Winters south to western and central Europe, Nigeria, Tanzania, Arabia, India, Philippines, Colombia and Guyana.

A.a.acuta Linnaeus breeds entire range except islands of south Indian Ocean.

RB or **MB**. Very scarce. Small numbers now breed regularly in at least two separate areas in eastern England (Cambridge/Norfolk and Kent), probably regularly in Aberdeen, Inverness and Caithness, and occasionally elsewhere in Scotland (notably in Kinross), northern England and Northern Ireland; some attempts at introduction, probably not lastingly successful. Very little is known of winter movements of the breeding population.

WV and **PV**. Immigrants from Iceland, northern Scandinavia, Russia and west Siberia, present September to April, distributed locally but widely throughout Britain and Ireland, chiefly in sandy or muddy estuaries, though also recorded annually in most inland counties. There is some onward movement to France, Spain, and occasionally beyond.

Garganey A
Anas querquedula Linnaeus

Palaearctic. Breeds England, southern Scandinavia and Finno-Karelia south in Europe to France, north Italy and the Black Sea, also in the Caucasus and Iran, and across middle Asia to Sakhalin and Kamchatka; between 64°N and 35°N. Usually winters far to the south of the breeding range in subtropical and tropical Africa and Asia, reaching as far south as the Transvaal and Philippines, and even (though perhaps not regularly) New Guinea and Australia.

Monotypic.

MB. Very scarce. Small, vary variable numbers breed regularly in southeast England from Sussex and Kent north to Cambridge and Norfolk, and (at present) also in Somerset and Yorkshire, and sporadically in many other English counties, in the period 1958–68 west to the Isles of Scilly, Monmouth, Cardigan and Lancashire, and north to Northumberland; has bred at least once in Scotland (1928) and Wales (1936) and twice in Ireland (Armagh 1956, Kerry 1959). Resident from March to September.

PV. Numbers in spring are often considerably larger than the likely nesting population, but the scale of passage in late summer and autumn is obscure; occurs regularly at both seasons in parts of England and Wales where does not breed, also in very small numbers in Scotland and Ireland. Individuals have occasionally been recorded in winter.

Blue-winged Teal A
Anas discors Linnaeus

Eastern Nearctic. Breeds from central plains of the United States and the Canadian prairie provinces east to Nova Scotia and North Carolina; between 50°N and 36°N. Winters from the southern United States and West Indies south to Peru and Guyana.

Monotypic. (Two doubtful races have been distinguished.)

SV. At least 29 (two 1858 to about 1860, five 1910–40, remainder 1949–68); all September to January apart from one February, one April–May, and one April–August. Records from Ireland (ten), England (nine, widely scattered), Scotland (eight, six of these in Outer Hebrides, including two together twice; the others Orkney and Dumfries) and Wales (two).

Shoveler A
Anas clypeata (Linnaeus)

Holarctic. Breeds Iceland (recent, small numbers only), and from Scandinavia, British Isles and France east through Europe and Asia to the Kolyma and Kamchatka, south to the Caucasus, northwest China and Sakhalin; also in western and central North America; between 73°N and 35°N. Winters from west, central and southeast Europe south to tropical (occasionally southern) Africa, Ceylon, Philippines, Costa Rica and Antilles.

Monotypic.

MB and **RB.** Scarce. Widely but somewhat locally distributed throughout Britain and Ireland, though extremely scarce or absent in central and western Scottish Highlands, also very sparsely distributed in Wales and over much of central and western southern England. Most breeding birds emigrate, to or through the Netherlands and France and to Iberia, Italy and Morocco (and from Britain to Ireland).

WV and **PV.** Immigrants from northwest Russia and the south Baltic countries, arriving November, remaining till March or April, are widely distributed in winter in Britain and Ireland north to southern Scotland. Numbers are increased in spring by returning natives and probably by passage migrants.

Genus NETTA Kaup

Palaearctic, Ethiopian and Neotropical genus of three species, one breeding in Europe and wandering to the British Isles.

Red-crested Pochard   A
Netta rufina (Pallas)

Southern Palaearctic. Breeds very locally in Europe from the Netherlands and Denmark south to Spain and the Balkans, in Asia from the northern Caucasus east to Mongolia and south to the Pamirs and Chinese Turkestan; isolated groups occur farther south, including in northwest Africa; between 55°N and 30°N. Winters in the south of the breeding range, around the Mediterranean, and in Iraq, Iran, India and Burma.

Monotypic.

CB. Bred Lincoln 1937, Essex 1958; but both cases probably refer to pairs which had escaped from captivity.

SV. Scarce vagrant, recorded very infrequently prior to 1948 but annually since then, in very small numbers; particularly numerous 1951–61 when 30–50 seen each year, principally in Essex, but some of these probably 'escapes'; most early records September to March, but recently noted in all months, especially September to December; recorded from at least 26 counties in England, two in Wales, seven in Scotland and six in Ireland.

Genus AYTHYA Boie

Holarctic, Australasian, Ethiopian and Oriental genus of twelve species, five in Palaearctic, four breeding in Europe, two regularly and one occasionally in the British Isles, where the fourth is a scarce visitor and a fifth, from the Nearctic, has also been recorded.

Pochard   A
Aythya ferina (Linnaeus)

Palaearctic. Breeds Iceland (recent, very few), British Isles, southern Fenno-Scandia and central Russia south to France, Hungary, and the north shore of the Black Sea; in Asia east to the Baikal region, mainly between 60°N and 45°N; sporadic breeding occurs farther south, including northwest Africa. Largely migratory; winters within the breeding range and south to northwest Africa, Nigeria, Sudan, Arabia, Iran, India, Burma, southeast China and Japan.

Monotypic.

MB and **RB**. Scarce. Widely but very locally distributed on shallow lakes chiefly in the eastern half of Britain from Kent north to Inverness and Moray, regularly also at one or two waters in western Britain (Somerset, perhaps Anglesey, Lancashire, Renfrew) and at one in Ireland (Roscommon); very erratic elsewhere, though has bred in most English counties, many in Scotland north to Sutherland and Orkney, and on a few occasions in south Wales and Ireland. Few breeders are resident at their breeding waters, but the extent of their movements is not known.

WV and **PV**. Immigrants, from the Baltic area, central Europe, Russia and west Siberia, arrive September to November and leave March to April; they are distributed widely in all parts of Britain and Ireland in winter, mainly on inland waters. Probably very few passage migrants occur in autumn, but there are more in spring.

Ring-necked Duck   **A**
Aythya collaris (Donovan)

Nearctic. Breeds in North America from British Columbia, northern Mackenzie, Quebec and Newfoundland south to east California, Colorado, northern Iowa and Maine; between 62°N and 40°N. Winters on the Atlantic and Pacific coasts of the United States, and from the southern states south to Panama and Cuba.

Monotypic.

SV. Nine or more: Gloucester (March 1955), Berkshire (April (1959), Armagh (March–May 1960, and almost certainly the same individual in most subsequent winters to at least 1968, with a second bird nearby in Down in 1966 and 1967, and in Armagh, at times with the first bird, in 1968), Norfolk (April 1962), Inverness (January 1963), Berkshire/Oxford (January–March 1967, again in February 1968), Pembroke (February–March 1967), Cambridge (January 1968). The original description of the species was of a specimen found in Leadenhall Market, London, in January 1801, said to have been taken in Lincoln.

Ferruginous Duck   **A**
Aythya nyroca (Güldenstädt)

Central and southwestern Palaearctic. Breeds very locally (in decreasing numbers in western and central Europe) from Spain through southern and central Europe (north to Poland) east through southern Russia, Asia Minor, and southwest Siberia to Tibet; also in northwest Africa; between 60°N and 30°N. Winters in southern parts of the breeding range and beyond it reaching as far south as Nigeria, Kenya, Arabia, India and the Yangtse in China.
Monotypic.
SV. Over 200 recorded, nearly all September to April, and most in central and southern England, particularly East Anglia; very few in Scotland, Wales or Ireland. Recent records average about five each year (though some may refer to escapes from captivity).

Tufted Duck   **A**
Aythya fuligula (Linnaeus)

Palaearctic. Breeds Iceland, British Isles, and from Scandinavia through northern Eurasia to Kamchatka, south to Belgium, north Germany, the Ukraine, Russian Altai, Amur basin, and north Japan; between 70°N and 45°N. Mostly migratory, wintering in the south of the breeding range and beyond it to north Africa, Arabia, India, Vietnam and the Philippines.
Monotypic.
RB. Not scarce. Widely distributed following a marked increase and spread over the last 80 years; now breeds regularly throughout the country except in parts of southwest England, Wales, northwest Scotland, and the extreme south of Ireland; large breeding concentrations occur on Lough Neagh (Northern Ireland) and Loch Leven (Kinross). Some breeding birds are perhaps sedentary, but most move away from the breeding sites, though there is little evidence of emigration.
WV. Immigrants present throughout the country, September to April, those from Iceland wintering in Ireland and Scotland, those from northern Europe (chiefly Finland and northwest Russia) and middle Europe (Netherlands to Czechoslovakia and Baltic) wintering mainly in southeast England.

Scaup A
Aythya marila (Linnaeus)

Northern Holarctic. Breeds Iceland, Fenno-Scandia, northern Russia and Siberia, Aleutian Islands, Canada east to Hudson Bay, nearly everywhere south to 60°N; sporadically farther south, in Faeroes, Britain, around the south Baltic and in eastern Canada; between 74°N and 50°N. Winters British Isles, coasts of Europe, the Black and Caspian Seas, Persian Gulf, north India, Korea, North America south to Mexico, Florida, and Cuba.

Monotypic.

CB. Has bred Caithness, Sutherland, west Ross, the Outer Hebrides and Orkney; perhaps breeds in Scotland annually but not known to be regular anywhere and numbers are very small; also bred Lincoln in 1944, while infertile clutches were laid in Suffolk in 1967 and 1968.

WV and **PV**. Some are present throughout the year but substantial numbers occur only from October to March, chiefly around coasts of northern Ireland, Scotland, and north and east England; scarcer and mostly irregular inland (though numbers occur on Lough Neagh, Northern Ireland) and on southwestern coasts. Scale of passage not known but visitors from Iceland also reach France and the European North Sea coast. Ringing recoveries show that there is some immigration from Russia and Fenno-Scandia.

Genus SOMATERIA Leach

Holarctic genus of three species, all in Palaearctic, two breeding in Europe, and one in the British Isles, where the other occurs as an irregular visitor.

Eider A
Somateria mollissima (Linnaeus)

Northern Holarctic. Breeding distribution almost circumpolar on arctic coasts and islands, and south to Iceland, Faeroes, British Isles, Brittany, Baltic region, Aleutians, south Alaska, Maine and south Greenland; between 82°N and 45°N. Mostly sedentary, though some move south in winter.

S.m.mollissima (Linnaeus) breeds British Isles and northern continental Europe; also Novaya Zemlya.

RB. Not scarce. Breeds regularly around northern coasts from Northumberland north to Moray, in Sutherland, Caithness, Orkney, Shetland, the Outer Hebrides, most Inner Hebrides, Bute, Arran and the west coast of Scotland from southwest Ross to Wigtown (scarcer in the southwest), also on Walney Island (Lancashire), and in northern Ireland from Sligo to Down. Non-breeders occur throughout the year off many other parts of England and in south Wales and have generally increased, like the breeders, in recent years. Some local movements but no evidence of long-distance migrations. Very rare inland.

WV. Ringing recoveries show that some birds from the Netherlands and Denmark reach the east and northeast coasts of Britain.

King Eider A
Somateria spectabilis (Linnaeus)

Northern Holarctic. Breeding distribution circumpolar on coasts of Spitsbergen, arctic Russia and Siberia, Alaska, Canada and Greenland; between 83°N and 60°N; has bred north Norway. Largely sedentary, some moving south and occasionally wandering to northwest Europe and the United States.

Monotypic.

SV. About 70 (mostly males—females probably overlooked), perhaps more numerous 1870–1900 than since, and only eight records 1958–68. Noted in all months, most often November–December; chiefly in Scotland (especially Shetland, Orkney, Angus and Fife), where there is a tendency for recent records to be in May–July, also on the English east coast (Northumberland, Yorkshire, Norfolk, Kent) and around Ireland (Antrim, Down, Cork, Mayo); none Wales.

Genus POLYSTICTA Eyton

Holarctic monospecific genus, breeding marginally and sporadically in Europe, and occurring as a rare vagrant in the British Isles.

Steller's Eider A
Polysticta stelleri (Pallas)

Northern Palaearctic, northwestern Nearctic. Breeds on coasts of northeast Siberia (west to the Lena delta and sporadically west to south Novaya Zemlya and Finnmark), west and north Alaska, and extreme

northwest Canada. Winters chiefly in the Bering Sea area, off northern Norway (where occurs also in summer), and in the Baltic.
Monotypic.

SV. Five records involving six birds: Norfolk (February 1830), Yorkshire (August 1845), Orkney (two in January 1947; November 1949), Sutherland (September 1959).

Genus HISTRIONICUS Lesson

Monospecific genus of discontinuous circumpolar distribution, breeding in Greenland and Iceland, but occurring only as a vagrant in the British Isles and continental Europe.

Harlequin Duck A
Histrionicus histrionicus (Linnaeus)

Holarctic. Breeds Greenland, Iceland, eastern Siberia south to Sakhalin and inland to the Lena and Lake Baikal, Commander and Aleutian Islands, western North America from Alaska to California, islands of northeast Canada south to Hudson Bay and central Labrador; between 70°N and 40°N. Partly migratory, moving south within or just beyond the breeding range in winter, reaching Korea, California and Massachusetts and occasionally farther south still.
Monotypic.

SV. Seven records involving nine or eleven individuals: Yorkshire (autumn 1862), Northumberland (December 1886, two records involving three birds), Lancashire (winter 1914–15 or 1915–16), Outer Hebrides (February 1931), Roxburgh (January 1954), Fair Isle (January–February 1965, two), Caithness (April–May 1965, two, believed to have been the Fair Isle birds).

Genus CLANGULA Leach

Monospecific genus of circumpolar distribution, breeding in northern Europe but only sporadically in the British Isles, where it occurs chiefly as a winter visitor.

Long-tailed Duck A
Clangula hyemalis (Linnaeus)

Northern Holarctic. Breeding distribution circumpolar, Iceland, Spitsbergen, Scandinavia, tundra of Russia and Siberia, islands of Bering Sea, Alaska, arctic Canada south to Hudson Bay and Labrador, and Greenland; mainly between 83°N and 60°N. Winters at sea south to northern France, and the Baltic, Caspian and Bering Seas; also on the Great Lakes and Atlantic coast of America south to Maryland.

Monotypic.

CB. Is believed to have bred on three occasions in Shetland in the 19th century; bred Orkney 1911, probably also in 1912 and 1926, but not recently.

WV. Apparently most numerous November to February, fewer in autumn and spring and very few in summer; principally off the Northern Isles and British east coast, also in northwest Scotland and north and northwest Ireland; but rather scarce in west and southwest Britain; accidental inland, though has been recorded at least once in practically every British county in recent years. Status as passage migrant is uncertain, but the species sometimes occurs in very small numbers with eastward movements of Common Scoters *Melanitta nigra* in the English Channel in spring.

Genus MELANITTA Boie

Holarctic genus of three species, two in Palaearctic, both breeding in Europe and one in the British Isles, where the other European species occurs as a non-breeding visitor and the Nearctic species as a scarce vagrant.

Common Scoter   **A**
Melanitta nigra (Linnaeus)

Northern Palaearctic and northwestern Nearctic. Breeds Iceland, Faeroes, British Isles, Scandinavia east to the Taimyr Peninsula; northeast Siberia, Aleutian Islands, western Alaska, and occasionally northern Canada; between 75°N and 50°N. Winters on Atlantic coasts south to South Carolina and northwest Africa, on Pacific coasts south to east China and California, in the North, Baltic, Mediterranean, Black and Caspian Seas, and on the Great Lakes.

M.n.nigra (Linnaeus) breeds from Iceland east to the Taimyr Peninsula.

RB or **MB.** Scarce. Small numbers breed regularly in north Scotland in Sutherland, Ross and south to north Perth, irregularly in Shetland, Orkney, the Inner Hebrides and Caithness; has bred Fife; also breeds regularly in Fermanagh and Mayo in Ireland. It is not known where the breeding population winters.

WV and **PV**. May be seen in large numbers offshore for most of the year, many males assembling in late summer, particularly off east Scotland, joined later by females and juveniles; generally more numerous on the east coast than the west, and in the northeast English Channel the species is especially numerous on eastward passage in spring (chiefly April); an apparent decline off Irish coasts in very recent years has not been evident elsewhere.

Surf Scoter   A
Melanitta perspicillata (Linnaeus)

Nearctic. Breeds northern North America from Alaska to Labrador, principally in Mackenzie District; also found in summer from northeast Siberia to Greenland; but breeding not recorded. Winters on coasts of North America south to California and Florida, and on the Great Lakes.

Monotypic.

SV. Under 100 recorded (females and immatures ordinarily indistinguishable from *M.fusca* when swimming, so accepted records are nearly all of males), August to May, with no clear seasonal peaks, nor trends in abundance during this century. Records are chiefly from Shetland and Orkney, also the Outer Hebrides, Kirkcudbright, Cumberland and Lancashire on the west coast, Caithness south to Yorkshire on the east coast, and Sussex to the Isles of Scilly on the south coast; only seven or eight in Ireland; none Wales.

Velvet Scoter   A
Melanitta fusca (Linnaeus)

Northern Holarctic. Breeds from Fenno-Scandia (including Baltic coasts) east across northern Eurasia to Kamchatka, south to Estonia, 53°N in western Siberia and Lake Baikal; and from Alaska east to Manitoba, south to Washington and North Dakota; between 71°N and 48°N; may also breed at least occasionally as far south as Armenia and Transcaucasia. Winters along Atlantic, North Sea and Baltic coasts of Europe, on American Atlantic coast to South Carolina, the Great Lakes, and on Pacific coasts south to California and east China.

M.f.fusca (Linnaeus) breeds western Palaearctic part of range.

WV and **PV**. Widespread, usually only in small groups, around British north and east coasts, south to the eastern English Channel, where variable (but generally small and decreasing) numbers occur on passage, October–November and March–May, as well as in winter; elsewhere recorded chiefly October to May, but some remain throughout the summer. It is scarce on western coasts and in most counties is irregular; rare in Ireland and inland. Breeding in north Scotland has been suspected, notably in Shetland in 1945, but there are no confirmed records.

Genus BUCEPHALA Baird

Holarctic genus of three species, two in Palaearctic and breeding in Europe (one of them in Iceland only), one occurring mainly as a winter visitor to the British Isles, where the purely Nearctic species has also been recorded on a few occasions.

Bufflehead   A
Bucephala albeola (Linnaeus)

Northern Nearctic. Breeds in wooded regions of northern North America, from southern Alaska east to Hudson Bay, south to British Columbia; between 66°N and 46°N. Winters in the United States and northern Mexico.
Monotypic.
SV. Five: Norfolk (about 1830), Yorkshire (winter 1864–65), Isles of Scilly (January 1920), Norfolk (February 1932), Buckingham (February–March 1961).

Goldeneye   A
Bucephala clangula (Linnaeus)

Holarctic. Breeds Scandinavia, south Baltic States, north Russia and Siberia between about 67°N and 50°N, east to Kamchatka; also in southern Alaska south to the northern United States and across Canada south of Hudson Bay to Newfoundland; between 70°N and 45°N. Winters from the British Isles and Baltic south to the Mediterranean and Black Seas, Iraq and Iran; also in central Asia, east China, Japan, and in North America south to the southern United States.
B.c.clangula (Linnaeus) breeds Palaearctic part of range.

CB. Said to have bred in Cheshire in 1931 and 1932, and breeding suspected in Scotland, where a few remain each summer.

WV and **PV.** Winter visitors, from Scandinavia and perhaps farther east, arrive mainly October to November and depart March to early May, and occur in all parts of the British Isles except southwest Ireland, where irregular. Particularly numerous and in largest flocks in Northern Ireland, eastern Scotland and Essex. Largest numbers are recorded in autumn and March, suggesting onward passage of some British visitors to undetermined wintering places.

Genus MERGUS Linnaeus

Palaearctic, Nearctic, Neotropical, Oriental and Australasian genus of seven species, four in Palaearctic, three breeding in Europe and two in the British Isles, where the third is a regular winter visitor and a fourth, Nearctic, species has also been recorded.

Hooded Merganser   A
Mergus cucullatus Linnaeus

Nearctic. Breeds from southeast Alaska in a broad band across North America at the latitude of the Canadian-United States border, south to Oregon in the west and Florida in the east; between 65°N and 30°N. Winters in the southern United States and Mexico, particularly along the Atlantic and Pacific coasts.

Monotypic.

SV. Four records concerning five birds: Menai Strait, north Wales (winter 1830–31), Cork (two in December 1878), Kerry (January 1881), Armagh (December 1957).

Smew   A
Mergus albellus Linnaeus

Northern Palaearctic. Breeds in extreme north of Fenno-Scandia and across parts of Russia and Siberia to Anadyrland and Kamchatka; between 69°N and 54°N. Winters in the British Isles, France, around the Mediterranean and Black Seas, Iraq, Iran, north India, east China and Japan.

Monotypic.

WV. Winter visitors of unknown origin are resident from November to April (exceptionally in other months) and are usually most plentiful in January and February. Noted chiefly on waters in southern England, particularly on reservoirs around London, though numbers always rather small; elsewhere scarce and irregular, and rare in Ireland. No evidence of passage.

Red-breasted Merganser A
Mergus serrator Linnaeus

Northern Holarctic. Breeds Iceland, Faeroes, British Isles, Scandinavia, Denmark, Baltic States, across northern Russia and Siberia south to Lake Baikal and beyond, on islands of the Bering Sea, in much of Alaska and Canada south to the northern United States, and southern Greenland; between 75°N and 45°N. Winters on coasts from Iceland to northwest Africa, south Iran, eastern Asia south to south China, and North America south to Baja California and Florida.

Monotypic.

RB. Not scarce. Breeds regularly in all counties in Scotland north and west of the Tay, including all the major islands and southwest Scotland (Ayr, Wigtown, Kirkcudbright and Dumfries); since about 1950 has spread into Cumberland, Westmorland, north Lancashire and west Yorkshire in northern England (also bred Lincoln 1961), and to Anglesey, Caernarvon, Merioneth and probably north Cardigan in north Wales, while a pair probably bred in Glamorgan in 1967; breeds regularly in most northern and western counties in Ireland, and in some central counties east to Dublin and southeast to Wexford. Most breeding haunts are deserted in winter, but there is no evidence that British or Irish birds emigrate.

WV. Immigrants from Iceland and probably Scandinavia present September to May, when the species is widespread and common in Scotland, chiefly around coasts; frequent but less numerous on the east, south and northwest coasts of England and in north Wales and Ireland; scarcer in south Wales and southwest England; casual inland in England, though it has occurred in recent years in all counties, annually on reservoirs around London. No evidence of passage.

Goosander A
Mergus merganser Linnaeus

Holarctic. Breeds Iceland, British Isles, Scandinavia south to east France,

Switzerland and Rumania, eastwards through Russia and Siberia to Anadyrland, Kamchatka and Sakhalin, with a central Asian stock in Afghanistan, the Altai and Tibet; also widely in North America south to Mexico in the west and New York in the east; between 71°N and 30°N. Mainly migratory, wintering south to the Mediterranean, Persian Gulf, north India, east China, north Mexico and Florida.

M.m.merganser Linnaeus breeds Europe and northern Asia.

RB. Scarce. Scotland was first colonized about 1871; the species now breeds regularly from Sutherland south to Angus and Perth in the east and to Wigtown, Kirkcudbright and Dumfries in the west, and also in Selkirk; absent from eastern-central Scotland and the Hebrides (has bred Inner Hebrides); in England breeds regularly in Northumberland, Cumberland, Westmorland and north Lancashire. Mainly resident, moving only short distances outside the breeding season to sheltered estuaries or large fresh-water lakes.

WV. Immigrants from Scandinavia and northwest Russia supplement residents in Scotland and provide most winter visitors to central and southeast England, from October to April; scarce in extreme south and southwest England, irregular in the Isle of Man, west Wales and Ireland. No evidence of passage.

Genus OXYURA Bonaparte

Cosmopolitan genus of six species, one in Palaearctic, breeding also in Europe; one introduced American species now breeds in the British Isles.

Ruddy Duck C
Oxyura jamaicensis (Gmelin)

Nearctic and Neotropical. Breeds from British Columbia and probably northern Manitoba south through the western United States, Central America, and northwest South America to Peru and Bolivia; also in the Antilles. Sedentary and migratory, northern populations wintering south to Mexico and Florida.

O.j.jamaicensis (Gmelin) breeds in the West Indies and (this or very poorly marked race '*rubida*') northwest central North America.

IB. Introduced; apparently now firmly established. Within recent years small numbers have begun to breed regularly in Gloucester and

Somerset, the original colonists having escaped from captivity; also bred Hertford in 1965 and Stafford in 1969, while birds have been seen at various times of the year in several other parts of central and southern England.

Order FALCONIFORMES

Family PANDIONIDAE

Genus PANDION Savigny

Cosmopolitan monospecific genus, breeding in Europe and in small numbers in the British Isles.

Osprey   **A**
Pandion haliaetus (Linnaeus)

Cosmopolitan. Breeds Scotland, Fenno-Scandia, Germany and the Mediterranean, east across Eurasia to Kamchatka, Japan, China and the Himalayas; North America south to Baja California and West Indies; and, mainly in coastal areas, northwest and east Africa, Arabia, Philippines and Indonesia south to Australia and Tasmania; between 69°N and 44°S. Migratory and sedentary, northern populations wintering south to the Mediterranean, Africa, India, Philippines, Sundas and South America.

P.h.haliaetus (Linnaeus) breeds throughout the Old World range, except the Philippines, Indonesia and Australasia.

MB. Extremely rare. One or two pairs have nested Inverness since 1954 or 1955 after an increase of summer records in Scotland during the previous few years; a third pair nested elsewhere in Scotland in 1967; in 1968 three pairs nested and two others built but did not lay. Bred more numerously in Scotland in the 19th century; reduced to two pairs by 1900, one breeding till 1916. Resident from April to August or early September.

PV. Passage, probably mainly of Scandinavian birds (nine Swedish-ringed birds have been recovered in England and Scotland), April to

May and August to October, occasionally March, June, July and November, very rarely December to February. Small numbers only—usually not more than 10 to 15 records in spring and 25 to 30 in autumn. Most regular in southern England, but has occurred in most British and Irish counties.

Family ACCIPITRIDAE

Genus PERNIS Cuvier

Palaearctic and Oriental genus of three species, two in Palaearctic, one breeding in Europe and, locally, in the British Isles.

Honey Buzzard A
Pernis apivorus (Linnaeus)

Western Palaearctic. Breeds Europe and western Asia from southern Fenno-Scandia, France and Iberia east through Russia and Asia Minor to western Siberia; between 67°N and 37°N. Winters in tropical and southern Africa.

Monotypic.

MB. Extremely scarce. Breeds very locally in southern England (Hampshire) north at least occasionally to the Welsh border and central England, as well as almost certainly in Fife in 1949; formerly perhaps more widespread, though still rare, nesting being recorded from Hereford north to Durham, Ross and Aberdeen in the 19th century. Resident from May to September.

PV. Recorded April to November, chiefly May to June and September to October, in very small numbers; probably annually in eastern Britain (though not in any one county), but only very occasionally elsewhere; only three records in Ireland during the 1950s and 1960s.

Genus MILVUS Lacépède

Palaearctic, Oriental, Ethiopian and Australasian genus of two species, both breeding in Europe and one in very small numbers in the British Isles, the other occurring here as a rare visitor.

Black Kite A
Milvus migrans (Boddaert)

Palaearctic, Oriental, Ethiopian and Australasian. Breeds throughout Eurasia, except Iceland, Britain and the adjacent Continent, Scandinavia, some Mediterranean islands, southern Greece, arctic and northeast Asia and Indonesia; also breeds through most of Africa, Arabia, and from Celebes and New Guinea to northern Australia; between 64°N and 34°S. Sedentary and migratory; European breeders winter in the Mediterranean area, Arabia and tropical and southern Africa.

M.m.migrans (Boddaert) breeds northwest Africa and Europe east to east Russia and southwest Asia.

SV. Ten, all but one April–May and including four in 1966 (though the same individual was possibly involved in two or three of these records): Northumberland (May 1866, May 1947), Aberdeen (April 1901), Isles of Scilly (September 1938, May 1942, April 1966), Norfolk (May 1966), Orkney (May 1966, May 1968), Shetland (May–June 1966). Race determined only in first four cases, but presumably all were *M.m.migrans*.

Red Kite A
Milvus milvus (Linnaeus)

Western Palaearctic. Limited breeding range in Europe from Britain, France and Iberia to southern Sweden and the Baltic States in the north, and Mediterranean islands, Italy, the Balkans and west Russia in the south; also Asia Minor, northwest Africa, Canary and Cape Verde Islands; between 60°N and 15°N. Sedentary and migratory, northern populations wintering south to the Mediterranean.

M.m.milvus (Linnaeus) breeds throughout the range except the Cape Verde Islands.

RB. Very scarce. Breeds locally in central Wales where an average of about 20 pairs in the late 1960s, an apparent increase from four to ten pairs in the first 40 years of this century and about 15 pairs in the early

1950s; also nested Devon 1913 and Cornwall 1920; formerly common in many parts of Britain. Breeding population is mostly resident, but some evidence of migration south across southwest England in autumn, and perhaps for return in spring; one ringed in central Wales reached Oxford in its first autumn. Elsewhere a rare vagrant in southern England, rarer still in the north and Scotland, and recorded only three or four times in Ireland, including one in Cork, November 1968. Such vagrants have been recorded in almost every month of the year, and their origin is not known.

Genus HALIAEETUS Savigny

Holarctic, Oriental, Ethiopian and Australasian genus of eight species, three in Palaearctic (possibly still a fourth), two breeding in Europe (one marginally) and one formerly in the British Isles but now only a scarce visitor.

White-tailed Eagle A
Haliaeetus albicilla (Linnaeus)

Palaearctic and marginally Nearctic (known as Gray Sea Eagle in North America). Breeds Eurasia from Iceland, Scandinavia, Germany and the Balkans east through Russia and Siberia, Asia Minor and northern Iran to Anadyr, Kamchatka, Japan and Manchuria; also southwest Greenland; formerly Faeroes, British Isles, Corsica, Egypt and China; between 75°N and 34°N. Adults chiefly sedentary, but young wander south to southern Europe, northwest Africa, Egypt and Iraq to northwest India and southern China.

Monotypic.

FB. In the 18th century was widespread in Scotland and Ireland and also bred in the English Lake District, Isle of Man and (probably) Isle of Wight, but towards the end of the 19th century was reduced to a few pairs in the Scottish Highlands and islands and Ireland; became extinct as a breeding species in Ireland (Kerry, Mayo) in the early 1900s, on the Scottish mainland after 1911, Shetland after 1910, and finally Skye after about 1916. Attempted reintroduction (four birds) at Fair Isle in 1968.

SV. Now rare and irregular, October to April, occasionally September and May, chiefly on the east coast, more rarely in the south and west, and only four records in Ireland in 50 years. Declining in Scandinavia and Iceland and so becoming rarer still in Britain: only four or five records in the last decade.

Genus NEOPHRON Savigny

Palaearctic, Oriental and Ethiopian genus of one or two species; one breeding in Palaearctic and Europe, and recorded in the British Isles as a rare vagrant.

Egyptian Vulture   B
Neophron percnopterus (Linnaeus)

Palaearctic, Oriental and Ethiopian. Breeds Eurasia from Iberia through Mediterranean Europe north to Rumania and the southern Ukraine, through Asia Minor, the Caucasus and Arabia to Iran, Turkestan and India; also in much of Africa and the Canary and Cape Verde Islands; between 48°N and 35°S. Sedentary and migratory, northern populations wintering in Africa, Iran and India.

N.p.percnopterus(Linnaeus) breeds throughout the range except most of India.

SV. Two: Somerset (October 1825) and Essex (September 1868).

Genus GYPS Savigny

Palaearctic, Oriental and Ethiopian genus of four to six species; two to four in Palaearctic, one breeding in Europe and recorded in the British Isles in the past as a rare vagrant.

Griffon Vulture   A
Gyps fulvus (Hablizl)

Palaearctic, Oriental and Ethiopian. Breeds Eurasia from Iberia and locally in Mediterranean Europe north to the southern Ukraine and east through Asia Minor, the Caucasus and Middle East to Iran, Afghanistan, Turkestan and northern India; also in northwest, northeast and (this species or close ally) southern Africa; between 48°N and 20°N, apart from the south African population. Mainly sedentary, but some winter south to Arabia and Somaliland.

G.f.fulvus (Hablizl) breeds throughout the range except India and the Himalayas, and south Africa.

SV. Two records involving three birds: Cork (spring 1843), Derby (two, June 1927).

Genus CIRCUS Lacépède

Cosmopolitan genus of nine or ten species, five in Palaearctic, four breeding in Europe and three in the British Isles where the fourth has occurred as a rare visitor.

Marsh Harrier **A**
Circus aeruginosus (Linnaeus)

Palaearctic, Ethiopian and Australasian. Breeds from southern Fenno-Scandia, Britain, France, Iberia and Morocco through much of Europe and Russia south to Asia Minor, Israel and Jordan east across Iran, Afghanistan and Siberia to Amurland and Japan; also in New Guinea, Australia, Tasmania, New Zealand and Pacific Islands east to Fiji, as well as in Madagascar, the Comoro Islands and Reunion; between 60°N and 47°S. Sedentary and migratory; Eurasian populations mostly winter south to tropical Africa, Arabia and Iran to China, Philippines, Borneo and Sumatra.

C.a.aeruginosus (Linnaeus) breeds Eurasia east to Lake Baikal and northwest Mongolia.

MB and **RB**. Very scarce, with up to five or six pairs in Suffolk and one other area; there was an increase after 1939–45 to about 20 pairs, mainly in Suffolk and Norfolk but including five or six other counties in England and one in Wales, followed by a sharp decline after 1958. Up to the mid-19th century it was more widespread, including in Ireland where it last bred in 1917. Most of the British population probably emigrate (ringing recoveries from France and northwest Africa), but some at least overwinter as indicated by a recovery in late December of a yearling near to where ringed in southern England.

PV, perhaps **WV**. Birds recently wintering in East Anglia and southern England may or may not belong to the British breeding population, though some evidently do. Otherwise, scarce visitor in various, mainly coastal, counties of England and Wales, chiefly September to November and March to May but also in other months, scarcer still in Ireland (chiefly in eastern coastal counties) and Scotland (various counties north to Shetland). Birds ringed as nestlings in Denmark and Germany have been recovered here (in Orkney and Gloucester respectively) in subsequent springs.

Hen Harrier   A
Circus cyaneus (Linnaeus)

Holarctic. Breeds Eurasia from Fenno-Scandia, British Isles and northern Iberia eastwards through Europe (except extreme south) and Siberia to at least the Kolyma, possibly Anadyr and Kamchatka, Sakhalin and northern Mongolia and Manchuria; also in North America (where known as Marsh Hawk) from Alaska and Baja California across to Newfoundland and Texas; between 70°N and 30°N; replaced by a close ally, perhaps race, in South America. Sedentary in southern parts of the range, but northern birds move south in winter and the species then reaches the Mediterranean basin, Middle East, northern India, Burma and China, as well as Central America, Colombia and the northern Antilles.

 C.c.cyaneus (Linnaeus) breeds throughout Eurasian range.

 RB and **MB**. Scarce. Until 1940 confined to Orkney and the Outer Hebrides (though much more widespread in the 19th century); has since colonized many parts of the Scottish Highlands, south also to Ayr, Galloway and elsewhere in southern Scotland, and now also nests in six counties in Ireland, one or two in Wales and two in England. Mainly sedentary; some Scottish birds move south within that country or to Ireland, a few disperse as far as the Continent, ringed birds having been recovered in northern Norway, Denmark, Netherlands and southern France.

 PV and **WV**. Passage mainly of immatures (or females), with some wintering, September to April and occasionally August and May, in many coastal and moorland parts of the British Isles, also Cambridge, but otherwise only irregularly in inland and western coastal counties of England. Birds ringed in Belgium (as adult, November) and Finland (as nestling) have been recovered here, in February and March.

Pallid Harrier   A
Circus macrourus (Gmelin)

Central Palaearctic. Breeds eastern Europe and western Asia from central Russia and Rumania south to northern Iran through Siberia and Turkestan east to Lake Baikal and perhaps northwest Mongolia; mainly between 60°N and 35°N; has also bred Czechoslovakia, Germany and southern Sweden. Winters Africa (south of the Sahara and down to Cape Province), Arabia and southern Iran to southern India, Ceylon and Burma.

Monotypic.

SV. Three, two males in spring and an immature in autumn: Fair Isle (April–May 1931), Dorset (April 1938), Yorkshire (October 1952).

Montagu's Harrier   A
Circus pygargus (Linnaeus)

Western and central Palaearctic. Breeds from northwest Africa, Iberia, British Isles, Denmark and southernmost Sweden east through Europe and west Asia to the Yenisei and the Russian Altai, south to north Italy, Rumania, Ukraine and through the Caucasus into northern Iran; between 60°N and 34°N. Winters in tropical and southern Africa, Iraq, southern Iran, India and Ceylon, but also in southern Europe and the Mediterranean basin.

Monotypic.

MB. Very scarce. About 20 to 30 pairs breed in widely separated parts of England and Wales, and probably one or two pairs in Ireland in at least some years since 1955; also nested in Scotland (Perth, Kirkcudbright) during 1952–55. Increased markedly during 1946–55 and in about 1950 Devon and Cornwall alone had 20 pairs, but there was a sudden decline after that (though currently perhaps increasing again). During 1956–65 nested at least once in 20 counties, but since 1960 annually in only three to six counties in England and Wales. Resident from May to August or September.

PV. Passage April into June and August to September, occasionally October, very rarely November, and exceptionally in winter months. Regularly in East Anglia, Sussex and Kent, occasionally in many other counties in England and Wales, more rarely in Ireland and very rarely in Scotland. Extent of involvement of Continental birds uncertain, but one ringed as a nestling in the Netherlands was recovered in Suffolk in June a year later.

Genus ACCIPITER Brisson

Cosmopolitan genus of 45 species, only seven in Palaearctic, four breeding in Europe (one marginally) and two in the British Isles (one irregularly).

Goshawk A
Accipiter gentilis (Linnaeus)

Holarctic. Breeding distribution circumpolar, in Eurasia and north-west Africa from Scandinavia, France, Iberia and Morocco, through continental Europe, the Mediterranean islands and Asia Minor, across Siberia to Anadyr, Kamchatka and Japan; also western China, Tibet and Himalayas; and in North America from Alaska and Newfoundland south in the west to northern Mexico; between 70°N and 30°N. Mainly sedentary, but some wander south even to Egypt, Jordan, Iran, northern India and Burma, and the southeastern United States.

A.g.gentilis (Linnaeus) breeds northwest Africa, Mediterranean (except Corsica and Sardinia) and Asia Minor east to Russia and north throughout Europe except in the far north from about 60°N.

A.g.atricapillus (Wilson) breeds North American range except Queen Charlotte and Vancouver Islands.

CB (possibly extremely rare **RB**). Status uncertain; up to three pairs nested Sussex for many years to 1951 or later and breeding has occurred in at least two and possibly six or more other quite separate parts of Britain in recent years. Bred sporadically in the 19th century and perhaps regularly in earlier times. *A.g.gentilis*.

SV. Probably annual in England and Scotland, March to May and August to November, chiefly in the south, east and north and much rarer in the west and Ireland, but not certain whether these represent visitors from abroad, wanderers from undiscovered breeding areas in Britain or even falconers' escapes. Race not determined in recent years, but past specimens were all *A.g.gentilis* with the exception of the following. *A.g.atricapillus* recorded four times in Ireland (Tipperary, Offaly, Tyrone, Galway) and once in England (Isles of Scilly).

Sparrowhawk A
Accipiter nisus (Linnaeus)

Palaearctic. Breeds Eurasia from Scandinavia, British Isles and Iberia east throughout Europe and Asia Minor across Siberia to the Kolyma, probably Kamchatka, Japan and northern China; also in northwest Africa, Madeira and the Canaries; and from Baluchistan, the Himalayas and Tibet into western China; between 70°N and 25°N. Sedentary and migratory, northernmost populations moving south and some wintering south to northeast Africa, Arabia, India and Burma.

A.n.nisus (Linnaeus) breeds Europe (except Corsica and Sardinia) east to west Siberia and Iran.

RB. Not scarce. Breeds widely in Britain and Ireland except the Northern Isles and Outer Hebrides (scarce and irregular Inner Hebrides), but has decreased markedly since 1955, particularly in eastern England, and is now virtually extinct as a breeding bird in several counties from Lincoln and Leicester south to Essex and Oxford. British birds are sedentary and none ringed as a nestling has been recovered abroad.

PV and **WV**. Passage September to November, March to April, chiefly on the British east coast but perhaps elsewhere as well, with recoveries of foreign-ringed birds in January and February suggesting that some immigrants winter; in all, 14 foreign-ringed ones have been recovered here from Finland, Norway, the Netherlands (five) and Germany (six).

Genus BUTEO Lacépède

Holarctic, Ethiopian and Neotropical genus of 27 species, only four in Palaearctic, three breeding in Europe and one in the British Isles with a second a scarce winter visitor.

Buzzard   **A**
Buteo buteo (Linnaeus)

Palaearctic. Breeds from southern Fenno-Scandia, the British Isles and Iberia through most of Europe, Russia and Asia Minor, then in a narrower band across Siberia to the Sea of Okhotsk and Japan; also in Madeira, the Azores, Canary and Cape Verde Islands; and Tibet and western China; between 66°N and 15°N. Largely sedentary in the west, though some northern birds migrate to the Mediterranean, and only partly migratory in the far east, but highly migratory in northeast Europe and western Asia, wintering south to Arabia and eastern Africa south to Cape Province.

B.b.buteo (Linnaeus) breeds Atlantic Islands, and western Europe north to southern Norway and Sweden, east to Poland and the Balkans.

B.b.vulpinus Gloger breeds from central Fenno-Scandia and Russia to the Yenisei in Siberia and south to the Caucasus, Kirghiz Steppes and the Tian Shan.

RB. Not scarce. Breeds widely in the Hebrides, Scottish Highlands and western Lowlands, northwest England, Wales and borders, and southwest England, with present eastern limits of range in southern half of England in west Stafford, west Worcester, Gloucester, Wiltshire, Hampshire, west Sussex and probably Surrey; formerly more widespread, but in eastern England now breeds irregularly—most recently in Kent, Derby and Northumberland, and for a time in the 1950s in Cheshire, Warwick and probably Huntingdon; absent Isle of Man; in Ireland extinct at end of the 19th century, but, after isolated nestings in 1930s, up to ten pairs bred in Antrim during 1950s and 1960s. *B.b.buteo.*

PV. Irregular passage occurs in August and September, chiefly on the British east coast, and vagrant in variable numbers in non-breeding areas in all months, mostly August to April; in Ireland scarce visitor March to April and August to November. Extent of immigration from Continent uncertain, but probably small and no recoveries here of foreign-ringed birds.

SV. At least one record of *B.b.vulpinus*: Wiltshire (September 1864).

Rough-legged Buzzard   A
Buteo lagopus (Pontoppidan)

Holarctic. Breeding distribution circumpolar, in Eurasia mainly north of 63°N (but further south in Scandinavia and Kamchatka), and in North America south to Labrador and Newfoundland; between 75°N and 47°N. Winters south to central Europe, the Caucasus, Turkestan, Manchuria and the northern United States, some wandering farther south still.

B.l.lagopus (Pontoppidan) breeds Eurasia east to about the Yenisei.

WV. October to April or May, usually scarce, but commoner in some years and at intervals in considerable numbers as in 1915/16 and 1966/67; chiefly in Scotland and eastern England south to East Anglia, but sometimes in other parts of England and rarely Wales and Ireland. Evidence of passage in some years, chiefly in autumn.

Genus AQUILA Brisson

Holarctic, Ethiopian and Australasian genus of nine or ten species; six or seven in Palaearctic, five breeding in Europe and one in the British Isles with a second recorded in the past as a rare vagrant.

Spotted Eagle **B**
Aquila clanga Pallas

Palaearctic and perhaps, marginally, Oriental. Breeds eastern Europe from southern Finland to Rumania across Russia and Siberia to northern Mongolia, Manchuria and Amurland; may at times breed farther south in the Balkans, Caucasus and even northwest India; between 64°N and 45°N. Partly migratory, wintering south and west to Spain, southern France, Italy, Egypt, Iraq, Iran and southern China.
Monotypic.

SV. About 12 records (14 birds), but recorded only twice in the 20th century: Essex (April 1908), Hereford (November 1915). Earlier, at least eight records in England and one record of two birds in Ireland, probably also one in Scotland, all September to January.

Golden Eagle **A**
Aquila chrysaetos (Linnaeus)

Holarctic, marginally Oriental, fringing on Ethiopian and Neotropical. Breeds Eurasia from Scotland and Fenno-Scandia across Russia and Siberia to Kamchatka in the north and, with an almost continuous gap in between, from Iberia and southern France through Italy, the Balkans and Asia Minor to Iran, Afghanistan, northern India and the Himalayas, northern Burma, China and Japan in the south; also in northwest Africa, Mauritania and Ahaggar; and in North America from Alaska to Baja California and central Mexico, across to Quebec and the northeastern United States; between 70°N and 20°N. Mainly sedentary, but some young wander south, particularly in the eastern United States.

A.c.chrysaetos (Linnaeus) breeds in the western Palaearctic south to the Pyrenees and east into west Siberia as far as the Yenisei.

RB. Scarce; about 200 breeding pairs. Breeds Scottish Highlands and Western Isles with a few pairs in southwest Scotland; non-breeders are resident in the English Lake District and one pair bred in Northern Ireland (Antrim) from 1953 to 1960. In former times it was resident in northern England, south to Derby, in Wales and various parts of Ireland. Sedentary. Noted as very rare vagrant to northern parts of Ireland and northern England with isolated examples south to Sussex, Berkshire, Northampton, Norfolk, Lincoln and Caernarvon, but not in recent years.

Family FALCONIDAE

Genus FALCO Linnaeus

Cosmopolitan genus of 39 species, 15 in Palaearctic, ten breeding in Europe and four in the British Isles where three others have also been recorded.

Lesser Kestrel A
Falco naumanni Fleischer

Southern Palaearctic. Breeds generally to the south of the Red-footed Falcon *F.vespertinus* but has a comparable range in Eurasia (and north-west Africa) from Iberia and Morocco through Mediterranean Europe and its islands, southern Russia, and Asia Minor, across north Iran, the Kirghiz Steppes, Afghanistan and Turkestan to northern Mongolia; also, after a gap, perhaps in Manchuria and northern China; between 56°N and 35°N. Winters in Africa south of the Sahara down to Cape Province.

Monotypic.

SV. About twelve, chiefly adult males and only one more recent than 1926: Yorkshire (November 1867, April 1892, October 1909), Kent (May 1877), Dublin (February 1891), Isles of Scilly (March 1891, February 1926), Isle of Wight (November 1895, April 1903), Aberdeen (October 1897), Lancashire (before 1901), Cornwall (May 1968). It is curious that, with two exceptions, all the dates are early in spring or late in autumn and the February, March and November ones (five in all) are particularly surprising.

Kestrel A
Falco tinnunculus Linnaeus

Palaearctic, Oriental and Ethiopian. Breeds throughout Eurasia and Africa with the exception of Iceland and a high arctic strip from northern Scandinavia and the Kola Peninsula across to Anadyr and Kamchatka, and with the exception also of parts of India and the region southeast of Burma, plus in Africa the most arid zone of the Sahara and the equatorial rain forest, but including Madeira and the Canary and Cape Verde Islands; between 70°N and 34°S. Mainly resident, but northern populations winter south to central Africa, Arabia, India and China.

F.t.tinnunculus Linnaeus breeds north Africa and throughout the Eurasian range except the extreme east from Japan and China to Burma and the Himalayas, and southern and western India.

RB and **MB**. Fairly numerous. Breeds in all parts of the British Isles except Shetland (where ceased about 1905), but marked decline during 1959–63 in eastern England east of a line from Lincoln to Hampshire; slight recovery from 1964 onwards in some areas. Nesting in urban districts increasingly common after about 1930. British birds are generally fairly sedentary, but some, especially from northern districts, move southwards in autumn and winter, a proportion of these reaching the Continent, as shown by ringing recoveries from Germany and the Netherlands south to north Spain, but mainly in the northern half of France.

PV and **WV**. Passage of Continental birds August to November, March to May, well marked in the Northern Isles and down the east coast, less well marked in western Britain and eastern Ireland. Recoveries here of foreign-ringed birds have included ones from Finland, Sweden, Norway, Poland, the Netherlands and Belgium. Some evidently pass inland and remain as winter visitors, while others continue south across the southern North Sea and English Channel.

Red-footed Falcon A
Falco vespertinus Linnaeus

Central and eastern Palaearctic. Breeds Baltic States, Poland, Hungary and Rumania (occasionally or in the past also Finland, east Sweden, Germany, Austria, Yugoslavia and Bulgaria) east across Russia and Siberia (with a gap in eastern Siberia) to Amurland, Manchuria and south to northern China; between 63°N and 35°N. Highly migratory, some perhaps wintering in India and southeast Asia, but most of even the easternmost populations travel to eastern and southern Africa from Kenya to Cape Province, with some also farther west.

F.v.vespertinus Linnaeus breeds entire range except in the far east.

SV. Over 160 recorded, more than one-third of these during 1958–1968, when identified annually. Chiefly in spring, April to June, occasionally July to October, rarely March and November, once January and February. Mainly in southern and eastern England, occasionally north to Yorkshire and Lancashire, with about four records in Wales, about twelve in Scotland and only two in Ireland (Wicklow, summer 1832 and Galway, September 1966). Most records refer to single individuals and there is only one of a small party (five in Hampshire, May 1959).

Merlin   A
Falco columbarius Linnaeus

Holarctic. Breeding distribution circumpolar, from Iceland, Faeroes, British Isles, Fenno-Scandia and Estonia across Russia and Siberia to Anadyr, with a southward extension in central Asia, and across northern North America (where known as Pigeon Hawk) from Alaska to Newfoundland and Nova Scotia; between 72°N and 43°N. Generally winters to the south of the breeding range, in northwest Africa, Egypt and central and southern Europe through Asia Minor and southern Russia to northern India and China; and in the southern United States, Mexico, northern South America and the West Indies.

F.c.aesalon Tunstall breeds from Faeroes east to the Yenisei in west Siberia, except in western and central Asia south of about 55°N.

F.c.subaesalon (Brehm) breeds Iceland.

F.c.columbarius Linnaeus breeds eastern North America.

RB and **MB**. Scarce. Thinly distributed, chiefly in upland areas. over much of Scotland (including the Northern and Western Isles), northern England (south to north Derby), Wales, southwest Shropshire. southwest England (irregular Cornwall), and many parts of Ireland. Generally decreasing, but recent increases on some Scottish islands, Exmoor and perhaps also Dartmoor. Birds on higher ground move down or southwards in winter; a small proportion of the population emigrates as indicated by the recoveries of four ringed birds from Yorkshire and Devon in western France and Spain. *F.c.aesalon*.

PV and **WV**. August to November, chiefly September–October, through to April and May. Following some dispersal of breeding stock in autumn, the species becomes fairly widely distributed in small numbers, particularly on moorland, coastal marshes and low ground generally; these appear to be augmented by Continental migrants, also

F.c.aesalon, particularly in northern Scotland and down the east coast, although there have been no recoveries here of Fenno-Scandian birds. Also augmented by birds from Iceland, *F.c.subaesalon* (especially in northern Scotland, Lancashire and Ireland in October–December and April), but most records relate to October (when Icelandic birds are trapped regularly at Fair Isle, for example) and probably most of these are passage visitors only (as suggested by the subsequent recovery of some ringed birds to south on the Continent).

SV. One record of *F.c.columbarius*: Outer Hebrides (November 1920).

Hobby A
Falco subbuteo Linnaeus

Palaearctic and marginally Oriental. Breeds most countries of Europe (but only in the south of England and Sweden and not at all in Iceland and some Mediterranean islands) extending north into the southern half of Finland and south into Asia Minor, thence right across Asia to the Kolyma, the Sea of Okhotsk and south Kamchatka south to China and Laos; also northwest Africa; between 68°N and 16°N. Winters in tropical Africa, northern India, Burma and southeast China.

F.s.subbuteo Linnaeus breeds entire range except southern and eastern China south to Laos.

MB. Very scarce; total breeding population probably just under 100 pairs. Largely restricted to southern England, chiefly Hampshire, Sussex, Surrey, Wiltshire, Dorset and Berkshire. Breeds less regularly west to Cornwall and Radnor, north to Warwick and Northampton, and east to Huntingdon and Kent, and has nested exceptionally west to Glamorgan and Brecon, north to Cheshire, Derby, Yorkshire and Northumberland (also Perth, 1887). Resident April or May to September.

PV. April or May to June, less frequently August to October; exceptional November to March. Occurrences west to Wexford, Cork, Kerry and six other counties of Ireland, and north to various parts of Scotland including Shetland, plus others in eastern England in spring and to a lesser extent autumn, suggest that some Continental birds may at times pass through the British Isles, and there has been one autumn recovery (in Norfolk) of a Swedish-ringed nestling.

Gyr Falcon A
Falco rusticolus Linnaeus

Holarctic. Breeding distribution circumpolar, in arctic Eurasia from Iceland and northernmost Fenno-Scandia east to the Bering Strait, probably south to Kamchatka, in arctic North America from Alaska to Labrador north to Baffin, Victoria, Devon and Ellesmere Islands; and on both sides of Greenland where it reaches its northernmost limits; mainly between 82°N and 65°N, with some down to about 55°N. Mainly resident, but irregular wanderer south to Britain, France, Iberia, Italy, about 60°N in Russia and Siberia, northern Manchuria, Japan and the northern United States.

Monotypic.

SV. Irregular visitor October to December and March to April, with records in January, February, May, June and September. A very few (an average of two records each year, 1958–68) still recorded in most years in Scotland and western England, but scarcer now than formerly in Ireland (only four records during 1950–68). The '*candicans*' (white) type has always been the most regular and this is the form which predominates in Greenland and arctic Canada; the '*islandus*' (grey) type has been recorded on a number of occasions, but the brown '*rusticolus*' only twice: Sussex (January 1845), Suffolk (October 1867).

Peregrine A
Falco peregrinus Tunstall

Cosmopolitan and circumpolar. The most wide-ranging bird of prey, breeding in every continent and from western Greenland in the north to Tierra del Fuego in the south; also one of the most widely sub-speciated with at least 15 races. Breeds throughout Eurasia except Iceland, the Taimyr Peninsula and a relatively narrow band across central Asia from the southern Urals to northern China; also in the Philippines, Greater Sundas, New Guinea, Australia, New Caledonia, New Hebrides, and Fiji; in northwest, tropical and southern Africa; in west and southeast Greenland; in much of North America (but has recently ceased to breed in many eastern parts); and in South America from Chile to Tierra del Fuego and the Falkland Islands; between 76°N and 54°S. Resident and migratory; northern populations winter south to southern Africa, India, Malaya and South America.

F.p.peregrinus Tunstall breeds in most of the western Palaearctic (but not in the Mediterranean region or Eurasian tundras, where replaced by other races) and extends east across Asia to Mongolia, Amurland and Manchuria,

F.p.anatum Bonaparte breeds Greenland and North America except the islands off Alaska.

RB. Scarce. Apart from very small numbers in southwest England, Wales, the Lake District and southwest Scotland, is now largely confined to the Scottish Highlands and to coasts and inland mountains of Ireland; previously more widely distributed on the south coast of England and in northern England and Wales, but declined drastically after about 1955; has also declined markedly in Ireland. Mainly sedentary, but some birds, particularly immatures, wander to inland and eastern parts of Britain outside the breeding season, and one nestling ringed in north Scotland reached southern Ireland in its first winter. *F.p.peregrinus.*

PV and **WV**. Ringing evidence shows that some Scandinavian birds (Sweden and Norway) pass through Britain in autumn and that some occur here in winter (November–January). *F.p.peregrinus.*

SV. American birds, *F.p.anatum*, have been identified twice: Leicester (October 1891), Lincoln (September 1910).

Order GALLIFORMES

Family TETRAONIDAE

Genus TETRAO Linnaeus

Palaearctic genus of two species, one breeding in Europe and the British Isles.

Capercaillie   BC
Tetrao urogallus Linnaeus

Western and central Palaearctic. Breeds Eurasia in Scotland and from the Pyrenees west into northern Spain, and from Fenno-Scandia, Germany, France and northern Italy east through the Baltic States and northern Balkans, across Russia and Siberia to the upper Lena River, Lake Baikal and northwest Mongolia; between 69°N and 43°N. Sedentary, with local movements in northern part of range.

T.u.urogallus Linnaeus breeds in the western and northern part of the range (except the Pyrenees and northern Spain) east to about the Yenisei.

FB, IB. Not scarce. Breeds mainly in the eastern Scottish Highlands, from Stirling and Fife north to southeast Sutherland, after introductions in the 19th century from 1837 onwards. Formerly indigenous, but became extinct in Scotland and Ireland about 1770 and before 1800 respectively, and in England in the 17th century.

Genus LYRURUS Swainson

Palaearctic genus of two species, both breeding in Europe (one marginally), and one in the British Isles.

Black Grouse
A
Lyrurus tetrix (Linnaeus)

Palaearctic. Breeds Eurasia from Britain, Netherlands, Belgium, France and northern Italy, through Fenno-Scandia, central Europe and the northern Balkans, across Siberia to the Lena River, south to the Kirghiz Steppes, Turkestan, north Mongolia and North Korea; between 68°N and 42°N. Mainly sedentary.

L.t.britannicus Witherby and Lönnberg breeds Britain only.

RB. Fairly numerous. Breeds many parts of Scotland (including the Inner Hebrides), northern England (north Stafford, north Derby and east Cheshire northwards), most counties of Wales, possibly southwest Shropshire, and Devon and Somerset, where a few remain on Exmoor and the Quantocks. Formerly more widespread in the southern half of England.

Genus LAGOPUS Brisson

Holarctic genus of three species, two in Palaearctic, both breeding in Europe and the British Isles.

Ptarmigan
A
Lagopus mutus (Montin)

Holarctic. Breeding distribution circumpolar, in Eurasia in Iceland, Spitsbergen, Scotland, Alps, Pyrenees, Fenno-Scandia and Kola Peninsula, then, after a gap, continuously from the northern Urals across Siberia to Anadyr, Kamchatka and the Chukotski Peninsula, south to the Russian Altai, Mongolia and Japan; also in northern North America from Alaska north to northern Ellesmere Island and south to Newfoundland; and in northwest Greenland; between 83°N and 43°N. Mainly sedentary; at times flocks migrate south in Greenland, North America and probably Siberia.

L.m.millaisi Hartert breeds Scotland only.

RB. Fairly numerous. Restricted to the Scottish Highlands from Ben Lomond northwards and in Mull and Skye; also seen recently in Rhum (where became extinct in the 19th century) and the Outer Hebrides (where extinct since 1938). Formerly bred Orkney, Arran, Jura, Islay, southwest Scotland and the English Lake District, but extinct there since the 19th century.

Red Grouse (Willow Grouse) A
Lagopus lagopus (Linnaeus)

Holarctic. Breeding distribution circumpolar, in Eurasia from the British Isles and Fenno-Scandia (also introduced Belgium) across Russia and Siberia to Anadyr and Kamchatka, south to the Kirghiz Steppes, Mongolia, probably northern Manchuria, and Sakhalin; also northern North America (where known as Willow Ptarmigan) from Alaska to Newfoundland; between 74°N and 47°N. Mainly sedentary, but mountain populations move to lower ground in winter and some wander slightly south of breeding areas.

L.l.scoticus (Latham) breeds British Isles; also eastern Belgium, where introduced.

RB. Numerous. Widespread in moorland areas of Scotland (including Hebrides and Orkney, but only as a result of introduction in Shetland), northern England (from central Stafford northwards), Wales (and border counties of Shropshire, Hereford and Monmouth), southwest England (Dartmoor and Exmoor, where introduced in the 19th century) and Ireland.

Family PHASIANIDAE

Genus ALECTORIS Kaup

Palaearctic and marginally Oriental and Ethiopian genus of five to seven species; five in Palaearctic, four breeding in Europe and one in the British Isles, where introduced.

Red-legged Partridge C
Alectoris rufa (Linnaeus)

Southwestern Palaearctic. Breeds indigenously only in southwest Europe, west of a line from northwest France to northwest Italy into Elba, Corsica and Iberia; formerly in the Channel Islands, western

Switzerland and German Rhineland; between 48°N and 36°N. Sedentary with local wandering. Introduced successfully in Britain, the Balaearic Islands, Madeira, Canaries and Azores.

A.r.rufa (Linnaeus) breeds Britain, France, northwest Italy, Elba, Corsica and the Balearic Islands.

IB. Numerous. Introduced many places from 1770 onwards and now breeds in east and south England west to Somerset (formerly Devon and Glamorgan, but declined after 1930s), northwest to Shropshire (some recent introductions in Manchester area) and north to north Yorkshire.

Genus PERDIX Brisson

Palaearctic genus of three species, one breeding in Europe and the British Isles.

Partridge A
Perdix perdix (Linnaeus)

Western and central Palaearctic. Breeds from the British Isles, France and northern Spain east through Europe and western Asia to west Siberia and Chinese Turkestan, north to Fenno-Scandia, south to Italy, some Mediterranean islands, the Balkans and northwest Iran; between 66°N and 36°N. Chiefly sedentary, but extensive southward migrations at times in Russia and western Germany. Introduced North America.

P.p.perdix (Linnaeus) breeds British Isles, parts of France, Norway and Sweden through central Europe to north Greece.

RB. Numerous. Breeds widely in Britain and Ireland, though it is very local or absent in the west Scottish Highlands and southwest Ireland, and absent from Scottish islands with the exception of Arran, Bute and Islay. Has decreased markedly in many areas in recent years.

Genus COTURNIX Bonnaterre

Palaearctic, Oriental, Ethiopian and Australasian genus of ten to twelve species, two in Palaearctic, one breeding in Europe and the British Isles.

Quail A
Coturnix coturnix (Linnaeus)

Palaearctic, Oriental and Ethiopian. Breeds Eurasia from the British

D

Isles (and irregularly Faeroes and south Fenno-Scandia) east throughout continental Europe, Mediterranean islands, Russia, Asia Minor and Middle East to upper Lena River, Lake Baikal, north Mongolia, west Chinese Turkestan and north India; also in northwest Africa, Madeira, Canary and Cape Verde Islands and Azores; and in eastern and southern Africa south to Cape Province, together with Madagascar, the Comoro Islands and Mauritius; between 64°N and 34°S. Migratory, except on the Atlantic Islands and in south and east Africa, wintering in the Mediterranean area, Africa between the Sahara and equator, Arabia and India.

C.c.coturnix (Linnaeus) breeds throughout Palaearctic range except the Atlantic Islands.

MB. Scarce. Breeds regularly in about eight counties of southern England (Cornwall, Wiltshire, Hampshire, Sussex, Berkshire, Oxford, Hereford and Cambridge) and two or three in southeast Ireland (Kildare, Carlow and probably Offaly), less regularly in several others and sporadically north to Shetland; in 1954–66 probably bred at least once in every English county except Middlesex, in six counties of Wales, in seven in south Scotland and in Caithness, Orkney, Shetland and Hebrides, as well as up to possibly 16 counties of Ireland. Subject to considerable fluctuations and 1964 was a year of exceptionally high population. Resident from May or June to about September. Noted on passage in many counties, mainly in spring, late May to early June, also September to October, but numbers erratic. Recorded only exceptionally in winter.

Genus PHASIANUS Linnaeus

Palaearctic and Oriental genus of two species, both in Palaearctic, one breeding in Europe (entirely as a result of introductions except in extreme southeast Russia) and the British Isles.

Pheasant   C
Phasianus colchicus Linnaeus

Palaearctic and Oriental. Breeds indigenously from the Volga delta, Caucasus and Caspian region east through Turkestan and north Iran to Mongolia, Amurland, south through Manchuria, Korea, China and Formosa to north Burma and north Indo-China; between 52°N and 17°N. Sedentary, but some migratory movements in Manchuria and Amurland. Introduced most of Europe except in the extreme north and south; also introduced northwest Africa, North America, Hawaii, Japan and New Zealand.

P.c.colchicus Linnaeus of the Transcaucasian region was the form originally introduced in the British Isles, but subsequently *P.c.torquatus* Gmelin was introduced from eastern China and followed by other races until the population became completely mongrel.

IB. Numerous. First introduced before 1059 in England and in the 16th century in Scotland and Ireland; *P.c.torquatus* and other races were introduced from 1785. Now breeds throughout Britain and Ireland, including very locally in the Northern Isles, Outer Hebrides, northwest Scotland, Isle of Man, Cornwall, Isles of Scilly, northwest and southwest Ireland; the populations in many of these western areas (and in some places elsewhere) survive only or mainly through artificial rearing or the constant reintroduction of fresh stock.

Genus CHRYSOLOPHUS Gray

Palaearctic genus of two species, restricted to China and extreme northeast Burma, but introduced locally in Europe and the British Isles.

Golden Pheasant C
Chrysolophus pictus (Linnaeus)

Southeastern Palaearctic. Indigenous population restricted to mountains of central China; between 34°N and 24°N. Sedentary. Introduced to parts of Europe.

IB. Scarce. Feral populations have survived in Breckland (west Norfolk/west Suffolk) and Kirkcudbright (perhaps also elsewhere in Britain) for several decades, and have recently shown signs of increase and spread.

Lady Amherst's Pheasant C
Chrysolophus amherstiae (Leadbeater)

Southeastern Palaearctic. Indigenous population restricted to mountains of south-central China and northeastern Burma; between 31°N and 23°N. Sedentary.

IB. Very scarce. A small, feral population survives in parts of Buckingham/Bedford/Hertford, the ancestors of these birds having originated from a collection at Woburn, Bedford.

Order GRUIFORMES

Family GRUIDAE

Genus GRUS Brisson

Holarctic, Oriental, Australasian and perhaps Ethiopian (but not Neotropical) genus of ten or eleven species; eight in Palaearctic, one breeding in Europe and occurring (formerly breeding) in the British Isles.

Crane   A
Grus grus (Linnaeus)

Palaearctic. Breeds Eurasia from Fenno-Scandia, Denmark, north Germany, Poland and perhaps Rumania east through Russia and across Siberia to perhaps the Kolyma, south to the Ukraine, Kirghiz Steppes, Turkestan, Mongolia and northern Manchuria; also isolated colonies in Turkey, Caucasus, Armenia and perhaps north Iran; formerly more widespread in Europe; between 69°N and 38°N. Winters in the Mediterranean area west to Spain, north and northeast Africa, Asia Minor to India, and south China to north Indo-China, Burma and Assam.

    G.g.grus (Linnaeus) breeds Europe east to east Russia.

    FB. Bred in East Anglia until about 1600 and perhaps in Ireland until the 14th century.

    SV. In the 19th and first half of the 20th centuries it was a rare visitor recorded at least once in most counties of England and on a handful of occasions in Wales, Scotland and Ireland, but it became so rare about the 1930s that isolated occurrences were thought mainly to involve escapes from captivity. During 1957–62 there were rather more records, including several parties of up to six, in more than a dozen

counties in England, seven in Scotland and one or two in Wales and
Ireland; then in October–November 1963 came an unprecedented
invasion of 500 or more in Sussex and Hampshire and to a lesser extent
in Dorset and Somerset, with a few in other counties north to Cambridge and west to Cornwall; 1964–68 produced a further 21 or more
records. Most recent occurrences have been in autumn, but a few in
winter and spring, and the species has been recorded in all months of the
year. Some individuals or small parties have made prolonged stays of
several weeks or months. All specimens examined have been *G.g.grus*.

Family RALLIDAE

Genus RALLUS Linnaeus

Cosmopolitan genus of 14 species (plus a further five, believed extinct,
on Pacific islands); one only in Palaearctic, breeding in Europe and the
British Isles.

Water Rail   A
Rallus aquaticus Linnaeus

Palaearctic and perhaps marginally Oriental. Breeds from Iceland,
southern Fenno-Scandia, British Isles, France, and Iberia east through
continental Europe and the larger Mediterranean islands to Turkey,
then in a narrow band across western Siberia and northern Kazakhstan
to about the River Ob; again in eastern Siberia, south to northern China
and Japan; and, separately, from the Aral Sea and eastern Iran east to
southern China and south to northwestern India; also to an uncertain
extent in north Africa, the Middle East and Turkey; between 67°N and
27°N. Sedentary and migratory, the northern populations wintering
south to the Mediterranean area, Egypt, Middle East and Arabia, Iran,
northern India, Burma, southern China and the Indo-Chinese countries.

R.a.aquaticus Linnaeus breeds throughout the European range (except Iceland and possibly Faeroes) into western Siberia, and in north Africa and the Middle East.

R.a.hibernans Salomonsen breeds Iceland and possibly Faeroes.

RB. Not scarce. Locally distributed throughout much of the British Isles, but perhaps commonest in Ireland (where breeds every county) and East Anglia; known to nest regularly in fewer than half the counties of England (absent particularly from many parts of the Midlands), Wales and Scotland, but doubtless overlooked. Probably largely sedentary, but early autumn wanderers, late July and August, in coastal areas are probably of British origin and some perhaps emigrate. *R.a.aquaticus.*

PV and **WV**. Continental passage migrants and winter visitors arrive September to November and depart March to May, with hard-weather movements December to February; at these times likely to occur in any county, most noticeably in coastal areas and on islands. There have been recoveries here of birds ringed in Denmark, Germany, the Netherlands and Czechoslovakia, while British-ringed birds have been recovered in France, the Netherlands, Germany, Czechoslovakia and Sweden. *R.a.aquaticus.* Birds of the Iceland race, *R.a.hibernans,* have been identified in north Scotland and particularly in Ireland where this form is considered to be both a passage migrant and a winter visitor.

Genus CREX Bechstein

Palaearctic monospecific genus, breeding in Europe and the British Isles.

Corncrake   A
Crex crex (Linnaeus)

Palaearctic. Breeds British Isles and France east through Europe north to southern Fenno-Scandia and south to northern Italy and northern Balkans, across Russia and Siberia to Lake Baikal, the Altai and Chinese Turkestan, also through Asia Minor to Iran; between 64°N and 33°N. Winters mainly in central, eastern and southern Africa, also Madagascar, though a few remain in Europe, the Mediterranean area and east to Iran.

Monotypic.

MB. Not scarce. Greatly decreased, formerly breeding over the whole of Britain and Ireland, but now numerous only in the Hebrides and northwest, west and southwest Ireland; otherwise breeds regularly in small numbers in Shetland, Orkney and north, west and southwest Scotland, Northumberland, Cumberland, Westmorland, Anglesey, Caernarvon and most counties of Ireland, irregularly in central Scotland, Durham, Yorkshire and several counties of Wales, and sporadically south to the Isles of Scilly, Cornwall, Hampshire and Suffolk. Resident mid-April to September, also exceptionally in winter.

PV. Mid-April to early June and late July to early October with stragglers to early November. On passage recorded in small numbers in most counties, more in the west than east. No ringing evidence of passage migrants of Continental stock, but it is suspected that some later arrivals in eastern Britain in spring move on to Scandinavia and there may be a small return movement.

Genus PORZANA Vieillot

Cosmopolitan genus of 12 or 13 species, seven or eight in Palaearctic, three breeding in Europe; these three are, respectively, a local breeder, a former breeder and a scarce visitor to the British Isles, where a fourth has also occurred rarely from the Nearctic.

Little Crake   A
Porzana parva (Scopoli)

Western and central Palaearctic. Breeds Europe and western Asia from Germany, parts of France and northern Italy east to about the region of Lake Balkhash, north to Estonia and central Russia, and south to northern Greece, the Caucasus and Aral Sea; between 59°N and 41°N (possibly also in northwest Africa). Winters in the Mediterranean area, north and east Africa and from Arabia to northwest India.

Monotypic.

SV. Just over 80 recorded, irregularly at the present time, with an average of about one record each year over the last decade. Noted in all months, including rare evidence of wintering in December and January, but chiefly March to May and September to November, mainly in eastern England from Yorkshire southwards, but as far west as the Isles of Scilly, Cornwall, Devon, Somerset, Shropshire, Lancashire and Cumberland, as well as three to five records each in Wales, Scotland and Ireland (north to Shetland and west to Cork).

Baillon's Crake   **A**
Porzana pusilla (Pallas)

Palaearctic, Ethiopian and Australasian. Breeds from France and Iberia
east through southern Germany, southern Czechoslovakia, northern
Italy, northern Balkans, across Kazakhstan, Manchuria and northern
China to the Amur and Ussuri Rivers and Japan; also northwest Africa,
eastern and southern Africa, Madagascar, and Australasia; between
58°N and 47°S. Palaearctic populations winter in Africa south to the
equator, Iraq, Iran, India, Ceylon, southern Japan, China, Malay
Peninsula and Indonesia.

    P.p.intermedia (Hermann) breeds northwest Africa and Europe east
to the northern Balkans.

    FB. Breeding proved on three to five occasions during 1858–89;
Cambridge (June and August 1858), Norfolk (probably June and July
1866, certainly May 1889). Since these records all involved nests and
eggs actually found, this elusive species doubtless bred on other occasions in East Anglia in the 19th century.

    SV. Chiefly March to May and September to November, but
exceptionally in other months, including winter; particularly Norfolk,
but most other east and south coast counties from Durham to Dorset,
and Derby, Nottingham, Hertford, Surrey, Cornwall, Somerset,
Gloucester, Cheshire, Lancashire, and Cumberland; Merioneth and
Caernarvon; Wigtown, Dumfries, Renfrew, Sutherland, Caithness and
Shetland; Isle of Man; and Cork and Waterford. Formerly more
frequent than Little Crake *P.parva*, but recently much rarer (only two
records in the period 1948–68).

Spotted Crake   **A**
Porzana porzana (Linnaeus)

Palaearctic. Breeds from southern Fenno-Scandia, British Isles (irregularly), France and perhaps Spain east through Europe and west Asia to
the Yenisei, south to northern Italy, northern Balkans, perhaps Asia
Minor, the Caucasus, and northern Kazakhstan; between 64°N and
40°N. Migratory, wintering in the Mediterranean area, north Africa,
east Africa south to Lesotho (Basutoland), Arabia, Iran and northern
India.

    Monotypic.

    MB. Extremely rare and little known, but probably an annual nester in scattered parts of England, Wales and Scotland, perhaps also formerly in Ireland where, however, proved only once (about 1851). Decreased through drainage of breeding habitats, mainly before mid-19th century, but during 1926–37 probably bred in about ten counties of England and Wales; more recently, certain or probable breeding in one or more years in Somerset, Hertford, Suffolk, Sutherland and perhaps three other southern counties and two northern ones.

PV (and occasionally **WV**). March to May and August to November, particularly mid-August to October, with individuals occasionally recorded in winter. All parts, but perhaps least common in northern Scotland and most frequent in England with a majority of records in coastal counties.

Sora Rail B
Porzana carolina (Linnaeus)

Nearctic. Breeds North America from British Columbia, Ontario, and Nova Scotia south to northern Baja California, Kansas, and Pennsylvania; between 61°N and 31°N. Winters from California, Texas and Florida through the West Indies and Central America south to Peru and Guyana.

Monotypic.

SV. Five, but none for over 50 years: Berkshire (October 1864), Glamorgan (1888), Inner Hebrides (October 1901), Outer Hebrides (November 1913), Galway (April 1920).

Genus GALLINULA Brisson

Cosmopolitan genus of three or four species, one in Palaearctic, breeding in Europe and the British Isles.

Moorhen A
Gallinula chloropus (Linnaeus)

Nearly cosmopolitan (not Australasian). Breeds over the greater part of Europe and central and southern Asia, from southern Fenno-Scandia, the British Isles, France and Iberia east through Russia and southwest Asia to the upper River Ob and Chinese Turkestan, thence east through India, Indo-China and eastern China north to Japan and Sakhalin; also in the Azores, northwest Africa, Egypt, Arabia, much of Africa south of the Sahara, Madagascar, Indonesia, Philippines, various islands in the Indian and Pacific Oceans, and in the Americas from Ontario and the northern United States to Argentina; between 64°N and 38°S. Largely sedentary, but the northernmost populations (except in western Europe) move south in winter into the more temperate parts of the breeding range, extending a little farther south into the northern Sudan.

G.c.chloropus (Linnaeus) breeds throughout Eurasia and in northwest Africa and Egypt.

RB. Numerous. Breeds throughout Britain and Ireland, including most major islands except some of the Inner Hebrides. British and Irish populations are largely sedentary.

WV (perhaps **PV**). Winter visitors, and probably also some passage migrants, from the Continent are widespread, September–November to March–April. Birds ringed particularly in Denmark and the Netherlands, but also in Belgium, Germany and Sweden, have been recovered here and a few ringed in Britain (chiefly in winter) have been found in Norway, Denmark, the Netherlands, Belgium and France.

Genus PORPHYRULA Blyth

Nearctic, Neotropical and Ethiopian genus of three species (if *Porphyrula (Porphyrio) alleni* of Africa is included), none in Palaearctic, but two recorded as vagrants in Europe and one in Britain.

American Purple Gallinule A
Porphyrula martinica (Linnaeus)

Nearctic and Neotropical. Breeds from the southern and southeastern United States south through Mexico, Central America and the West Indies to Peru, Bolivia and the northern Argentine; between 32°N and 25°S. Winters mainly in South America, though a few remain in the extreme south of Florida and Texas. Vagrant north to Newfoundland and across Atlantic to Norway, Azores and Cape Province; almost regular on Tristan da Cunha.

Monotypic.

SV. One, Isles of Scilly (November 1958).

Genus FULICA Linnaeus

Cosmopolitan genus of ten species, two in Palaearctic, both breeding in Europe and one in the British Isles.

Coot A
Fulica atra Linnaeus

Palaearctic, Oriental and Australasian. Breeds over the greater part of Eurasia from Iceland (irregularly), British Isles, southern Fenno-Scandia, France and Iberia east through Europe, Asia Minor and the Middle East, and thence right across Siberia to Sakhalin and Japan, south to Iraq, Iran, India, Ceylon and the Yangtse Basin (but apparently absent from a large area of southern Mongolia and central and western China); also in the Azores, northwest Africa, Egypt, New Guinea, Australia and Tasmania; between 65°N and 44°S. Sedentary and partially migratory, the northern populations (except in western Europe) moving into the central and southern parts of the breeding range and beyond it to the southern Sahara, Sudan, southern Arabia and southeast Asia.

F.a.atra Linnaeus breeds throughout the range except New Guinea, Australia and Tasmania.

RB. Fairly numerous. Breeds throughout Britain and Ireland, but scarce in the northwest Highlands and now absent or only occasional in the Inner Hebrides and Shetland where formerly not uncommon. This local decrease is offset by an evident increase in eastern England. Essentially sedentary but populations from higher and more northerly breeding areas within the British Isles move down and south, often to large reservoirs or lakes and coastal districts.

WV. Winter visitors (with perhaps some transient visitors in spring and autumn) are widespread in the British Isles from October to April. Birds ringed in the Baltic States, Denmark, Germany, Netherlands, Belgium and Channel Islands have been recovered here, and there are also numerous recoveries of others ringed in Britain (many of them in winter) across middle Europe and the Baltic area east to 39°E in Russia.

Family OTIDIDAE

Genus OTIS Linnaeus

Palaearctic genus of two species, both breeding in Europe and one formerly in the British Isles where both are now vagrants.

Little Bustard   A
Otis tetrax Linnaeus

Southwestern and central Palaearctic. Breeds northwest Africa, Iberia and France east through Sardinia, southern Italy, Sicily, the Balkans and western Turkey, and from southern Russia eastwards through the Kirghiz Steppes to western Siberia and western Altai, south to Turkestan, as well as Iran and southern Transcaspia; between 55°N and 33°N. Sedentary and migratory, the northern populations wintering irregularly south to the Mediterranean area, the Nile delta, Transcaucasia, Iran, Afghanistan and northwest India.

Monotypic.

SV. Probably more than 100 recorded, irregularly now, with only eight records during 1958–68. Noted chiefly October–January, but there have been occurrences in all months, the recent ones being in April, June, July, October, November and December (three). Most in Yorkshire, Norfolk, Suffolk and Cornwall, rather fewer in other southern counties and still more occasional elsewhere in England and in Wales; eight have been recorded in Scotland and eight in Ireland.

Great Bustard   A
Otis tarda Linnaeus

Palaearctic. Breeds across Eurasia with a broken and relict distribution in Iberia, northern Germany and Poland, and from southeast Europe, southern Russia, Asia Minor, the Caucasus and southern Transcaspia eastwards to western Siberia, the Altai, Tien Shan and Turkestan, then more patchily still farther east to Lake Baikal, Mongolia, northern Manchuria and southern Ussuriland; between 57°N and 36°N; perhaps also in northwestern Morocco. Mainly sedentary, but also partly migratory, wintering south to southern Europe, Syria, Iraq, Iran and northern Afghanistan, and in Inner Mongolia, Korea and western, central and northern China.

O.t.tarda Linnaeus breeds Europe and western Asia east to the western Altai, Tien Shan and Turkestan.

FB. Formerly bred in many parts of England and even southeast Scotland (Berwick before 1526). Last bred Norfolk in 1830 and Suffolk in 1832; females lingered until at least 1838 and some may have remained in Norfolk until 1845.

SV. In winters of 1870/71, 1879/80 and 1890/91 a number of migrants were noted and there were single birds in several other years up to 1910, but in the last 50 years only six records (nine birds): Orkney (January 1924), Cork (December 1925), Suffolk (four in December 1925), Yorkshire (December 1925 to March 1926), Shetland (May 1936), Norfolk (March 1963).

Genus **CHLAMYDOTIS** Lesson

Palaearctic and marginally Oriental monospecific genus, just reaching Europe (southeast Russia); has occurred as a vagrant in Britain.

Houbara Bustard   A
Chlamydotis undulata (Jacquin)

Palaearctic and marginally Oriental. Breeds from the eastern Canaries across northern Africa to Egypt, the Sinai Peninsula, southern Israel, the Syrian Desert, eastern Turkey and southern Armenia through Iraq to Iran, Afghanistan and Baluchistan, north through Transcaspia and Turkestan to the southern Kirghiz Steppes and eastwards to the Altai and Mongolia; between 52°N and 22°N. The African population is mainly sedentary, but the Asiatic one winters south to Arabia, Iraq, Iran and northwest India.

C.u.macqueenii (Gray) breeds throughout the Asiatic (and marginally European) range from east of the Nile to Mongolia.

SV. Five, all 1847–98 except one in 1962: Lincoln (October 1847), Yorkshire (October 1892, October 1896), Aberdeen (October 1898), Suffolk (November–December 1962). *C.u.macqueenii* in the first four cases, but not determined in the last.

Order CHARADRIIFORMES

Family HAEMATOPODIDAE

Genus HAEMATOPUS Linnaeus

Cosmopolitan genus of four to seven species; only one in Palaearctic, breeding also in Europe and the British Isles.

Oystercatcher   A
Haematopus ostralegus Linnaeus

Palaearctic. Breeds Iceland, Faeroes, British Isles and coasts of Europe from northern Russia to Portugal, discontinuously in the area of the northern Mediterranean east to Turkey; also inland in southern Russia and Asia from the Black Sea to western Siberia and Russian Turkestan; again locally on the Pacific coasts of Asia; between 71°N and 36°N. Sedentary and migratory, northern populations wintering south to the Mediterranean area, the Red Sea, Ceylon, southeast China and Japan.

 H.o.ostralegus Linnaeus breeds Europe east to the Pechora in northern Russia.

 RB and **MB**. Fairly numerous. Breeds around almost the entire coastline of Britain and Ireland, and widely inland (usually along or near rivers) in Scotland and northern England south to north Yorkshire. Inland breeding grounds are deserted after the breeding season when birds move to the coast and some emigrate, reaching as far south as Iberia and even Morocco in winter.

 PV and **WV**. Passage mainly July to October, March to May, chiefly coastal but also overland. Winters all coasts, the largest concentrations occurring in northwest England and south Wales. Wintering populations include birds from Iceland, Faeroes and northwest Europe as well as British and Irish residents.

Family CHARADRIIDAE

Genus VANELLUS Brisson

Nearly cosmopolitan (not Nearctic) genus of 24 species, six in the Palaearctic, three breeding in Europe (two marginally) and one in the British Isles, where another has occurred as a straggler.

Sociable Plover   A
Vanellus gregarius (Pallas)

Central Palaearctic. Breeds from southeast Russia, east of the Volga, through the Kirghiz Steppes to Semipalatinsk south to the Aral Sea and Lake Balkhash; between 55°N and 47°N. Winters Iraq and northeast Africa.
Monotypic.
 SV. Ten records: Lancashire (autumn 1860), Meath (August 1899), Waterford (December 1909), Orkney (November 1926), Northampton (October 1951), Dorset (April 1961), Hertford (October 1961), Devon (September–November 1963), Kent (September–November 1968), Suffolk (October 1968).

Lapwing   A
Vanellus vanellus (Linnaeus)

Palaearctic. Breeds Faeroes, British Isles, throughout most of Europe, and eastwards across Asia mainly between 60°N and 40°N to the Pacific coast; extreme limits 68°N and 36°N. Sedentary and migratory; winters in central and western Europe, the Mediterranean region, Iraq, northwest India and southeast China.
Monotypic.
 RB and **MB**. Numerous. Widespread, breeding in every county,

though rather locally in west Cornwall, northwest Scotland and southwest Ireland. Partially migratory, some British birds wintering west to Ireland, south to Iberia and Morocco.

PV and **WV**. Passage and weather movements may take place in all months, and on the English east coast, for example, immigration occurs from early June to December (sometimes into January), emigration from January to May. Widespread in winter, but scarce or absent parts of north Scottish mainland (especially inland), and during severe weather absent also from much of Britain farther south. Wintering population includes many birds from northern and eastern continental Europe, especially Scandinavia, Germany and the Netherlands.

Genus PLUVIALIS Brisson

Holarctic and Australasian genus of four species, three in the Palaearctic, two breeding in Europe and one in the British Isles, where another occurs as a regular visitor and a third as a vagrant.

Grey Plover   A
Pluvialis squatarola (Linnaeus)

Northern Holarctic. Breeds arctic tundras of Eurasia from the Kanin Peninsula in Russia, east across Siberia to Anadyr; and in North America (where known as Black-bellied Plover) from Alaska east to southwest Baffin Island; between 75°N and 64°N. Virtually cosmopolitan in winter, south as far as South Africa, Australia and Brazil.

Monotypic.

PV and **WV**. Passage mainly late July to November, March to June (a few non-breeders remain in summer), all coasts except northern Scotland and Northern Isles (where irregular); rarely inland. Winters on coasts of nearly all maritime counties, north to Ayr (occasionally Inner Hebrides) in the west, and Aberdeen (occasionally Caithness) in the east.

Golden Plover   A
Pluvialis apricaria (Linnaeus)

Northwestern Palaearctic. Breeds Iceland, Faeroes, British Isles and Scandinavia east through the Baltic States, northern Russia and Siberia to the Taimyr Peninsula; between 72°N and 51°N. Winters west and southwest Europe, Mediterranean basin and south Caspian.

P.a.apricaria (Linnaeus) breeds British Isles, Denmark, west Germany and southern Scandinavia.

P.a.altifrons C. L. Brehm breeds Iceland, Faeroes and from northern Scandinavia eastwards.

RB and **MB.** Fairly numerous. Widespread from southern Pennines and northeast Yorkshire north through northern England and Scotland to the Outer Hebrides and Shetland, more locally in Wales (Brecon, Cardigan, Montgomery, Merioneth, Denbigh; perhaps Pembroke and Radnor; irregular Anglesey), Devon (Dartmoor only) and Ireland (Galway, Mayo, Cavan, Fermanagh, Antrim; occasionally Donegal). Probably mainly resident, though some at least winter south of the English Channel. Breeding grounds are generally deserted from about late August to end February. Breeding race is *P.a.apricaria*, but small numbers resembling *P.a.altifrons* also nest in parts of Scotland and Ireland.

WV and **PV.** Passage to some extent in most months but mainly March to May, August to October; chiefly on or near coasts. Regular in winter on all coasts and also inland in many counties of England, Wales and southern Scotland. Winter visitors and migrants include both *P.a.apricaria* and *P.a.altifrons*, in unknown proportions (the latter most conspicuous in April when in summer plumage). Immigrants include many from Iceland (also Faeroes), especially in Ireland, as well as from the Continent.

Lesser Golden Plover   **A**
Pluvialis dominica (P. L. S. Müller)

Northeastern Palaearctic and northern Nearctic. Breeds northern Siberia eastwards from the Yamal Peninsula, and in northern North America from Alaska east to southern Baffin Island; between 75°N and 60°N. Nearctic population winters southern South America; Siberian one in Hawaii, south and southeast Asia and Australia.

P.d.dominica (P. L. S. Müller) breeds North American range.

P.d.fulva (Gmelin) breeds Siberian range.

SV. Fourteen, all in autumn: Surrey (November 1870; *P.d.fulva*), Orkney (November 1887; *P.d.fulva*), Mayo (September 1894; *P.d. dominica*), Essex (August 1896; *P.d.fulva*), Meath (November 1952; *P.d.dominica*), Fair Isle (September 1956), Isles of Scilly (September–October 1962), Kerry (September 1963), Cork (three in September–October 1966), Roscommon (October 1966), Gloucester (October

1967), Cornwall (October 1968). Probably *P.d.dominica* in cases where subspecies not determined, as mostly in western areas and associated with other American vagrants.

Genus CHARADRIUS Linnaeus

Cosmopolitan genus of 24 species, nine in Palaearctic, only three breeding in Europe and two of these (the third formerly) in the British Isles, where single species from Asia and North America have been recorded as scarce vagrants.

Ringed Plover A
Charadrius hiaticula Linnaeus

Northern Palaearctic and northeastern Nearctic. Breeds Iceland, Faeroes, British Isles and coasts and tundras of entire northern Eurasia east to Chukotski and Anadyr; also eastern Ellesmere and Baffin Islands eastwards to Greenland; between 82°N and 48°N. Migratory and sedentary; winters south to southern Africa and western India.

C.h.hiaticula Linnaeus breeds entire range except Russia and Siberia; intergrades with *C.h.tundrae* in northern Scandinavia and Kola Peninsula.

C.h.tundrae (Lowe) breeds Russia and Siberia.

RB and **MB**. Not scarce. Breeds around almost entire coastline (but only very locally in some areas, e.g. Devon and north Wales, and absent from Cheshire and probably now also from mainland of Cornwall) and inland in the Brecks (East Anglia), in parts of northern England, Scotland and Ireland, and occasionally elsewhere. Mainly resident but some winter south of English Channel. *C.h.hiaticula*.

PV and **WV**. Passage of Continental birds, also some from Iceland and Greenland, mainly March to May, August to October, all coasts, and regularly in small numbers in most inland counties. Winters around entire coastline, and is only occasionally found inland at this season. Mainly *C.h.hiaticula*, but *C.h.tundrae* has been recognized on a few occasions and probably occurs regularly.

Little Ringed Plover A
Charadrius dubius Scopoli

Palaearctic, Oriental and Australasian. Breeds over the whole of the first two of these regions, mainly south of the range of *C.hiaticula*, in Europe north to southern Fenno-Scandia and 65°N in northeast Russia; also in New Guinea and New Ireland; between 66°N and 10°S. Sedentary except for the northern populations which winter south to about the equator in Africa and Asia; European birds winter in Africa.

C.d.curonicus Gmelin breeds Palaearctic part of range.

MB. Scarce. First bred 1938 (Hertford), next in 1944 (Middlesex) and regularly since. Has increased and spread and by 1967 about 230 pairs were breeding in all counties in eastern and central England from Kent, Surrey, Hampshire and Berkshire north to Durham, west to Gloucester, Warwick, Stafford and Cheshire; the species breeds occasionally or irregularly in Suffolk, Sussex and Lancashire. The breeding range extended to Northumberland and the Clyde region of Scotland in 1968. Resident from late March to October.

PV. Mainly April to June, August to October, chiefly within breeding range but also regularly in Somerset, Shropshire and Flint; has occasionally been recorded west to Cornwall, Carmarthen, Pembroke, Merioneth and Anglesey, also twice in Ireland (Dublin and Cork), and seven times in Scotland (west and north to Skye, Fair Isle and Shetland) apart from breeding in the Clyde area in 1968. Formerly known only as scarce vagrant.

Kentish Plover A
Charadrius alexandrinus Linnaeus

Cosmopolitan. Breeds on European coasts south of southern Sweden, across southern Russia and central Siberia to Transbaicalia, and south to Africa, Arabia, southern Asia, Australia and Tasmania, as well as in North and South America; between 57°N and 42°S. Sedentary and migratory; Eurasian birds winter south to tropical Africa and India.

C.a.alexandrinus Linnaeus breeds Eurasia.

FB. Very small numbers bred locally in Kent (less often Sussex) until about 1930, occasionally thereafter until the last pair nested (in east Sussex) in 1956; also bred Suffolk, 1952.

PV. Late March to May, August to October, regularly in Norfolk (very small numbers), irregularly on other parts of east and south coasts from Yorkshire to the Isles of Scilly; only rarely inland and elsewhere, but has been recorded west to Ireland, north to Scotland. Exceptional in other months but has been noted in winter, e.g. Norfolk, December 1968.

Killdeer A
Charadrius vociferus Linnaeus

Nearctic and Neotropical. Breeds from British Columbia, south Mackenzie and New Brunswick south to Mexico and Florida; also West Indies and Peru; between about 62°N and 18°S. Northern populations winter in the southern United States and Caribbean area. *C.v.vociferus* Linnaeus breeds from Canada south to Mexico.

SV. Sixteen recorded, usually singly, all November to March apart from one April and one undated: four Isles of Scilly, two Kerry, two Cork, and one in each of Cornwall, Devon, Hampshire, Huntingdon, Derby, Aberdeen, Dublin and Down.

Caspian Plover B
Charadrius asiaticus Pallas

Central Palaearctic. Breeds from northern Caucasia eastwards through the Kirghiz Steppes to Semipalatinsk, south to the Caspian and Aral Seas, also in northeast Iran; between 51°N and 37°N. Winters in eastern and southern Africa.

Monotypic.

SV. Two, Norfolk (May 1890).

Genus EUDROMIAS C. L. Brehm

Palaearctic and Neotropical genus of two species; one species in Palaearctic, breeding in Europe and the British Isles.

Dotterel A
Eudromias morinellus (Linnaeus)

Northern Palaearctic. Breeds (discontinuously, mainly in mountains) Scotland, Netherlands (locally, at sea-level), Fenno-Scandia, Poland, Austria, Czechoslovakia, Rumania and possibly Italy; in Asia as far east as the Kolymski Mountains and south to the Russian Altai; between 75°N and 42°N. Winters from northwest Africa and the Mediterranean east to the south Caspian and Persian Gulf.

Monotypic.

MB. Very scarce. Virtually confined to the central Scottish Highlands (north Perth, northwest Angus, west Aberdeen, south Banff,

Inverness) and perhaps to a few sites in Ross; has bred in Sutherland and southwest Scotland; now nests only irregularly in the English Lake District. Resident May to August.

PV. Mainly April to May, September to October (rarely to December); recorded regularly in Norfolk and Cambridge, fairly regularly in southwest England, occasionally elsewhere (rarely in Ireland). That some autumn migrants may originate from well to east is indicated by the recovery in June on the Yenisei in west Siberia of one ringed on passage in Wexford in the previous September.

Family RECURVIROSTRIDAE

Genus HIMANTOPUS Brisson

Cosmopolitan monospecific genus, breeding in Europe and wandering to the British Isles where it has bred on one occasion.

Black-winged Stilt   A
Himantopus himantopus (Linnaeus)

Cosmopolitan south of 50°N. Breeds discontinuously in Iberia (except northwest), southwest and south France (irregularly north to the Low Countries), north Africa, central and southeast Europe east through Asia to Inner Mongolia; also in India and southeast Asia, the southwestern United States and Central America, southern South America, central, eastern and southern Africa, Australia and New Zealand; between 50°N and 47°S. Sedentary or, where migratory, the more northerly populations winter south within the breeding range.

H.h.himantopus (Linnaeus) confined to Palaearctic, Oriental and Ethiopian regions.

CB. Two pairs bred in Nottingham in 1945.

SV. About 150 (recorded almost annually in recent years) in all months April to November but chiefly April to June and August to September, also, more rarely, December to February. Most have occurred in ones and twos (occasionally up to five together) on the south and east coasts north to Norfolk, some inland in central and southern England, and a few north to Scotland, west to Wales and Ireland.

Genus RECURVIROSTRA Linnaeus

Cosmopolitan genus of four species, one in the Palaearctic, breeding in Europe and the British Isles.

Avocet   A
Recurvirostra avosetta Linnaeus

Palaearctic and Ethiopian. Breeds southern Sweden, Denmark, the Low Countries, eastern England, and on the Atlantic and Mediterranean coasts of western Europe, again from central and southeast Europe east to Inner Mongolia; also in north Africa, Kenya and South Africa; between 57°N and 35°S. Sedentary and migratory, the more northerly populations wintering in southwest and southern Europe, southwards to South Africa, western India and southeast China.

Monotypic.

RB and **MB**. Very scarce. Bred regularly, mainly in eastern England from Sussex to the Humber, until the early to mid-19th century. Then no further breeding till nested Ireland in 1938 (two pairs, Wexford) and sporadically in Essex and probably Norfolk from 1941 to 1946. Re-established in Suffolk in 1947, subsequently increasing to over 100 pairs at Havergate Island with smaller numbers at Minsmere, also other parts of Orford area. Has not spread permanently outside this county, although pairs bred in Kent in 1958, probably in Essex in 1953, and in one or more undisclosed counties in the 1960s. Resident April to September (part of breeding population may winter in southwest England).

PV. Late March to June, July to September. Regular in small numbers on coasts of southeast England (Sussex to Norfolk), irregular elsewhere on coasts and inland in southern England, rarely north to Scotland and west to Ireland.

WV. Regular wintering flock of about 60 birds on Tamar Estuary (Devon/Cornwall) and small numbers locally elsewhere in southwest

England, north Kent and southwest Ireland (Cork); infrequent in winter in other parts, but has been recorded occasionally north to Anglesey and Lincoln as well as in various parts of Ireland.

Family SCOLOPACIDAE

Genus BARTRAMIA Lesson

Nearctic monospecific genus, which has wandered to Europe and the British Isles.

Upland Sandpiper*   **A**
Bartramia longicauda (Bechstein)

Nearctic. Breeds from southern Alaska, southern Manitoba and Maine, south to Washington, north Texas and Maryland; between 62°N and 34°N. Winters in southern South America.
Monotypic.
SV. Twenty-three recorded, usually singly, all September to December (nine 1851–1901, two 1922–33, twelve 1956–68). Thirteen England (eight in Cornwall and the Isles of Scilly; also one each in Somerset, Suffolk, Cambridge, Warwick, Northumberland), four Wales (Pembroke, Flint), one Scotland (Dumfries), and five Ireland (Cork, two Wexford, Galway, Sligo).

Genus NUMENIUS Brisson

Holarctic genus of eight species, five in Palaearctic but only two breeding in Europe and the British Isles, where another formerly occurred as a scarce vagrant.

* Bartram's Sandpiper of 1952 List; Upland Plover of AOU List.

Eskimo Curlew   **B**
Numenius borealis (Forster)

Northern Nearctic. Breeds very sparsely in northern Mackenzie, Canada; verging on extinction. Winters in southern South America. Monotypic.

SV. Seven, all in 19th century: Suffolk (two in November 1852), Kincardine (September 1855), Ireland (October 1870, probably Sligo), Aberdeen (September 1878), Aberdeen (September 1880), Isles of Scilly (September 1887).

Whimbrel   **A**
Numenius phaeopus (Linnaeus)

Northern Holarctic. Breeds Iceland, Faeroes, Scotland, Scandinavia and eastwards across north Russia and west Siberia to the Yenisei; again in northeastern Siberia, and from northern Alaska to northwestern Mackenzie and Hudson Bay; between 71°N and 55°N. European birds winter mainly in Africa south to Cape Province; also found in winter in India, southeast Asia, Australia, New Zealand and South America.
    N.p.phaeopus (Linnaeus) breeds Eurasia east to the Yenisei.
    N.p.hudsonicus Latham breeds Alaska and Canada.
    MB. Very scarce. Confined to Shetland and (a very few pairs) Lewis, Outer Hebrides; has bred sporadically elsewhere in Scotland, but the only recent records are from west Sutherland (1960), St. Kilda (1964), and probably Orkney (at least two pairs in 1968). Resident from May to August. *N.p.phaeopus.*
    PV (also **WV**). Mainly mid-April to mid-June, July to October, all coasts (where some non-breeders remain in summer), also fairly frequently overland, though relatively few birds alight inland. Exceptional in winter, when recorded occasionally in Ireland and on British coasts north to Lancashire and Yorkshire. *N.p.phaeopus.*
    SV. *N.p.hudsonicus* has been identified twice: Fair Isle (May 1955), Kerry (October 1957).

Curlew   **A**
Numenius arquata (Linnaeus)

Palaearctic. Breeds from northwest France, the British Isles and Scandinavia east across Eurasia to central Manchuria, north to about the

Arctic Circle in west Siberia, south to Switzerland, Crimea and the Aral Sea; between 70°N and 46°N. Winters from northwest Europe (including Iceland) south to southern Africa, India and southeast China.

N.a.arquata (Linnaeus) breeds Europe east to the Urals.

RB and **MB**. Fairly numerous. Widely distributed in Ireland and in western and northern Britain (but absent from the Outer Hebrides apart from the recent colonization of Lewis by a pair or two), and has extended its range this century to lowland areas so that it now breeds at least locally in every county except seven in southeast England (Kent, Essex, Middlesex, Hertford, Bedford, Cambridge—where has bred— and Huntingdon). Partially migratory, some British birds wintering south to Iberia. Resident on breeding grounds approximately March to July or August.

PV and **WV**. Passage mainly July to October, March to May, chiefly coastal (all areas) but also frequently overland. Non-breeders remain in some numbers on all coasts throughout the summer. Widespread on all coasts and in many inland areas in winter, native birds being augmented by many from northwest Europe.

Genus LIMOSA Brisson

Holarctic genus of four species, two in Palaearctic, breeding also in Europe, one breeding in the British Isles, where the other occurs as a common visitor.

Black-tailed Godwit   A
Limosa limosa (Linnaeus)

Palaearctic. Breeds Iceland, British Isles, and from the Low Countries, southern Baltic and Ukraine east across Eurasia to Kamchatka and Ussuriland; between 65°N and 47°N. Winters from southern British Isles and southern Europe to tropical Africa, India, southeast Asia and Australia.

L.l.islandica C. L. Brehm breeds Iceland.

L.l.limosa (Linnaeus) breeds Europe and Asia east to the Ob.

MB. Very scarce. Bred regularly (mainly in eastern England, Yorkshire to Suffolk) until the early 19th century. Nested occasionally in East Anglia 1937–49. Re-established as a British breeding bird on the Ouse Washes (Cambridge/Norfolk), where increased from one pair in 1952 to 41 pairs in 1969. Has also bred occasionally in at least eight other counties since 1940, from Suffolk, and probably Somerset, north to Shetland. Resident on breeding grounds from March to July. Probably *L.l.limosa* in East Anglia, but north Scottish records may refer to *L.l.islandica*.

PV and **WV**. Passage mainly late March to May, July to September, but also recorded in June and a few birds remain on some coasts throughout the summer. Regular on passage on coasts of all Irish and most English and Welsh maritime counties, more locally in east Scotland (north to Orkney); occasional inland and on coast of west Scotland. Winters regularly on all coasts of Ireland south of Mayo and Dublin, on the English south coast, also in Somerset, Suffolk, Pembroke and Lancashire, and occasionally elsewhere north to Fife and south Argyll. Migrants and winter visitors include both *L.l.islandica* and *L.l.limosa*, the former occurring everywhere and being the predominant race in Ireland and west and north Britain, the latter being probably largely confined to the English east and south coasts, where numbers of Black-tailed Godwits wintering have greatly increased since 1950.

Bar-tailed Godwit A
Limosa lapponica (Linnaeus)

Northern Palaearctic and northwestern Nearctic. Breeds from northern Fenno-Scandia east across northern Eurasia and into western Alaska; between 76°N and 60°N (south only to 66°N in Eurasia). Winters from the British Isles south to South Africa, India, southeast Asia, Australia and New Zealand.

L.l.lapponica (Linnaeus) breeds northern tundras of Europe and Siberia east to the Taimyr Peninsula.

PV and **WV**. Passage mainly late July to October, March to end May (a few non-breeders remain on coasts in summer). Occurs on passage and in winter on coasts of virtually every maritime county in Britain and Ireland, most numerously in estuarine areas. Seldom noted inland.

Genus **TRINGA** Linnaeus

Holarctic genus of twelve species, of which nine are in the Palaearctic; six breed in Europe, three now nest regularly in the British Isles and a fourth has done so; the two scarcest of these four occur here as regular passage visitors, as does a third, while four others have occurred as stragglers, including three from the Nearctic.

Spotted Redshank A
Tringa erythropus (Pallas)

Northern Palaearctic. Breeds from northern Fenno-Scandia east across northern Russia and Siberia to Anadyr; between 72°N and 65°N. Winters mainly from the Mediterranean basin (and in small numbers north to the British Isles) south to the equator in Africa, eastwards to India and southeast China.

Monotypic.

PV. April to June, and much more commonly July to October; chiefly on coasts of East Anglia and southeast England, but regularly also in most English and many Welsh and Irish counties, and locally in southwest and eastern Scotland and Orkney.

WV. Formerly occasional in winter; has increased, and small numbers now winter regularly but locally on east and south coasts from Norfolk to Cornwall (mainly from Hampshire westwards), in Cambridge, Gloucester, on the Cheshire Dee, and in southeast and southwest Ireland; irregular elsewhere, but occasionally recorded north to Northern Ireland and Scotland.

Redshank A
Tringa totanus (Linnaeus)

Palaearctic. Breeds Eurasia from Iceland, Faeroes, British Isles, Scandinavia and central Europe east across southern Siberia, western China and Mongolia to Ussuriland; also discontinuously in France, Iberia and northern Italy; between 71°N and 30°N, but in Asia mainly south of 53°N. Winters from Iceland and the British Isles south to the Mediterranean, tropical Africa, India and southeast Asia.

T.t.robusta (Schiøler) breeds Iceland, Faeroes.

T.t. britannica Mathews breeds British Isles.

T.t.totanus Linnaeus breeds continental Europe east to west Siberia.

RB and **MB**. Fairly numerous. Widely distributed. Breeds most commonly in flat coastal regions, but regularly also in every inland county except Hereford (where irregular) and Carlow, and in all coastal ones except Cornwall, Devon (fairly regular in extreme southeast until 1962, but not since), Carmarthen (may breed occasionally), Pembroke (irregular), Denbigh, Kilkenny, Waterford, Cork, and Kerry (has bred once). Mainly resident but some birds winter south of the English Channel, some perhaps reaching as far south as Morocco. *T.t.britannica*.

PV and **WV**. Passage mainly March to May, late June to October; chiefly coastal but also frequently in many inland areas. Winters all coastal areas (very locally inland). Passage and wintering populations include all three subspecies above, though *T.t.totanus* has not been identified in Ireland.

Lesser Yellowlegs   A
Tringa flavipes (Gmelin)

Northern Nearctic. Breeds from Alaska and central British Columbia east to Hudson Bay and Quebec; between 68°N and 53°N. Winters from the southern United States to southern South America.
Monotypic.

SV. Over 70 recorded, with up to six (on average, three) identified annually since 1958, chiefly singly between late July and September, but also through to November and December and again in spring. Records are mainly from the coasts of southern England (a few inland) but they include some from Wales and northern England and also four from Scotland and 15 from Ireland.

Marsh Sandpiper   A
Tringa stagnatilis (Bechstein)

Central and eastern Palaearctic. Breeds southeast Europe and west Asia from Bulgaria, Rumania and the Ukraine east across the Kirghiz Steppes to Zaisan Nor; also discontinuously in Transbaicalia and possibly Ussuriland; between 57°N and 45°N. Winters from the eastern Mediterranean south to South Africa, India, Indo-China and Australia.
Monotypic.

SV. Eighteen (one 1887, two 1937, nine 1947–56, six 1963–68), nearly all singly but once two and once three together. Six April–May, one July, ten August–September, one October. Chiefly in southeast England, Sussex to Lincoln, but also recorded in Cheshire, Lancashire, Durham, Northumberland and Caithness.

Greenshank   A
Tringa nebularia (Gunnerus)

Palaearctic. Breeds Eurasia from Scotland, Fenno-Scandia and north Russia eastwards across Siberia (mainly between about 65°N and 55°N) to Kamchatka and Amurland; extreme limits 70°N and 52°N. Winters from the British Isles and Mediterranean south to South Africa, India, Indo-China and Australia.

Monotypic.

MB. Scarce. Restricted to central and north Scottish Highlands (south to northern Argyll, northern Perth and Aberdeen), Skye and the Outer Hebrides. Bred Orkney 1951, and has bred occasionally (not recently) in Scotland to the south of the present breeding range. Resident from about April to July.

PV. April to early June, late June to October; most numerous in autumn when widespread all coastal areas and occurs regularly and frequently inland.

WV. Small numbers winter regularly on the coasts of southwest England (Hampshire and Gloucester to the Isles of Scilly), southwest and northwest Wales, western Scotland, and on all coasts of Ireland, in very small numbers in Essex and Suffolk and in eastern Scotland north to Caithness, and irregularly elsewhere.

Greater Yellowlegs A
Tringa melanoleuca (Gmelin)

Northern Nearctic. Breeds from Alaska and British Columbia east across Canada to Labrador and Newfoundland; between 60°N and 47°N. Winters from the southern United States to Patagonia.

Monotypic.

SV. Seventeen (two 1906–27, nine 1939–55, six 1957–68). Three April–May, three (all Irish) December–January, the rest July to October; in Isles of Scilly (three), Cornwall/Devon, Kent, Essex, Northampton, Flint, Aberdeen, Shetland, Cork (two), Down, Antrim (two), Donegal; also one from an unknown Irish locality.

Green Sandpiper A
Tringa ochropus Linnaeus

Palaearctic. Breeds Eurasia from central and southern Fenno-Scandia, east Germany and the Ukraine east to the Kolyma in eastern Siberia, north to the Arctic Circle, south to about 50°N on the Kirghiz Steppes, Russian Altai and Amurland; between 68°N and 49°N, and sporadically farther south. Winters mainly from the Mediterranean south to tropical Africa, India and southeast Asia.

Monotypic.

CB. Only two proved breeding records, in Westmorland (1917) and Inverness (1959).

PV. Mainly March to May, and (more numerously) late June to November, annually in nearly all counties in England and Wales, but much less common and widespread in Scotland and Ireland, and seldom in the west and northwest of either.

WV. Small numbers winter locally but regularly in about 20 (chiefly coastal) counties in England and Wales south of Denbigh and Lincoln, also in eastern and southern Ireland (Dublin to Cork), and irregularly elsewhere, mainly in the southern half of England but occasionally north to south Scotland.

Solitary Sandpiper   A
Tringa solitaria Wilson

Northern Nearctic. Breeds from central Alaska and British Columbia, north to north Mackenzie, east to Labrador; between 69°N and 51°N. Winters from the southern United States south to Argentina.

SV. Eleven, all dated records being in autumn: Lanark (before 1870), Isles of Scilly (September 1882), Cornwall (October 1884), Kent (July 1908), Norfolk (August 1942; September 1947), Nottingham (August–September 1962), Lincoln (August 1963), Wiltshire (September 1966), Essex/Hertford (September–October 1967), Kerry (September 1968). Subspecies not determined.

Wood Sandpiper   A
Tringa glareola Linnaeus

Palaearctic. Breeds from Denmark and the Scandinavian peninsula eastwards across the whole of northern Eurasia to Kamchatka and Amurland; between 71°N and 51°N. Winters from the Mediterranean south to South Africa, India, southeast Asia and Australia.

Monotypic.

MB. Extremely scarce. Bred Northumberland 1853. No further records till 1959, since when a very few pairs have bred in northern Scotland, most often in Sutherland and Inverness, also elsewhere south to northern Perthshire and probably northern Argyll. Resident from May to July or August.

PV. Mid-April to early June, early July to mid-October, chiefly in autumn when recorded annually in most English counties (most numerously in the south and east) and much more locally in eastern and southern Ireland and eastern Scotland. Irregular elsewhere, and especially infrequent on passage in north and northwest Scotland. Rarely overwinters, the only recent record being one inland in Cheshire, 1958/59.

Genus XENUS Kaup

Palaearctic monospecific genus (sometimes placed in *Tringa*) breeding in Europe and occurring as a vagrant in the British Isles.

Terek Sandpiper A
Xenus cinereus (Güldenstädt)

Eastern and central Palaearctic. Breeds from Finland and western Russia east to eastern Siberia; between 70°N and 52°N. Winters from the Persian Gulf south to South Africa, India, southeast Asia and Australia.
Monotypic.
SV. Five: Sussex (May 1951), Suffolk (June 1951), Durham (September 1952), Cornwall (June 1961), Hampshire (May 1963).

Genus ACTITIS Illiger

Holarctic genus of two species, one Palaearctic and the other Nearctic, of which the former breeds in the British Isles and the latter occurs as a vagrant.

Common Sandpiper A
Actitis hypoleucos (Linnaeus)

Palaearctic. Breeds from Iberia, British Isles and Scandinavia east across Eurasia to Kamchatka, north to about the Arctic Circle (and beyond in Scandinavia), south to the Mediterranean, northwest India, Mongolia and Japan; between 71°N and 33°N. Winters mainly from the Mediterranean south to South Africa, India, southeast Asia and Australia.
Monotypic.
MB. Not scarce. Widely distributed, breeding in all counties in Scotland and most in Ireland (not Wexford, Kilkenny; doubtfully Limerick), Wales (not Glamorgan, doubtfully Pembroke, irregular

Anglesey), and northern and western England, locally south and east to
Yorkshire (not East Riding), north Derby, north Stafford, Shropshire,
west Worcester, Hereford, and north Monmouth; absent Isle of Man.
Breeds erratically in eastern and southern England (e.g. Norfolk 1962,
1963) apart from Dartmoor (Devon) where bred locally but regularly
till 1962, though doubtfully since. Resident from April to August.

PV. Late March to May, July to mid-October; all areas including
coasts, but found mainly beside inland waters. Extent of passage of
Continental birds is largely unknown, but ringing evidence shows that
Fenno-Scandian birds occur here in autumn.

WV. Small numbers are recorded regularly in winter in Cornwall,
Hampshire, Sussex, Essex, Pembroke and Dublin, and occasionally
elsewhere north to Lincoln, Lancashire and Antrim.

Spotted Sandpiper A
Actitis macularia (Linnaeus)

Nearctic. Breeds throughout North America except in extreme north
and south; between 68°N and 30°N. Winters from the southern United
States south to southern Brazil and northern Chile.

Monotypic.

SV. Fourteen (four 1866–99, one 1924, nine 1957–68), nearly all
singly but once two together. Particularly in recent years it has been
recorded chiefly in autumn, August to November (especially September–October), but also in February, May and June (two). One each in
Ireland (Westmeath) and Wales (Carmarthen), the remainder England,
in the Isles of Scilly (five, in four successive autumns, 1965–68), Cornwall (two), Somerset, Sussex (two), Norfolk and Yorkshire.

Genus ARENARIA Brisson

Holarctic genus of two species, one confined to Nearctic, the other
breeding in Europe and occurring as a non-breeding visitor to the
British Isles.

Turnstone A
Arenaria interpres (Linnaeus)

Northern Holarctic. Breeding distribution circumpolar on arctic
coasts of most of northern Eurasia and North America (not Iceland)

south in Europe to southern Sweden and Danish Islands; between 83°N
and 55°N. Winters south as far as South Africa, Australia, New Zealand,
Chile and Brazil; in Europe north to Iceland and south Norway.

A.i.interpres (Linnaeus) breeds Ellesmere Island, Greenland, east to
Siberia and northwest Alaska.

PV and **WV**. Passage on all coasts and occasionally inland, mainly
April to early June, late July to October (some non-breeders remain on
coasts in summer south even to the Isles of Scilly). Winters on all coasts,
chiefly on rocky ones in the west. Wintering and migrant populations
include birds from northeast Nearctic as well as Palaearctic breeding
grounds.

Genus LIMNODROMUS Wied

Nearctic and locally Palaearctic genus of three species, two occurring
as scarce visitors in Europe and the British Isles.

Short-billed Dowitcher   A
Limnodromus griseus (Gmelin)

Northern Nearctic. Breeds Alaska, central Alberta to west side of
Hudson Bay, and in the Ungava Peninsula. Winters southeastern United
States and south to the West Indies, Brazil and Peru.

L.g.hendersoni Rowan occupies central part of breeding range.

L.g.griseus (Gmelin) breeds Ungava Peninsula.

SV. Of 83 or more dowitchers recorded in the British Isles, 33
were identified specifically. Of these, 13 were referred to *L.griseus* but
this total includes seven in Ireland (including a party of five) which
should perhaps now be considered as 'dowitcher species' in view of the
difficulty of separating *L.griseus* and *L.scolopaceus* in the field. The six
British records are: Middlesex (autumn 1862; almost certainly *L.g.
griseus*), Hampshire (September 1872), Hampshire (October 1902;
L.g.hendersoni), Norfolk (October–November 1957), Lincoln/Norfolk
(September 1963) and Sussex (February–March 1965). The possible
Irish records are: Roscommon (October 1963), Galway (five together,
October 1963) and Cork (October 1966).

Long-billed Dowitcher   A
Limnodromus scolopaceus (Say)

Northeastern Palaearctic and northwestern Nearctic. Breeds extreme
northeast Siberia (Chukotski Peninsula and Anadyr) and northern and

western Alaska; between 70°N and 61°N. Winters in the southern United States and south to Guatemala.

Monotypic.

SV. Of 83 or more dowitchers recorded in Britain and Ireland up to 1968, 33 were identified specifically. Of these up to 20 were *L.scolopaceus* (six 1801–93, four 1943–51, ten 1959–68). Apart from one in May, all were noted between late September and early November (one remaining till late December and another through to April), chiefly on the English south coast (nine) and in Ireland (probably five); also four elsewhere in England and one each in Wales and Scotland.

Genus GALLINAGO Brisson

Nearly cosmopolitan (not Australasian) genus of about 13 species, seven in Palaearctic, two breeding in Europe and one in the British Isles, where the other occurs as a scarce visitor.

Great Snipe   A
Gallinago media (Latham)

Northwestern Palaearctic. Breeds Norway, Sweden, and from southern Finland and northern Poland across Russia and west Siberia to the Yenisei; between 68°N and 50°N. Winters in tropical (chiefly eastern) Africa, south to Natal.

Monotypic.

SV. Probably over 200 identified, but recorded barely annually in recent years. Formerly mainly in autumn, now mainly in autumn and winter: of the 20 most recent (1958–68) records nine were in autumn (August to November), while eight were in winter (December to February) and three in spring (March–May). Apart from three at Fair Isle and one in Ireland (Down), all were from widely scattered localities in England.

Snipe   A
Gallinago gallinago (Linnaeus)

Nearly cosmopolitan (absent Australasia and perhaps South America, very local Oriental). Breeds, in Palaearctic, from western Europe (Lapland to Pyrenees) east through Siberia to Anadyr, Kamchatka and Sakhalin, south locally to India; in Nearctic, in Alaska, Canada and the northern United States; mainly between 71°N and 43°N; also (this species or close allies) in South America and southern and eastern Africa. Sedentary and migratory, becoming in winter virtually cosmopolitan (absent Australasia).

G.g.delicata (Ord) breeds North America.

G.g.faeroeensis (C. L. Brehm) breeds Iceland, Faeroes, some Scottish islands.

G.g.gallinago (Linnaeus) breeds over rest of Palaearctic.

RB (also **MB**). Fairly numerous. Widely distributed, breeding in every county exept Middlesex, but only very locally in extremely small numbers in many counties in central and southern England. Mainly resident (short-distance movements, chiefly westwards, within the British Isles), but some birds winter south of English Channel, especially in cold weather. Breeding race is *G.g.gallinago*, replaced by *G.g.faeroeensis* in Orkney, Shetland and on St. Kilda.

WV and **PV**. Passage mainly late August to November, March to April, largely inseparable from arrivals and departures of winter visitors. Widely distributed in winter (but absent or local inland in parts of northern Scotland) when population includes both *G.g.faeroeensis* from Iceland and *G.g.gallinago* from the Continent, the former being probably chiefly confined to Ireland although it has been identified in Scotland and England also.

SV. *G.g.delicata* recorded twice: Outer Hebrides (October 1920), Lancashire (September 1957).

Genus SCOLOPAX Linnaeus

Palaearctic and Australasian genus of four species, two in Palaearctic, one breeding in Europe and the British Isles.

Woodcock   A

Scolopax rusticola Linnaeus

Palaearctic. Breeds British Isles, western Europe (from the Arctic Circle to the Pyrenees and northwest Spain) and east across Eurasia mainly between 63°N and 50°N to Amurland and Japan; also in the Azores, Madeira, Canaries, Corsica, Caucasia and northern India; between 70°N and 28°N. Sedentary where ground does not freeze; migratory populations winter south to the Mediterranean and in southern and southeast Asia.

Monotypic.

RB (also **MB**). Fairly numerous. Widely but rather locally distributed over much of Britain and Ireland, but absent from southwest England (Somerset, Devon, Cornwall), Middlesex, Pembroke, Anglesey, the Outer Hebrides and Northern Isles, and not certainly known to breed Donegal. Mainly resident (some from Britain migrate to Ireland), but a few winter as far south as Iberia.

WV and **PV**. Continental immigrants arrive mainly mid-October to November, depart March to April. Widely distributed in winter except Shetland (where regular on passage), but in hard weather the population tends to concentrate in western and southern coastal districts. Extent of passage is unknown, but autumn migrants probably include transient as well as winter visitors.

Genus LYMNOCRYPTES Kaup

Palaearctic monospecific genus, breeding in Europe and occurring as a non-breeding visitor to the British Isles.

Jack Snipe   A
Lymnocryptes minima (Brünnich)

Northern Palaearctic. Breeds northern Fenno-Scandia east across northern Eurasia to the Kolyma; between 70°N and 53°N. Winters from western and southern Europe south to tropical Africa, India and southeast Asia.

Monotypic.

WV and **PV**. Winter visitors arrive September to November, depart March to May. Most numerous and widespread in autumn when passage migrants also occur, at least in eastern and southern Britain. Widely but rather locally distributed in winter, all areas, but apparently not regularly in some counties on the Welsh border, nor in several mainland counties of northern Scotland.

Genus CALIDRIS Merrem

Holarctic genus of 18 species, all breeding in high latitudes, and 15 of them in the Palaearctic; six of these breed in Europe (including Spitsbergen), but only one in the British Isles, where a further 13 have been recorded; of these 13, three occur mainly as winter visitors, three as passage migrants (one of which has bred here), and seven (six of which are mainly Nearctic) as stragglers.

Knot A
Calidris canutus (Linnaeus)

Holarctic. Breeding distribution circumpolar in high arctic latitudes: Spitsbergen, the northern Taimyr Peninsula, New Siberian Archipelago, Wrangel, Alaska and arctic islands east to Greenland; between 83°N and 64°N. Winters from the British Isles south to equatorial Africa, and elsewhere south as far as Australia, New Zealand, and the Argentine.

C.c.canutus (Linnaeus) breeds entire range except Victoria Island, Melville Peninsula and Southampton Island in North America.

PV and **WV**. Passage March to May, late July to November, all coasts, where a few non-breeders remain in summer. Winters on all coasts from the Outer Hebrides and Caithness southwards, but only locally in northern and western Scotland, and most numerously on some estuarine parts of the English east coast and the shores of the Irish Sea. Rarely inland, but small numbers have been recorded on passage or in winter on one or more occasions in the last ten years in all English counties.

Sanderling A
Calidris alba (Pallas)

Holarctic. Breeding distribution circumpolar: Spitsbergen, the northern Taimyr Peninsula, Severnaya Zemlya, Lena Delta, New Siberian Archipelago, and on northwestern Nearctic coast and islands east to Greenland; between 83°N and 64°N. Highly migratory; virtually cosmopolitan in winter.

Monotypic.

WV and **PV**. Widespread on passage, mainly on sandy coasts from Shetland southwards, March to mid-June, mid-July to October; a few non-breeders remain in summer. Rather less widely distributed around coasts in winter from the Outer Hebrides and Caithness southwards (but irregular or absent from some parts of the west coasts of Scotland, Wales and Ireland). Has been recorded in most inland counties, and occurs annually in some in spring or autumn, but numbers are always small and birds rarely remain for more than a few days at the most.

Semi-palmated Sandpiper A
Calidris pusillus (Linnaeus)

Northern Nearctic. Breeds arctic coasts of North America south to the south coast of Hudson Bay; between 71°N and 55°N. Winters from the southern United States to Chile and southern Brazil.

Monotypic.

SV. Fourteen recorded, all since 1953, twelve of them during 1964–1968, almost certainly owing to better identification rather than increased frequency. One November into December, the rest July to October (especially September–October), in Devon, Kent (two), Gloucester, Norfolk, Norfolk/Lincoln, Pembroke, Fife, Kerry (four, including three together) and Cork (two).

Western Sandpiper A
Calidris mauri (Cabanis)

Northeastern Palaearctic and northwestern Nearctic. Breeds northeast Siberia on the east coast of the Chukotski Peninsula, and in Alaska; between 71°N and 60°N. Winters from the southern United States to Central America and Peru.

Monotypic.

SV. Three: Fair Isle (May–June 1956), Wicklow (October 1960), Kerry (September 1961).

Little Stint A
Calidris minuta (Leisler)

Northern Palaearctic. Breeds from northeasternmost Norway and the Kola Peninsula eastwards across arctic Russia and Siberia to the Yana Delta and the New Siberian Archipelago; between 76°N and 66°N. Winters from the Mediterranean (small numbers only) south to southern Africa, southern Iran, Arabia and other parts of southern Asia.

Monotypic.

PV (also **WV**). Mid-April to early June (scarce), end July to mid-October; in variable numbers, chiefly in autumn, mainly on British southeast and east coasts (north to East Lothian), but also regularly in most maritime counties (and in several inland ones) of England, south Wales, and in east and southwest Ireland; rather irregular elsewhere. Recorded increasingly, and now perhaps regularly, in winter on coasts of England and Ireland, usually singly, but sometimes in small flocks.

Temminck's Stint A
Calidris temminckii (Leisler)

Northern Palaearctic. Breeds northern Eurasia, mainly to the south of *C.minuta* in west, from central and northern Norway east to the Bering Straits; between 74°N and 62°N. Winters from the Mediterranean basin south to equatorial Africa, Iraq, Arabia, southern Iran to India and southeast Asia.

Monotypic.

CB. Has attempted to breed on at least three occasions (in 1934, 1936, 1956) in the Cairngorms region of Scotland and once (1951) in Yorkshire, in every case unsuccessfully.

PV. May to mid-June, late July to October; annually in very small numbers in southeast England (Kent to Norfolk), less often elsewhere in England, and only rarely in Wales, Scotland and Ireland.

Least Sandpiper A
Calidris minutilla (Vieillot)

Northern Nearctic. Breeds from central Alaska, northern Mackenzie and Labrador, south to southern Hudson Bay, and Newfoundland; between 70°N and 47°N; also Sable Island (Nova Scotia). Winters from the western and southern United States south to Peru and Brazil.

Monotypic.

SV. Fifteen (four 1853–92, two 1955–57, nine 1962–67), all August to October, and all but two in Ireland or southwest England: one Isles of Scilly, three Cornwall, five Devon, one Lanark, one Shetland, one Kerry, two Cork, one Derry.

White-rumped Sandpiper A
Calidris fuscicollis (Vieillot)

Northern Nearctic. Breeds from northern Alaska and Baffin Island south to northwest Hudson Bay; between 74°N and 63°N. Winters in southern South America.

Monotypic.

SV. About 75, more than two-thirds of this total since 1955 during which time it has been recorded annually in autumn (July to November), mainly in September and October. About two-thirds of the records are from England (chiefly in southwestern and southern counties) and Wales, the remainder from Ireland apart from four in Scotland.

Baird's Sandpiper   A
Calidris bairdii (Coues)

Northeastern Palaearctic and northern Nearctic. Breeds extreme north-eastern Siberia and across northern North America from northern Alaska to Baffin Island and northwest Greenland; between 81°N and 62°N. Winters in inland South America, from Ecuador south to south Argentina.
Monotypic.
SV. Thirty (two 1903–11, three 1950–55, the remainder since 1961 including 16 in 1966–67). All August to October (mainly September) apart from one in each of July, November and May–June. Recorded from the Isles of Scilly (five), Dorset, Sussex, Kent/Sussex, Middlesex, Bedford, Suffolk (two), Norfolk (two), Norfolk/Lincoln, Gloucester (two), Pembroke, Lincoln, Cheshire, Yorkshire, Durham, Northumberland, St. Kilda, Kerry (three) and Cork (three).

Pectoral Sandpiper   A
Calidris melanotos (Vieillot)

Northeastern Palaearctic and northern Nearctic. Breeds on arctic coasts of northeast Siberia from the Taimyr Peninsula to the Bering Straits, and from Alaska to Hudson Bay; between 76°N and 55°N. Winters in southern South America and, in small numbers, in eastern Australia and New Zealand.
Monotypic.
SV. The most frequently recorded of all transatlantic vagrants; usually at least ten and often over 20 annually in recent years, usually singly but up to seven together. Mainly August to October, some July, and only rarely in spring. Now identified annually in Kerry and Cornwall, almost annually in Cork and the Isles of Scilly, and less frequently in many other counties (including some inland ones). A concentration of records in Ireland and southwest England, together with a strong tendency for birds to occur following westerly Atlantic gales, suggest that the great majority, if not all, are North American rather than east Siberian in origin.

Sharp-tailed Sandpiper   A
Calidris acuminata (Horsfield)

Northeastern Palaearctic. Breeds tundras of northeastern Siberia, but the extent of its range there remains practically unknown. Winters in Melanesia, Australia and New Zealand.

Monotypic.

SV. Eight: Norfolk (September 1848, September 1865, January 1868, August 1892), Lanark (October 1956), Bedford (September 1961), Durham (August 1963), Middlesex (September 1966).

Purple Sandpiper   **A**
Calidris maritima (Brünnich)

Northern Holarctic. Breeding distribution circumpolar: Iceland, Faeroes, northern and central Scandinavia, Kola Peninsula, Bear Island, Spitsbergen, Franz Josef Land, Novaya Zemlya, northern coast of the Taimyr Peninsula and southern island of Severnaya Zemlya; and in the Nearctic, discontinuously on arctic islands from Baffin Island to Greenland south to Hudson Bay; between 81°N and 56°N. Sedentary where coasts in the breeding range are ice-free, otherwise winters on Atlantic coasts south to west France (occasionally Iberia) in Europe and to Maryland (occasionally Florida) in North America.

Monotypic.

PV and **WV.** Passage, March to early June, mid-July to November (few till October), including small numbers away from rocky shores, but only extremely rarely inland. In winter widely but locally distributed on coasts, confined chiefly to rocky shores; hence is most numerous in the west and north of the British Isles, and most uncommon and local in east and southeast England.

Dunlin   **A**
Calidris alpina (Linnaeus)

Holarctic. Breeding distribution circumpolar, mainly on arctic tundras, though with a southerly extension of range into the Baltic coastal regions, Denmark and the British Isles; between 77°N and 50°N. Winters on Atlantic and North Sea coasts of Europe south to equatorial Africa, and elsewhere south to Arabia, northwest India, southeast China and the southern United States.

C.a.arctica (Schiøler) breeds northeast Greenland.

C.a.schinzii (Brehm) breeds southeast Greenland, Iceland, Faeroes, British Isles and the Baltic area.

C.a.alpina (Linnaeus) breeds from northern Scandinavia eastwards to the Taimyr Peninsula.

RB and **MB**. Not scarce. Breeds on coasts and moors of Shetland, Orkney and the Hebrides, and widely but sparsely on upland moors in most counties in Scotland (not known to breed now in Banff, Kincardine, Fife, Kinross, Clackmannan, West Lothian, Lanark, Roxburgh) and northern England south to north Derby; also locally in Wales (Denbigh, Merioneth, Cardigan; perhaps Brecon, Radnor, Montgomery), southwest England (Devon, occasionally Cornwall) and northwest Ireland (south to Galway, east to Antrim, Westmeath); very occasionally elsewhere, including single pairs, near sea-level, in Cheshire (1955) and Lincoln (1956). Breeding grounds occupied only in summer, some birds wintering south of the English Channel. *C.a.schinzii.*

PV and **WV**. Main passage, March to late May, mid-July to late October, all coasts (where some non-breeders remain in summer), also frequently inland. Distributed widely on all coasts in winter. In Scotland and northern England the wintering population comprises mainly *C.a.alpina*, and in southern England, Wales and Ireland it comprises both *C.a.alpina* and *C.a.schinzii*—the latter from Europe but probably not Iceland, though Iceland and European *schinzii*, as well as *alpina*, occur on passage. Recently, specimens of *C.a.arctica* have been identified on spring (May–June) and autumn (July–September) passage in southeast England and once (October 1968) in western Ireland (Kerry).

Curlew Sandpiper   A
Calidris ferruginea (Pontoppidan)

Northeastern Palaearctic. Breeds northern Siberia from the Taimyr Peninsula east to Khatanga Bay and locally as far as the Kolyma; between 77°N and 70°N. Winters in Africa from about Senegal and the Sudan southwards, and elsewhere south to Iraq, India, southeast Asia, Australia and New Zealand.

Monotypic.

PV. End April to early June, mid-July to mid-October. Scarce in spring, variable numbers in autumn (sometimes quite numerous), when recorded chiefly on or near the east and south coasts of England and Ireland, but regularly also on coasts of northwest England and east Scotland (north to Moray), and in several inland counties; mainly irregular elsewhere. Exceptional November to March, but since 1959–1960 a few have remained through each winter on one part of the Lancashire coast.

Genus MICROPALAMA Baird

Northern Nearctic monospecific genus, vagrant to the British Isles.

Stilt Sandpiper   **A**
Micropalama himantopus (Bonaparte)

Northern Nearctic. Breeds from northeast Alaska across northern Canada to west coast of Hudson Bay; between 70°N and 55°N. Winters in South America.

Monotypic.

SV. Seven, all in autumn: Yorkshire (August–September 1954), Sussex (September 1962), Lincoln/Norfolk/Cambridge (August 1963), Sussex (August 1963), Lincoln/Norfolk (August 1965), Lancashire (September–October 1967), Kerry (October 1968).

Genus LIMICOLA Koch

Northern Palaearctic monospecific genus, breeding in Europe and occurring as a vagrant in the British Isles.

Broad-billed Sandpiper   **A**
Limicola falcinellus (Pontoppidan)

Northwestern Palaearctic. Breeds Norway and Sweden to northern Finland and the Kola Peninsula, and probably also on the tundras of northern Siberia; between 70°N and 60°N. Winters from the eastern Mediterranean southeast to India, southeast China and Australia.

L.f.falcinellus (Pontoppidan) breeds Fenno-Scandia and Kola Peninsula.

SV. About 35, one-third of these since 1958. Recorded mainly August to September, but occasionally also May to July and in October. Chiefly on the English coast from Sussex to Norfolk, but noted four times in Scotland, three times in Ireland, and twice in Wales.

Genus TRYNGITES Cabanis

Nearctic monospecific genus, vagrant to Europe and the British Isles.

Buff-breasted Sandpiper   A
Tryngites subruficollis (Vieillot)

Northwestern Nearctic. Breeds arctic coasts from Alaska east to Mackenzie, north to Melville Island; between 74°N and 69°N. Winters in southern South America.

Monotypic.

SV. About 90 recorded, the great majority during 1952–68 when noted almost annually (with 17 or more in 1968); usually singly but occasionally two, three or even four together. Identified in all months May to November, with most in September, most of the remainder in October, and only three in spring. Twenty-nine Ireland (chiefly in the southwest and north), five Scotland (widely scattered), one Wales, the rest England (chiefly in the southwest and East Anglia).

Genus PHILOMACHUS Merrem

Palaearctic monospecific genus, breeding in Europe and very locally in the British Isles, where it also occurs as a passage and winter visitor.

Ruff   A
Philomachus pugnax (Linnaeus)

Northern Palaearctic. Breeds from eastern England, the Low Countries to northern Scandinavia and across Eurasia to the Bering Straits; between 73°N and 50°N, with an isolated population in southwest France. Winters mainly from the Mediterranean south to South Africa; also in southern Asia and locally in western Europe.

Monotypic.

MB. Extremely scarce. Formerly bred in many parts of England, in decreasing numbers in the 18th and 19th centuries, latterly mainly in East Anglia, till finally ceased to breed regularly, in Norfolk, in 1871. Thereafter bred occasionally, most often in Norfolk, until 1922. Then no further authenticated nest until 1963 since when very small numbers have nested, probably annually, in the Ouse Washes (Cambridge/ Norfolk).

PV. Mainly late March to early June, and (more numerously) mid-July to October. Occurs regularly on and near all coasts of England and Ireland, on the east coast of Scotland north to Shetland, and locally in almost every inland county in England; less frequent elsewhere, and especially infrequent in west Scotland (other than Solway) and Wales.

WV. Formerly only occasional in winter, has recently become more common. Small numbers now winter regularly (mainly at or near coasts, but also inland) in parts of southern, eastern and northwest England, southern Scotland and Northern Ireland.

Family PHALAROPODIDAE

Genus PHALAROPUS Brisson

Holarctic genus of three species, two in Palaearctic, both breeding in Europe and one in the British Isles where the other occurs as a passage visitor, and the third, Nearctic, species as a vagrant.

Grey Phalarope   A
Phalaropus fulicarius (Linnaeus)

Northern Holarctic. Breeding distribution circumpolar. Iceland, Spitsbergen, southern Novaya Zemlya and arctic Siberia east from the Taimyr Peninsula to Anadyr; in North America (where known as Red Phalarope) from Alaska and arctic islands of Canada east to Greenland; between 82°N and 60°N. Winters at sea off coasts of South America, west Africa and south Arabia.

Monotypic.

PV. Late August to December (mainly mid-September to November), occasionally January to March, rarely April to July. Annual in very variable numbers (hundreds in some years, exceptionally in flocks of up to 1,000) off coasts of southwest England and west Ireland, and (in much smaller numbers) on parts of English east and south coasts; less frequent elsewhere and rather scarce inland and in Scotland.

Red-necked Phalarope A
Phalaropus lobatus (Linnaeus)

Northern Holarctic (known as Northern Phalarope in the New World). Breeding distribution circumpolar in tundra and boreal zones in and to the south of the range of *P. fulicarius*, south in Europe to Iceland, Faeroes, Scotland, Ireland, Scandinavia, and Estonia; between 74°N and 52°N. Winters at sea off coasts of western South America, west Africa, Arabia and southeast Asia, chiefly in the tropics.

Monotypic.

MB. Very scarce. Restricted to a few localities in the northern and western islands of Scotland (Shetland, Orkney, Tiree, Outer Hebrides), perhaps also on the north Scottish mainland, and in one locality in Ireland (Mayo). Resident May to August.

PV. Mid-July to October (mainly August–September), fewer April–June, occasionally in other months. Recorded annually in very small numbers in East Anglia, less frequently elsewhere on coasts and inland in England, Wales and Ireland, and only rarely in Scotland away from breeding haunts.

Wilson's Phalarope A
Phalaropus tricolor (Vieillot)

Nearctic. Breeds from central British Columbia and southern Ontario south to the central United States; between 55°N and 37°N. Winters in southern South America.

Monotypic.

SV. Thirty, all since 1954, all May to November, but most in June and September. Occurrences widely scattered on coasts and inland, in Isles of Scilly, Cornwall (four), Somerset (two), Bedford, Northampton, Lincoln/Norfolk (two together), Anglesey, Flint (two,) Nottingham, Derby, Cheshire, Lancashire, Yorkshire (two), Durham, Northumberland, Fife (two), Dunbarton, Kerry (two together), Cork (two), Wexford.

Family BURHINIDAE

Genus BURHINUS Illiger

Nearly cosmopolitan (not Nearctic) genus of seven species, two in Palaearctic, one breeding in Europe and the British Isles.

Stone Curlew   A
Burhinus oedicnemus (Linnaeus)

Southwestern Palaearctic and Oriental. Breeds from Germany, eastern England and Iberia east through Europe, the Middle East and southwest Asia to the Zaisan basin, south to northern Africa, Arabia, India, Ceylon and Burma; between 55°N and 6°N. Sedentary or, where migratory, the northern populations wintering in east Africa.

B.o.oedicnemus (Linnaeus) breeds Europe (except Greece where replaced by another race) east to southeast Russia and northwest Iran.

MB. Scarce. Restricted to southeast England where breeds very locally in all counties south of a line from Dorset to the Wash except in Surrey, Middlesex, Bedford, Huntingdon, and perhaps now Kent (where reduced to one pair, breeding irregularly, since 1965). Resident from March to October. Recorded only irregularly in England north and west of the breeding range, mainly March to May and August to September; very infrequent in Wales, Scotland and Ireland. Exceptional in winter.

Family GLAREOLIDAE

Genus CURSORIUS Latham

Ethiopian, Oriental and Palaearctic genus of four or five species, one in Palaearctic, not breeding in Europe, but occurring in the British Isles as a scarce visitor.

Cream-coloured Courser   A
Cursorius cursor (Latham)

Southern Palaearctic and Ethiopian. Breeds Cape Verde Islands, Canaries, Sahara east to Somaliland and south to Kenya; also Syria, Arabia, Iraq and Transcaspia east to Afghanistan and Baluchistan; between 40°N and the equator. Sedentary and partially migratory to southern Sudan, Somaliland, Socotra and northwest India.

C.c.cursor (Latham) breeds Canaries and Sahara east to Egypt and Arabia.

SV. About 30 recorded (only three since 1959), all September to December, chiefly October. Three Wales ('north Wales', Cardigan, Carmarthen), two Scotland (Lanark, East Lothian), one Ireland (Wexford), the remainder widely scattered in England, mainly in the south and east.

Genus GLAREOLA Brisson

Palaearctic, Ethiopian and Oriental genus of four species, two in Palaearctic, both breeding in Europe and occurring as vagrants in the British Isles.

Collared Pratincole A
Glareola pratincola (Linnaeus)

Southern Palaearctic and Ethiopian. Breeds from northwest Africa and Iberia, Mediterranean France and southeast Europe east through southwest Asia to Lake Balkhash; also lower Egypt, and west tropical, east and southeast Africa; between 50°N and 30°S. Sedentary or, where migratory, wintering in the region south of the Sahara.

G.*p.pratincola* (Linnaeus) breeds Palaearctic range of species.

SV. Probably fewer than 35 (five Scotland, one Ireland, the rest England). Of the twelve most recent (1955–68) records of pratincoles, only four (Essex, May 1958; Orkney, October 1963; Northumberland, July 1966; Wiltshire, May 1968) refer to this species, the remainder to G.*nordmanni*. This contrasts with pre-1955 records of pratincoles, most of which were reputed to be G.*pratincola*, and suggests the possibility that some were wrongly identified. A review of these older records (which are chiefly for the months of May and August) is required.

Black-winged Pratincole A
Glareola nordmanni Fischer

Central Palaearctic. Breeds from Rumania, the Ukraine and southeast Russia east across southwest Asia to the Zaisan basin; between 55°N and 40°N. Winters in eastern and southern Africa.

Monotypic. (Regarded as race or colour phase of G.*pratincola* by some authors.)

SV. At least ten. Of the twelve most recent (1955–68) records of pratincoles, seven or eight showed the characters of this species: Sussex (August 1955), Somerset (June 1957), Northampton (August 1959), Essex (August–September 1960), perhaps Kent (October 1962), Somerset (September 1964), Norfolk (July 1966) and Somerset (September 1968). Only three earlier records have been referred to this species— Yorkshire (August 1909), Fair Isle (May 1927), Mayo (August 1935)— but it seems possible that others were recorded as G.*pratincola* (*q.v.*).

Family STERCORARIIDAE

Genus STERCORARIUS Brisson

Bipolar genus of four or five species, four breeding in the northern Atlantic or adjacent Arctic Ocean, two in the British Isles, where the other two occur as passage visitors.

Great Skua   A
Stercorarius skua (Brünnich)

Northern Atlantic, southern oceans and Antarctic. Breeds Iceland, Faeroes, northern Scotland, coasts of southern South America, circumpolar islands of the southern oceans; between 65°N and 60°S; also (this species or close ally) on shores of Antarctic continent. Migratory; north Atlantic population winters south to the Tropic of Cancer, mainly in the east Atlantic.

S.s.skua (Brünnich) breeds Iceland, Faeroes, north Scotland.

MB. Not scarce. Formerly confined in Britain to Shetland, has increased there during the present century and spread to Orkney and, since about 1950, to Caithness, Sutherland, the Outer Hebrides (Lewis) and St. Kilda. Resident late March to August–September. British birds disperse widely at sea after the breeding season, some have crossed the Atlantic, but most perhaps winter off coasts of Europe from Denmark southwards, with the majority of winter recoveries of ringed birds coming from west Iberia. A surprising number of Shetland juveniles have been recovered in autumn well inland in middle Europe (France to western Russia).

PV. Passage of Icelandic and probably Faeroese, as well as Scottish, birds, mainly March–April and August–October, noted regularly along North Sea, Irish Sea and Atlantic coasts, with the largest numbers

generally in autumn off western Ireland. Birds are recorded not infrequently in summer at sea well to the south of the breeding range.
Irregular or accidental in winter (though some possibly present well
offshore) and inland.

Pomarine Skua   A
Stercorarius pomarinus (Temminck)

Northern Holarctic. Breeding distribution almost circumpolar, from
the Kanin Peninsula and Novaya Zemlya in Russia east through the
tundras of northern Eurasia and North America (where known as
Pomarine Jaeger) to west Greenland, north to about 76°N (New
Siberian Archipelago; Melville Island), south to about 63°N (both sides
of North America). Winters south to Guyana, southwest Africa, east
Australia, New Zealand and Peru.
  Monotypic.
  PV. Small numbers (rarely more than ten together), mainly April to
June, August to November; occasionally December, and rarely in other
months. All coasts but recorded most frequently off parts of British
east coast (especially north Norfolk), Cornwall, and around Ireland.
Accidental inland.

Arctic Skua   A
Stercorarius parasiticus (Linnaeus)

Northern Holarctic. Breeding distribution circumpolar on northern
moors, coasts and islands of Eurasia and North America (where known
as Parasitic Jaeger), north to 80°N (and beyond in Franz Josef Land),
south to north Scotland, southern Fenno-Scandia, Kamchatka, Aleutians, Hudson Bay, north Labrador and south Greenland; between 82°N
and 52°N. Winters at sea south as far as the southern capes of South
America and Africa, Australia and New Zealand.
  Monotypic.
  MB. Not scarce. Restricted to northern Scotland where breeds in
small numbers in the Inner Hebrides (Coll and Jura) and Caithness, and
in rather larger numbers in the Outer Hebrides and, especially, Orkney
and Shetland; bred west Sutherland 1968. Resident late April to early
September. British birds winter probably mainly in the Atlantic off
west Africa; pre-breeders range widely, Shetland-ringed immatures
having been recovered in the breeding season as far apart as Brazil and
Greenland.

PV. Rather scarce passage migrant in spring, April into June, but much more numerous in autumn, August to October, when regular along all coasts. Accidental inland.

Long-tailed Skua   A
Stercorarius longicaudus Vieillot

Northern Holarctic (called Long-tailed Jaeger in American List). Breeding distribution circumpolar on northern coasts, alpine tundras and islands, north to about 72°N (but to beyond 80°N in Greenland), south to Jan Mayen, Scandinavia, Gulf of Ob, Kamchatka, west Alaska and north Quebec; extreme limits 83°N and 52°N. Winters at sea in the Atlantic and Pacific south to about 50°S.

Monotypic.

PV. Scarce passage migrant (usually single birds), chiefly August to November, less often May–June, rarely in other months. Identified more or less annually in autumn along coasts of Northumberland and Norfolk, occasionally elsewhere on east coast, and irregularly or rarely on other coasts of Britain and Ireland. Odd birds have been known to visit the Arctic Skua *S.parasiticus* colony on Fair Isle. Accidental inland.

Family LARIDAE

Genus PAGOPHILA Kaup

Northern Holarctic monospecific genus, breeding on arctic islands ot Europe and occasionally wandering south to the British Isles.

Ivory Gull   A
Pagophila eburnea (Phipps)

Northern Holarctic. Breeding distribution circumpolar in scattered colonies on arctic coasts and islands of northwest Canada, Greenland,

Spitsbergen, Franz Josef Land, Novaya Zemlya, and islands off north Siberia; between 82°N and 72°N. Winters on open waters of Arctic Ocean.

Monotypic.

SV. About 80 recorded, but very few in recent years (only four since 1958, three in the winter of 1961–62—in Sussex, Outer Hebrides and Shetland—and one in December 1967 in Shetland). Recorded chiefly in winter, especially December–February, though has been identified in all months except July. Most records are from Scotland, especially Orkney and Shetland, but several have been noted in England and Wales south to the English Channel, and there are six records from Ireland.

Genus **LARUS** Linnaeus

Cosmopolitan genus of approximately 35–40 species, more than half these in Palaearctic, eleven breeding in Europe and six in the British Isles, where four others (including one Nearctic species) occur as regular visitors, and four more (two Nearctic, two Palaearctic) as scarce visitors.

Common Gull A
Larus canus Linnaeus

Palaearctic and northwestern Nearctic. Breeds Iceland, Faeroes, British Isles, and from Scandinavia and the Netherlands across northern Eurasia to Anadyrland, Kamchatka and Sakhalin, south to central Russia, the Kirghiz Steppes and Lake Baikal; also north Iranian region; and in North America (where known as Mew Gull) in Alaska and northwest Canada; mainly between 70°N and 50°N, locally south to 37°N. Some populations migratory; winters south to the Mediterranean basin, Persian Gulf, Indo-China and California.

L.c.canus Linnaeus breeds from Iceland to White Sea, south to the British Isles and Netherlands.

RB. Not scarce. Breeds thinly but widely through the Scottish Highlands and Scottish western and northern isles, more locally in southwest Scotland and in north and west Ireland, with a few pairs in southeast Scotland (Berwick) and at single localities in England (Dungeness, Kent) and Wales (Anglesey); in recent years odd pairs have also bred in Yorkshire, Durham, Nottingham and Norfolk. Resident; native birds winter mainly in the British Isles, some Scottish birds going to Ireland, but there is little evidence of any regular emigration to the Continent.

WV and **PV**. Immigrants, chiefly from Scandinavia-Baltic area, arrive in numbers on east (especially northeast) coasts, August to October, and depart March to April. These winter widely inland as well as on coasts of Britain and, less especially, Ireland. Movements in spring and autumn, especially in southern England, probably include transient visitors from northwest Europe wintering south of the English Channel.

Herring Gull   A
Larus argentatus Pontoppidan

Holarctic. Breeds Iceland, Faeroes, British Isles, and from Scandinavia and northwest France across northern Eurasia to northeast Siberia; separate groups breed northwest Africa (including the Atlantic Islands), Mediterranean basin, and from the Black and Caspian Seas east through central Asia to Manchuria, and in North America from Alaska and Baffin Island south to Montana and New York; between 78°N and 40°N. Sedentary and migratory; in winter reaches south to the Gambia, Red Sea, northwest India, east China, Panama and Barbados.

L.a.argentatus Pontoppidan breeds northwest Europe, from Brittany north to Iceland and White Sea.

RB. Numerous. Widely distributed, breeding in colonies mainly on coastal cliffs, stacks and islands, also sand-dunes, around much of the British and Irish coastline, though not on the English east coast from Essex to south Yorkshire (except for the recent establishment of a colony in Suffolk). In recent years has colonized the roofs of houses and other buildings in many seaside towns (notably in southern and northeast England and south Wales), and has occupied a few sites inland, especially in western Ireland, but also, for example, in southwest England and now even in central London (Regent's Park). Mainly sedentary, with limited juvenile and post-breeding dispersal, some birds from southern colonies reaching northern and western France.

WV. Immigrants from northwest Europe (especially Murmansk coast of Russia, Norway, Denmark, Netherlands) arrive in some numbers from July to December (mainly September–October) and winter chiefly in the eastern half of Britain; ringed birds from Faeroes and north France have also reached Britain. Most immigrants probably return March–April, and passage movements in both spring and autumn may include transient visitors. Herring Gulls belonging to other races—notably *L.a.taimyrensis* Buturlin, *L.a.michahellis* Naumann and perhaps *L.a.heuglini* Bree—may have occasionally wandered to Britain and Ireland, but we are unaware of any record definitely assignable to any subspecies other than *L.a.argentatus*.

Lesser Black-backed Gull   A
Larus fuscus Linnaeus

Northwestern Palaearctic. Breeds Iceland, Faeroes, British Isles, northwest France, Denmark, Fenno-Scandia and northwest Russia (Kola Peninsula); between 71°N and 47°N. Winters south to coasts of tropical Africa, Arabia and Persian Gulf, with small numbers as far north as the British Isles and southern Baltic.

L.f.fuscus Linnaeus breeds from Kola Peninsula southwest to Denmark.

L.f.graellsii A. E. Brehm breeds Iceland, Faeroes, British Isles, Brittany and locally or sporadically in the Netherlands and northwest Germany.

MB (also **RB**). Fairly numerous. Widely but locally distributed on coasts of Britain and Ireland, mainly on western and northern coasts and islands from the Isles of Scilly north to Shetland, and with only a few pairs or colonies (in Cornwall, Devon, Sussex, Suffolk, and irregularly in Dorset, Isle of Wight and Essex) on the English south and east coasts between Cornwall and Northumberland (Farne Islands). There are also a few scattered—and sometimes large—colonies well inland, notably in Lancashire, Stirling and on several lakes in western and central Ireland. Some birds remain here throughout the year, but most of the British population winters in Portugal, southern Spain and along the northwest coast of Africa. *L.f.graellsii*.

PV. Mid-February to May, July to November, most numerous and conspicuous in autumn when passage frequently noted inland as well as on coasts. As well as birds of British origin, migrants at both seasons include birds from Scandinavia (nominate *fuscus*), which pass mainly through eastern England and are identified only rarely as far west as Ireland, and from Iceland and Faeroes (*L.f.graellsii*), which probably pass mainly through western Britain and Ireland.

Great Black-backed Gull   **A**
Larus marinus Linnaeus

Northern Atlantic. Breeds eastern North America from northern
Quebec and Newfoundland to New York, also Greenland, Iceland,
Faeroes, British Isles, northwest France, Baltic and Atlantic coasts of
Fenno-Scandia, Murmansk coast, Spitsbergen and Bear Island; between
77°N and 42°N. Winters south to the Great Lakes, Mediterranean,
Black and Caspian Seas.

Monotypic.

RB. Fairly numerous. Breeds locally in practically all maritime
counties in Ireland, Scotland (though not south of Aberdeen on the east
coast except at some islands in the Firth of Forth) and Wales (not in
Carmarthen, Merioneth, Flint and Denbigh), also in the Isle of Man;
in England, apart from single colonies in Cumberland and Lancashire,
it is confined to the southwest, from the Isles of Scilly east to Monmouth and the Isle of Wight. Small numbers have bred inland in
Longford, Lancashire and Stirling, and in recent years a pair or two
have attempted to breed on the Suffolk coast. The native population
winters chiefly within the British Isles, but some immatures, especially
from southern colonies, reach the Atlantic coasts of France and Iberia.

WV. Immigrants from northwest Europe and Iceland arrive mainly
August to October and return March–April (perhaps also some passage
at these times), with some immature birds remaining through the
summer. In winter it is distributed widely inland as well as on coasts.
Evidence from ringing suggests that most immigrants come from coasts
of Norway and northwest Russia (wintering mainly in the eastern half
of Britain) and Iceland (wintering mainly in Ireland and Scotland).

Iceland Gull   **A**
Larus glaucoides Meyer

Northern Nearctic. Breeds southern Baffin Island and both coasts of
Greenland north to 75°N in west and 68°N in east; replaced by close
ally or race on islands in Canadian arctic. Partially migratory, winters
south to New Jersey, Iceland and the British Isles.

L.g.glaucoides Meyer breeds Greenland.

WV. Scarce visitor, chiefly in winter, November to April, though
has been identified in all months. Regular in Shetland, Outer Hebrides,
Aberdeen, Ayr and in recent years in Cork, fairly regular on coast of
northeast England; but inland and on coasts elsewhere, though some-

times reaching south to the English Channel and various parts of Ireland, it is irregular.

SV. Sight-record, Kerry (January 1958), of a bird showing the characters of *L.g.kumlieni* Brewster which breeds in southern Baffin Island and the northern Ungava Peninsula.

Glaucous Gull   A
Larus hyperboreus Gunnerus

Northern Holarctic. Breeding distribution circumpolar on arctic islands and tundras from high arctic south to Iceland, the Kola Peninsula, Pribilofs, Labrador and south Greenland; between 83°N and 60°N. Winters south to California, New York, France and Japan.

L.h.hyperboreus Gunnerus breeds range of species except Siberia east of Taimyr Peninsula and Alaska.

WV. Winter visitor, chiefly late October to March, occasionally in other months including the summer. Recorded regularly in small numbers on parts of the east coast between Shetland and Suffolk, and in the west in the Outer Hebrides, Firth of Clyde, Lancashire and in various parts of Ireland. Occasionally or rarely on other coasts south to Cornwall. Infrequent inland.

Great Black-headed Gull   A
Larus ichthyaetus Pallas

Central Palaearctic. Breeds discontinuously from the Crimea and south Russia across southern Siberia to Mongolia and north China, mainly between 50°N and 40°N. Winters Black Sea, eastern Mediterranean, and from Red Sea east to Burma.

Monotypic.

SV. Seven: Devon (May or June 1859), Sussex (January 1910, August 1932), Hampshire (November–December 1924), Norfolk (March 1932), Isle of Man (May 1966), Yorkshire (March–April 1967).

Laughing Gull   A
Larus atricilla Linnaeus

Nearctic and northern Neotropical. Breeds from Nova Scotia south along the Atlantic and Gulf coasts of the United States; also in southeast California, Mexico and Caribbean region; between 45°N and 12°N.

Winters in east from North Carolina south to the Amazon mouth, in west from Mexico to Peru.
Monotypic.
SV. Five: Sussex (July 1923), Essex (December 1957), Kent (May 1966), Isles of Scilly (October 1967), Cork (August 1968).

Mediterranean Gull A
Larus melanocephalus Temminck

South-central Palaearctic. Breeds Greece, Asia Minor and coasts of the Black Sea; between 46°N and 37°N; has bred exceptionally in the Netherlands and Hungary. Apparently winters mainly in the central Mediterranean, a few reaching the Baltic and coasts of western Europe.
Monotypic.
CB. A few birds have bred Hampshire, from 1968. These have included hybrid *Larus melanocephalus* × *ridibundus*, and mixed pairs have been formed with *L.ridibundus*.
PV and **WV.** Formerly irregular vagrant, now regular visitor in very small numbers, chiefly to parts of the English east and south coasts between Cornwall and Durham, occasionally or rarely elsewhere, including north to Fair Isle and west to Ireland. Identified in all months, though rather few from April to June, and most frequent August to October. Individuals sometimes over-winter in the same locality for several years in succession.

Black-headed Gull A
Larus ridibundus Linnaeus

Palaearctic. Breeds Iceland, Faeroes, British Isles, and across Eurasia from central Fenno-Scandia and France to the Kolyma, Kamchatka and Ussuriland, north to about the Arctic Circle, south to north Italy, Black and Caspian Seas, and Lakes Balkhash and Baikal; between 66°N and 40°N. Winters from southern parts of the breeding range south to the Canaries, Gambia, Nigeria and Nile valley in Africa, and to India and Malaysia in Asia; regular vagrant to eastern North America.
Monotypic.
RB and **MB.** Numerous. Widely distributed, breeding in scattered but often large colonies throughout Britain and Ireland, regularly in all coastal counties except those in southwest England (Monmouth and

Gloucester to Cornwall), East Lothian in east Scotland, and Kerry in southwest Ireland, and in nearly all inland counties except several in central southern England. British birds disperse widely within the British Isles outside the breeding season, and a substantial number migrate south through west France to winter in Iberia.

WV and **PV**. Immigrants from the northern half of Europe (Fenno-Scandia south to Belgium, north-central France and Czechoslovakia; also from Iceland) winter in large numbers throughout Britain and Ireland, arriving mainly August–December and returning mainly February to April. Some evidence of onward passage to southwest Europe during hard weather as well as in autumn.

Slender-billed Gull A
Larus genei Breme

Southern Palaearctic. Breeds very locally in north Mauritania, Tunisia, southern Spain, on the Black and Caspian Seas, and from Iraq along coasts of the Persian Gulf to Pakistan; also sporadically in southern France and on the Kirghiz and west Siberian steppes; between 50°N and 20°N. Winters within the breeding range and beyond it to Morocco and the Mediterranean and Red Seas.

Monotypic.

SV. Two, both Sussex (June 1960, April 1963).

Bonaparte's Gull A
Larus philadelphia (Ord)

Northern Nearctic. Breeds Alaska and in Canada from south Yukon and British Columbia east to Ontario; between 66°N and 50°N. Winters on the Great Lakes and the Atlantic, Gulf and Pacific coasts of the United States.

Monotypic.

SV. Nineteen (six 1848–90, five 1948–56, eight 1961–68); four January–February, two March–April, three June–July, three August–September, seven October–November. One Ireland (near Belfast), two Scotland (Dunbarton, Sutherland), the rest in England, in Cornwall (five), Devon, Somerset, Hampshire, Sussex (four), Norfolk, Lancashire, Yorkshire and Northumberland.

Little Gull   A
Larus minutus Pallas

Palaearctic; also recently in Nearctic. Breeds locally in Europe, mainly
in the north and east, from the Netherlands, Gulf of Bothnia and north
Russia, southeast and southwards at least occasionally to the Black Sea;
other discrete groups breed in central and eastern Siberia; a few have
bred in Ontario, Canada, since 1962; between 66°N and 46°N. Winters
on coasts of Europe and south to the Red Sea and Persian Gulf, also,
perhaps exceptionally, in west Africa (Sierra Leone).
    Monotypic.
    PV and **WV**. Passage and winter visitor, recorded in all months,
but mainly between July and mid-April, and most frequently and
widely in September–October. Usually singly or in small parties, but
occasionally in flocks of up to 100 or more, especially in Fife in late
summer. Recorded annually on many parts of the British east and south
coasts from Aberdeen to Cornwall, on coasts of Lancashire and
Cheshire, and fairly regularly in many inland counties of England (and
at least occasionally in all); less frequently on coasts or inland in west
and north Scotland, Wales and Ireland.

Sabine's Gull   A
Larus sabini Sabine

Northern Holarctic. Breeding distribution almost circumpolar, on
arctic and high arctic coasts and islands, south to about the Arctic
Circle, but not on continental coasts of western Eurasia; between
82°N and 62°N. Winters in the rich upwelling areas of cool water off
the coasts of southwestern Africa and Peru.
    Monotypic.
    PV. Scarce but regular passage or drifted migrant, ten or more
annually in recent years between June and December (chiefly August to
October); only rarely between January and May. Identified regularly
off Cornwall and southwest Ireland, less regularly elsewhere on coasts
of south and east England and around Ireland, and only very occasionally on other coasts or inland.

Genus RHODOSTETHIA MacGillivray

Northeast Palaearctic monospecific genus which has strayed to the
British Isles.

Ross's Gull   **A**
Rhodostethia rosea (MacGillivray)

Northeastern Palaearctic. Breeds extreme northeast Siberia; known to
have nested once in west Greenland. Winters probably in open waters
of Arctic Ocean; regularly migrates past north Alaska and through the
Bering Sea.

Monotypic.

SV. Six: Yorkshire (winter 1846–47), Shetland (April 1936),
Northumberland (April 1960), Yorkshire (February 1962), Dorset
(August 1967), Cork (September 1967).

Genus RISSA Stephens

Holarctic genus of two species, both in Palaearctic, one breeding in
Europe and the British Isles.

Kittiwake   **A**
Rissa tridactyla (Linnaeus)

Northern Holarctic. Breeding distribution circumpolar, on islands in
the Arctic Ocean and south to south Greenland, British Isles, northwest France, Scandinavia, northeast Siberia to Commander Islands,
west Alaska and Aleutians, and eastern Canada south to Newfoundland; between 81°N and 47°N. Winters mainly in the North Atlantic
between 60°N and 40°N.

Monotypic.

RB and **MB**. Numerous. Widely distributed, breeding in scattered
colonies mainly on coastal cliffs and islands around Scotland, Ireland,
the Isle of Man and west Wales; most numerous in eastern Scotland;
in England several colonies in the northeast (Northumberland, Durham,
Yorkshire) and southwest (Cornwall, Devon, Dorset), and single sites
occupied in Cumberland and Suffolk. Essentially oceanic outside
breeding season, many British-ringed birds having reached Greenland
and Newfoundland.

PV and **WV**. Large dispersive, weather or feeding movements
occur off most coasts, especially in spring and autumn (but sometimes,
or on a smaller scale, at other seasons). Not all these birds are necessarily
of British origin, as indicated by several recoveries here of birds ringed
in northwest Europe (northwest Russia to France) and one from Greenland. Occasional inland, with periodic winter wrecks, and stragglers

(occasionally small flocks) reaching several inland counties of England every year.

Genus CHLIDONIAS Rafinesque

Nearly cosmopolitan (not Neotropical) genus of three species, all breeding in Europe, one breeding occasionally (formerly regularly) in the British Isles, where the other two occur as scarce visitors.

Whiskered Tern   A
Chlidonias hybrida (Pallas)

Southern Palaearctic, Oriental, Ethiopian and Australasian. Breeds locally in northwest Africa, southern Europe from Iberia and southern France through the Balkans to southern Russia, and in the Near East, Iraq, Iran, Russian Turkestan, India, Manchuria, and parts of Australasia (including New Guinea and New Zealand); between 56°N and 47°S. Migratory; western Palaearctic population winters mainly in tropical west and east Africa, south to Kenya.

C.h.hybrida (Pallas) breeds northwest Africa, southern Europe, and in Asia east to Russian Turkestan.

SV. At least 36, about half of these during 1956–68. Identified in all months April to October, with most of the accepted records during May to July. One Scotland (Dumfries), three Ireland (Cork, Wicklow, Dublin), two Wales (Radnor, Cardigan); the rest England, chiefly on or near the east and south coasts between Yorkshire and the Isles of Scilly, also recorded in Somerset, Middlesex (two), Cheshire, Lancashire and Northumberland.

White-winged Black Tern   A
Chlidonias leucopterus (Temminck)

Palaearctic; sporadically Ethiopian. Breeds from western Russia, Hungary and Bulgaria through eastern Europe and central Asia east to Semipalatinsk, north to about 57°N, south to Iraq in the west, but only to Lake Balkhash in the east; also in eastern Siberia from eastern Transbaicalia to Sakhalin south to Manchuria; mainly between 55°N and 40°N (30°N in Iraq); also breeds sporadically or irregularly in western Europe (Belgium, Germany, France), Algeria, and in tropical east Africa. Winters mainly in tropical Africa and Asia, south to Cape Province, Madagascar, Ceylon, Indonesia and Australia.

Monotypic.

SV. About 165 recorded, nearly three-quarters of these in 1958–68, when identified annually and with increasing frequency (74 since 1964, including 26 in 1968). Usually singly, occasionally two or three together. Recorded in all months, March to November, but principally in May–June and August–September; most recent records have been in autumn. Most have been found in eastern and southern coastal counties of England between Yorkshire and Cornwall, with several in southern inland counties, while a few have reached as far west as Wales and Ireland, and six as far north as Scotland (Aberdeen, Caithness, Orkney, Shetland, two Outer Hebrides), four of these being in 1967.

Black Tern A
Chlidonias niger (Linnaeus)

Holarctic. Breeds western Eurasia from south Sweden and France east to the Yenisei, north to Lake Ladoga in Russia, south locally to southern Iberia, north Italy, Bulgaria, the Caucasus and Russian Altai; also widely in central North America; between 60°N and 36°N. Winters tropical Africa south to Angola and Tanganyika, and in South America.

C.n.niger (Linnaeus) breeds Palaearctic range of species.

FB, CB. Formerly nested in strength in East Anglia and also elsewhere in east and southeast England, but ceased to do so around the middle of the 19th century. Erratic thereafter, but has bred in East Anglia (Ouse Washes, Norfolk/Cambridge) again in recent years and may be on the point of re-establishing itself there. Somewhat remarkably, a pair bred successfully in Ireland in 1967. (The supposed breeding in Sussex in 1941 and 1942 is now discounted.)

PV. Mid-April into June, July to mid-October (rarely into November) in rather variable numbers. Recorded annually in practically all counties in England, most numerously on coasts between Norfolk and south Kent, though flocks of up to 50–100 or more are not infrequent at some inland waters in southern England. Occurs less commonly in Wales (regular only in the southeast) and Scotland (very rarely in north and northwest), but in Ireland, where formerly regarded as rare vagrant, it has occurred annually in recent years, sometimes in small flocks and in many parts of the country.

Genus GELOCHELIDON C. L. Brehm

Nearly cosmopolitan monospecific genus, breeding in parts of every continent, including Africa though not in Ethiopian region; has bred once in the British Isles, where otherwise occurs as a scarce visitor.

Gull-billed Tern   A
Gelochelidon nilotica (Gmelin)

Nearly cosmopolitan. Breeds very locally in Europe in Denmark, southern France, Iberia, the Balkans, southern Russia, formerly in the Netherlands, also in southwest Asia east to Zaisan Nor, in southern Iran, Pakistan, southeast China and probably elsewhere in south and east Asia, as well as in parts of northwest Africa, Mauritania, Australia and the Americas; between 57°N and 36°S. Sedentary or migratory; winters from the Mediterranean south to South Africa, and elsewhere south to India, the Greater Sundas and South America.

G.*n.nilotica* (Gmelin) breeds northwest Africa, Europe, east to central Asia and Pakistan.

CB. A pair bred at Abberton Reservoir, Essex, in 1950, and probably also in 1949.

SV. Over 140 recorded, nearly 90 of these in 1958–68, when identified annually, nearly always in ones and twos. Apart from one in March, all have occurred during April–October, with most from May to September; principally on coasts of eastern and southern England from Yorkshire to the Isles of Scilly; formerly mainly off East Anglia, now chiefly along the south coast, especially Kent and Sussex; only rarely on English coasts elsewhere and exceptional inland; one Wales (Flint), one Ireland (Antrim) and four Scotland (two East Lothian, West Lothian and Orkney).

Genus HYDROPROGNE Kaup

Nearly cosmopolitan (not Neotropical) monospecific genus, breeding locally in Europe and wandering to the British Isles.

Caspian Tern   A
Hydroprogne caspia (Pallas)

Nearly cosmopolitan, but local. In western half of Palaearctic, breeds

Tunisia, coasts of Baltic, Black and Caspian Seas, Kirghiz and western Siberian steppes; also locally in eastern, western and southern Africa, Persian Gulf, Ceylon, east China, Australia, New Zealand and North America; between 65°N and 45°S. Sedentary and migratory; European birds winter in Africa.

Monotypic.

SV. About 75 records (though some could refer to the same individuals seen in different places), more than half this total since 1958, including about 27 birds during 1966–68. Has been identified in all months between April and November, formerly mainly in May–June, now mainly in June–August. Recorded principally on (or inland near) the English east and south coasts from Yorkshire to Dorset (especially East Anglia), also in Northampton (two), Northampton/Leicester, Derby, Stafford, Lancashire (two), Nottingham (three) and Northumberland; only once in each of Wales (Brecon), Ireland (Donegal) and Scotland (Dumbarton/Stirling). The origin of most birds seen here is presumably Eurasia, but the only ringed bird found (Yorkshire, August 1939) had been marked in North America (as a chick in July 1927 on Lake Michigan).

Genus STERNA Linnaeus

Cosmopolitan genus of approximately 25–30 species, 14 (but several only marginally) in Palaearctic, five breeding in Europe and the British Isles, where three others have been recorded as scarce vagrants.

Common Tern   A
Sterna hirundo Linnaeus

Holarctic. Breeds from Norway, the British Isles and coasts of Spain east across Eurasia mainly south of the Arctic Circle to Kamchatka and Sakhalin, south to the Mediterranean, Iraq, Iran, Afghanistan and northern China; also in northern and western Africa, North America and the Caribbean region; between 70°N and 6°N. Winters south to southern Africa, Ceylon, Malaya, Indonesia and the southern tip of South America.

S.h.hirundo Linnaeus breeds over entire range of the species except in Asia to the east of Iran and of the Ob in Siberia.

MB. Fairly numerous. Widely distributed, breeding in scattered colonies on parts of all coasts of Britain and Ireland from the Isles of Scilly north to Shetland; colonies are very few and far between in

F

northwest, southwest and northeast England and especially in Wales (where largely confined to Anglesey). Also breeds inland along rivers and by lakes in some counties in Ireland and many in Scotland, and in recent years has begun to nest regularly at inland sites in Stafford, Nottingham, Lincoln, Norfolk, Huntingdon, Bedford, Essex and occasionally elsewhere in eastern, central and southern England. Resident from mid-April to September. British and Irish birds winter chiefly along coast of tropical west Africa.

PV. Mid-April into June, July to October (occasionally November, exceptionally in winter). All coasts and also, in small numbers, regularly and widely inland. Most seen on migration are probably native birds, but some come from continental Europe as shown by recoveries here of birds ringed in Norway, Baltic region, Germany and the Netherlands.

Arctic Tern   A
Sterna paradisaea Pontoppidan

Northern Holarctic. Breeding distribution circumpolar, from islands of high arctic south to south Greenland, Iceland, British Isles, Brittany, Baltic, north Siberian tundras, Aleutians, British Columbia, Hudson Bay and Massachusetts; between 83°N and 42°N. Winters in southern parts of the Atlantic, Indian and Pacific Oceans south to Antarctica.

Monotypic.

MB. Fairly numerous. Breeds somewhat locally around coasts (rarely now inland) of Scotland and Ireland and more locally still in northern England and north Wales. Outnumbers Common Tern *Sterna hirundo* in extreme north of Scotland and in a few localities farther south (for example, Farne Islands, Northumberland; Inishmurray, Sligo), but at most places is generally the scarcer of the two. No permanent colonies now exist in Britain south of Northumberland in the east and Anglesey in the west; small numbers breed occasionally in the Isles of Scilly (where formerly regular) and the odd pair or two nests sporadically elsewhere, most often in Norfolk. Resident from end April or May to about September. British birds are often recovered off southern Africa and probably winter much farther south than this, in Antarctic waters, where one ringed bird has been recovered.

PV. End April into June, mid-July to October (stragglers later). All coasts and, in small numbers, widely inland. Several recoveries here, chiefly on the east coast in autumn, of ringed birds from northwestern continental Europe (Baltic region and northwest Germany), and single recoveries of birds from Faeroes (in west Ireland), Greenland and North America, indicate that alien as well as native birds are involved.

Roseate Tern　　　　　　　　　　　　　　A
Sterna dougallii Montagu

Nearly cosmopolitan. Breeds very locally in Europe, regularly only in the British Isles and Brittany, also Azores, east coast Africa, Indian Ocean, Indonesia east to Australia, China, Philippines, Ryu Kyus, eastern North America and the Caribbean region; between 56°N and 35°S. Sedentary and migratory, wintering south to western and southern Africa, Madagascar and eastern South America.

S.d.dougallii Montagu breeds eastern America, Azores, Europe and east Africa.

MB. Not scarce. Very locally distributed; confined to about 20 breeding colonies, mainly on shores of Irish Sea (in Antrim, Down, Dublin, Wexford, Anglesey and north Lancashire), and in the Isles of Scilly, Northumberland and the Firth of Forth. Also breeds occasionally in southwest Scotland (though probably not at the present time) and west Ireland, and has nested once or twice in recent years in Dorset, Hampshire and possibly Aberdeen. The species is erratic in its occupation of some breeding sites. Spring arrivals are from late April into June, autumn departures from mid-July to September (stragglers later). British birds winter off coasts of west Africa, chiefly in the Gulf of Guinea.

PV. Noted on migration chiefly along parts of east coasts of Ireland and England, also in the English Channel; only rarely inland. Some migrants may originate from outside the British Isles but there is no certain evidence of this.

Bridled Tern　　　　　　　　　　　　　　A
Sterna anaethetus Scopoli

Oceanic. Breeds Caribbean region, northern Mauritania, Red Sea, Persian Gulf, Indian Ocean, tropical islands of the Pacific north to southeast China and Philippines, south to New Guinea and Australia; between 30°N and 34°S. Pelagic outside breeding season.

S.a.anaethetus Scopoli breeds range of species except Caribbean region, perhaps northern Mauritania (where subspecific status of breeding population is uncertain), and in an unknown area, probably in the

Pacific, where replaced by *S.a.nelsoni* (known only from two specimens from Central America).

S.a.melanoptera Swainson breeds Caribbean region.

SV. Four, all of which were found dead: Kent (November 1931), Dublin (November 1953), Glamorgan (September 1954), Somerset (October 1958). The first was referred to *S.a.anaethetus*, the second to *S.a.melanoptera*; the racial identity of the other two was not established.

Sooty Tern A
Sterna fuscata Linnaeus

Oceanic. Breeds, often in immense colonies, mainly on tropical islands in all oceans, from the Caribbean and mid-Atlantic islands and across the Indian and Pacific Oceans, also Red Sea; between 30°N and 34°S. Pelagic outside breeding season.

S.f.fuscata Linnaeus breeds Caribbean region and tropical Atlantic islands of Fernando Novonha, Ascension and St. Helena; also probably on islands in the Red Sea and Indian Ocean, though birds there have been separated by some authors.

SV. Twenty (seven 1852–1911, nine 1933–54, four 1961–66), the earlier records nearly all of birds found inland, the later ones mostly of birds seen along coasts. Dates scattered from March or April to October with most (seven, including two together) in June. Only two Scotland (Stirling, Orkney), one Wales (Merioneth), the rest in England in Cornwall, Somerset, Dorset (three, including two together), Hampshire, Sussex, Kent, Berkshire, Suffolk (two), Norfolk (two), Stafford, Lancashire, Cumberland, Northumberland.

Little Tern A
Sterna albifrons Pallas

Cosmopolitan (though very marginal in South America). Breeds Europe from the Baltic and Scotland south to the Mediterranean and Black Seas, chiefly on coasts but on lakes and rivers in Russia and in southwest Asia; also locally south and east to tropical west and east Africa, Persian Gulf, Ceylon, Malaysia, China, Manchuria, Japan, Australasia, North and Central America and islands off Venezuela; between 59°N and 37°S. Northern populations migratory, some reaching latitudes farther south than the breeding range.

MB. Not scarce. Rather more than 150 known colonies (containing about 1,600 pairs) scattered on almost all low-lying coasts of Britain and Ireland southwards from the Outer Hebrides and southeast Sutherland (also bred Caithness in 1968), though there is none in southern Wales and southwest England (between Cardigan and west Dorset) nor on the mainland of west Scotland north of Ayr; the largest numbers breed on the English east and south coasts between Dorset and Lincoln. Inland nesting is highly exceptional but it has taken place at Abberton Reservoir, Essex. Resident from mid-April to September.

PV. Noted on passage on many parts of the coast (but only as rare straggler in the Northern Isles) between mid-April and early October, mostly in May and August; rather scarce inland, though it is noted at least occasionally in all counties in England. Extent of passage of birds from Continental breeding grounds is uncertain but is probably slight.

Royal Tern A

Sterna maxima Boddaert

Southern Nearctic, marginally Neotropical, and very locally west African. Breeds coasts of north Mauritania and in North America from Maryland and Baja California south to the Caribbean region; between 38°N and 12°N. American birds winter south to Peru and the Argentine.

SV. Two: one found long dead Dublin (March 1954), the other seen Kent (July 1965). It is not known whether they belonged to the African or the American race.

Sandwich Tern A

Sterna sandvicensis Latham

Western Palaearctic, Nearctic and Neotropical. Breeds on coasts from southern Baltic and Scotland south to the Mediterranean, Black and Caspian Seas; also in southeastern North America, Mexico and the Bahamas; between 60°N and 12°N. Winters from the Mediterranean basin and Persian Gulf south to South Africa, and from the southern United States to the Argentine.

S.s.sandvicensis Latham breeds Eurasian range of species and formerly (perhaps still) in Tunisia.

MB. Not scarce, the total breeding population being of the order of 6,000 pairs. About 40 breeding colonies (some of them rather unstable), situated mainly on the British east coast and shores of the Irish

Sea, the largest usually in Suffolk, Norfolk, Northumberland, the Firth of Forth, Cumberland, north Lancashire, Wexford and Down; other, smaller, colonies exist at the present time in one county in England (Hampshire), six in Scotland (Angus, Aberdeen, Nairn, Caithness, Orkney, Ayr) and five in west Ireland (Kerry, Galway, Mayo, Sligo, Donegal). Sporadic breeding—usually by the odd pair or two—has occurred on the coasts of several other counties in Britain and Ireland north to Shetland. Numbers at all colonies tend to be erratic and sites are often changed. Resident from end March to September. British birds winter chiefly along the coast of west Africa from Senegal to South Africa.

PV. Mid-March to May, July to mid-October, all coasts (though scarce in northwest Scotland), also inland in very small numbers, annually to the London area, irregularly elsewhere, though it has occurred at least once in recent years in nearly all English counties. Most migrants seen are probably natives of Britain and Ireland, but several autumn recoveries of immatures (mainly in southeast England) ringed at colonies in Denmark, northwest Germany and Netherlands indicate that some Continental birds are involved at that season.

Family ALCIDAE

Genus ALLE Link

Holarctic monospecific genus, breeding in Europe and occurring in the British Isles as a scarce winter visitor.

Little Auk   A
Alle alle (Linnaeus)

Northern Holarctic (called Dovekie in North America). Breeds on arctic islands from eastern Ellesmere Island and Greenland east to Severnaya Zemlya, south to southernmost Greenland and north Iceland (Grimsey); between 82°N and 60°N. Winters regularly south to Nova Scotia, Faeroes and the northern North Sea, sometimes south to New England and the western Mediterranean, exceptionally farther south.

P.a.alle (Linnaeus) breeds range of species except Franz Josef Land and perhaps Severnaya Zemlya.

WV. Regular winter visitor off coasts of Northern Isles (especially Shetland), mid-September to mid-March, but mainly November to February (a few records April to August); also noted annually in variable but usually small numbers along parts of the east coast from Aberdeen to Norfolk, and irregularly on other coasts; straggler inland, though has been recorded most counties, usually following periodic winter 'wrecks' (last major one in 1950).

Genus PINGUINUS Bonnaterre

North Atlantic monospecific genus, now extinct.

Great Auk   B
Pinguinus impennis (Linnaeus)

North Atlantic; extinct since about 1844. Formerly bred on islands off Newfoundland, Iceland, probably Scotland and possibly elsewhere in the northern North Atlantic area.

Monotypic.

FB. Almost certainly bred St. Kilda (where the last British specimen was killed about 1840), probably Orkney, doubtfully Isle of Man and Lundy (Devon), and possibly elsewhere.

Genus ALCA Linnaeus

North Atlantic monospecific genus, breeding in the British Isles.

Razorbill   A
Alca torda Linnaeus

Holarctic. Breeds on coasts of North Atlantic from Labrador and west Greenland south to Maine, and from Iceland and northwest Russia (Kola Peninsula) south to Brittany and the Baltic; between 75°N and 44°N. Winters at sea south as far as New York (exceptionally Florida), the western Mediterranean and Morocco.

A.t.torda Linnaeus breeds North America, Greenland and continental Europe south to Scandinavia and south Finland.

A.t.islandica C. L. Brehm breeds Iceland, Faeroes, British Isles, Channel Islands, Brittany and Heligoland.

RB and **MB**. Numerous. Breeds colonially on rocky coasts around

Britain and Ireland, though not between southern Yorkshire and
eastern Isle of Wight, and only very locally in northeast England and
along the Irish Sea coasts of England and Ireland. It has decreased
markedly at its southernmost colonies in England and Wales in recent
years. Disperses outside the breeding season to coastal waters off all
parts of the British Isles, many birds (especially from Scotland) crossing
the North Sea to winter off coasts of Norway and Denmark, others
(especially from the general area of the southern Irish Sea) regularly
reaching the Atlantic and Mediterranean coasts of Iberia and, at least
occasionally, Italy and west Morocco. *A.t.islandica*.

WV. Eight records of *A.t.torda*, all February–March, from Cornwall, Kent, Flint, northeast England, East Lothian, Sutherland and
Wicklow; wide scatter of specimens (five of which refer to recoveries
of birds ringed in west Norway and Russia) suggests that this race
occurs quite frequently in winter. Birds from north France and Channel
Islands (*A.t.islandica*) probably also occur quite frequently off coasts of
southern England, as indicated by single recoveries of ringed birds
from both areas.

Genus URIA Brisson

Holarctic genus of two species, both in north Atlantic, one breeding
in and the other vagrant to the British Isles.

Brünnich's Guillemot   A
Uria lomvia (Linnaeus)

Northern Holarctic (called Thick-billed Murre in North America).
Breeds on coasts and many islands of the North Atlantic, west Arctic and
north Pacific Oceans, north of *U.aalge*, and overlapping with it south
to Iceland, north Norway, the Taimyr Peninsula, Sakhalin, central
Kuriles, Aleutians and Gulf of St. Lawrence; between 82°N and 47°N.
Winters at sea south to Norway, northern Japan, southern Alaska and
New England.

U.l.lomvia (Linnaeus) breeds eastern North America, Greenland,
Iceland east to Novaya Zemlya, north to Franz Josef Land.

SV. Five: East Lothian (December 1908), Wicklow (September
1938), Dublin (October 1945), Lancashire (April 1960), Shetland (March
1968). Subspecies not determined, but highly unlikely to have been
other than nominate *lomvia*.

Guillemot   A
Uria aalge (Pontoppidan)

Holarctic (called Common Murre in North America). Breeds coasts
and islands of North Atlantic, west Arctic and North Pacific Oceans,
locally south to Portugal, Hokkaido, California and Newfoundland;
between 76°N and 40°N. Winters at sea mainly within southern limits
of the breeding range.

U.a.aalge (Pontoppidan) breeds on Atlantic coasts of North America,
western Greenland, Iceland, Faeroes, Scotland (intergrades with
albionis in southwest), most of Norway (intergrades with hyperborea in
north) and in the Baltic; probably this race, though perhaps albionis,
on Heligoland.

U.a.albionis Witherby breeds British Isles (north to Ayrshire in the
west, Northumberland in the east), Channel Islands, Brittany, northwest Spain and Portugal (Berlengas).

U.a.hyperborea Salomonsen breeds northern Norway east to Seven
Islands, Bear Island and western Novaya Zemlya.

RB and **MB**. Numerous. Breeds colonially on coastal cliffs around
Britain and Ireland, but scarce or absent between south Yorkshire and
Isle of Wight, and only very locally in northeast and northwest England
and on the Irish east coast; often with Razorbills Alca torda, but usually
in far larger numbers where the two occur together, and in greatest
numbers in Orkney and Shetland. Disperses at sea outside the breeding
season, many birds reaching the coasts of continental Europe from
Norway south to north Spain. Two breeding races, U.a.aalge and U.a.
albionis (see above), the latter decreasing over much of its range during
the last 20 to 30 years.

WV. Status uncertain, but recoveries of several Heligoland and
single Norway and Faeroes ringed birds on British coasts point to
immigration of nominate aalge (or perhaps albionis; see above) from
these areas at least, presumably annually. Extent of passage unknown,
but frequent large-scale movements, mainly on western coasts of
Britain and Ireland, are perhaps chiefly composed of British birds.

SV. A bird ringed as a breeding adult on the Murmansk coast of
Russia, within the range of U.a.hyperborea, was recovered Durham,
May 1950; since December 1965 several specimens resembling this
race have been identified in Aberdeen, northeast England and Cornwall,
suggesting that the subspecies occurs regularly in small numbers.

Genus CEPPHUS Pallas

Holarctic genus of three species, one almost circumpolar and breeding in Europe and the British Isles.

Black Guillemot A
Cepphus grylle (Linnaeus)

Holarctic. Breeding distribution circumpolar, on arctic coasts and islands, south in Atlantic area to Maine, southern Greenland, Iceland, Faeroes, British Isles, eastern Denmark and the Baltic; between 82°N and 44°N. Mainly sedentary.

C.g.grylle (Linnaeus) breeds Faeroes (not Iceland) and British Isles east to the White Sea; also North America from Labrador to Maine and in southern Greenland.

RB. Fairly numerous. Breeds colonially (small groups) on rocky or broken coasts, inlets and islands of western and northern Scotland and Ireland; more local, but increasing, on east and south coasts of Ireland (now breeding in practically every county), but in eastern Scotland not south of Caithness; also a few pairs in Cumberland, and in recent years in Anglesey and perhaps Caernarvon. Mainly sedentary, though occasionally recorded outside breeding season on other coasts south to the English Channel, most often in eastern Scotland, Northumberland and Norfolk, where one recovered July had been ringed in southwest Sweden.

Genus FRATERCULA Brisson

Holarctic genus of two species, both in Palaearctic, only one in north Atlantic, breeding also in the British Isles.

Puffin A
Fratercula arctica (Linnaeus)

Northern Holarctic. Breeds North Atlantic and adjacent Arctic Oceans from northwest Greenland south to Maine in North America, and from Spitsbergen and Novaya Zemlya south to Brittany in Europe; between 79°N and 44°N. Disperses offshore from breeding stations and reaches south to Massachusetts, Iberia and the western Mediterranean.

F.a.arctica (Linnaeus) breeds from the Kola Peninsula south to about Bergen in Norway, also Iceland, Bear Island, Jan Mayen, and from Maine north to about 74°N in west Greenland.

F.a.grabae (C. L. Brehm) breeds Faeroes, British Isles, north France and southern Scandinavia.

MB and **RB**. Numerous. Breeds colonially mainly on western islands and coasts of Britain and Ireland from the Isles of Scilly north to Shetland, and only very locally on eastern and southern coasts (none between the Isle of Wight and Yorkshire); several once large colonies, mainly in the southern part of the range, have been abandoned or reduced to a negligible size during this century. Resident at breeding stations from about March to August; a few are recorded inshore off various parts of Britain and Ireland (accidentally inland) outside the breeding season, but most disperse well out to sea, two ringed birds having reached Newfoundland, one Greenland, three the western Mediterranean and northwest Africa, and many the coasts of continental Europe from south Norway to Portugal. *F.a.grabae.*

PV and **WV**. Status obscure, but spring and autumn passage movements (only on a small scale inshore, mainly off western coasts) and small numbers offshore in winter perhaps mainly concern birds of British origin, though ringed birds from the Channel Islands and north France (*F.a.grabae*) have reached southern England. Three birds ringed on the coast of western Norway within the range of *F.a.arctica* were recovered in Caithness (May 1958), Fife (September 1959), Norfolk (February 1962); other evidence that this race reaches the British Isles is scanty, though it seems probable that some occur annually.

Order COLUMBIFORMES

Family PTEROCLIDAE*

Genus SYRRHAPTES Illiger

Palaearctic genus of two species, one periodically reaching Europe and the British Isles during irruptive migrations, following which a few are known to have bred.

Pallas's Sandgrouse   A
Syrrhaptes paradoxus (Pallas)

Central Palaearctic. Breeds from the Aral-Caspian and Kirghiz steppes east to northwest Manchuria and south to northwest China; between 50°N and 37°N. Mainly sedentary but subject to irregular migration and irruptions, when may reach western Europe, India and Korea.

Monotypic.

SV and **CB**. The greatest invasions recorded were in May 1863 and May 1888, when small flocks reached many parts of the British Isles west to the Outer Hebrides, west Ireland and the Isles of Scilly, and following which pairs bred in Yorkshire in 1888 and in Moray in 1888 and 1889. Invasions also occurred in at least nine other years up to 1909, the last of any size being in 1908. In the last 60 years there has been only one positive record—a single bird in Kent in December 1964.

---

* The affinities of the sandgrouse are controversial. Maclean (1967, *J. Orn.* 108: 203–217) has argued that they are related to waders rather than to pigeons, but Stegmann (1969, *Zool. Jb.* (Syst.) 96: 1–51) has recently produced further evidence that the long-standing classification of the sandgrouse with the pigeons is correct.

Family COLUMBIDAE

Genus COLUMBA Linnaeus

Cosmopolitan genus of over 50 species, 13 in Palaearctic but only three breeding in Europe and the British Isles.

Rock Dove A
Columba livia Gmelin

Southern Palaearctic, Oriental and northern Ethiopian. Breeds Faeroes and British Isles, from Iberia across southern Europe, locally north to the Alps, east to Chinese Turkestan, India and Ceylon; also Arabia and Africa, including Canaries, south to Ghana and the Sudan; between 62°N and 7°N. Mainly sedentary. Feral populations virtually world-wide.

C.l.livia Gmelin breeds Europe, east to west Kazakhstan, south to Morocco and western Egypt.

RB. Fairly numerous. Pure, apparently pure, or predominantly pure wild populations are confined to rocky northern and western coasts and islands of Scotland and Ireland, although locally feral strains predominate in some areas (for example in Galway); coast-dwelling populations in southwest and northeast England, Wales, Isle of Man, southwest and eastern Scotland, and southeast and northeast Ireland are now extinct or very largely composed of feral birds. Mainly sedentary, though in some localities, for example Fair Isle, occurs chiefly as a summer visitor.

Stock Dove A
Columba oenas Linnaeus

Western Palaearctic. Breeds from central Fenno-Scandia south across

Europe to Iberia and the Mediterranean, east to western Siberia, and
Iran; also northwest Africa and the mountains of Turkestan; between
65°N and 34°N. Partially migratory, northern populations wintering
south to the Mediterranean basin and Iraq.

C.o.oenas Linnaeus breeds range of species except Turkestan.

RB. Fairly numerous. Confined to southern and eastern England
in early 19th century, but has gradually extended its range and now
breeds widely in probably all counties of Britain and Ireland, north to
southern Argyll in western Scotland, and through central and eastern
Scotland to eastern Ross and, until the last few years, eastern Sutherland. Mainly sedentary, but there is some evidence of southward
movements in winter by part of the population, and two British-
ringed birds have reached southern France and Spain in their first
winter.

PV and **WV**. Status obscure; two recoveries here of birds ringed
in Finland and the Netherlands, and a mainly irregular passage in
spring (well spread) and autumn (October–November) on various
parts of the east and south coasts from Shetland to southwest Ireland,
suggest that Continental birds occur at least occasionally.

Woodpigeon   A
Columba palumbus Linnaeus

Western Palaearctic. Breeds from central Fenno-Scandia south throughout Europe including most Mediterranean islands, east to west Siberia,
Iran and eastern Himalayas; also northwest Africa, Madeira and the
Azores; between 66°N and 28°N. Mainly sedentary, but northern
populations winter in the southern part of the breeding range or beyond.

C.p.palumbus Linnaeus breeds Europe, western Siberia and northwest Africa.

RB. Abundant. Widely distributed throughout Britain and Ireland, breeding in every county, though only locally in northwest
Scotland and very locally in the Outer Hebrides and Shetland. Mainly
sedentary, movements being largely limited to short-distance dispersal
and weather movements within the British Isles, though a few birds
ringed as nestlings in southern England have reached France.

WV. Immigrants from continental Europe probably reach Britain
regularly in small numbers, as indicated by recoveries of two from the
Netherlands, one each from Norway, Denmark and Germany, by a
regular but small spring and autumn passage at Fair Isle (where one

ringed July was recovered northwest Germany the following May), and perhaps by occasional larger movements, most often in November, on coasts elsewhere in Britain and Ireland.

Genus STREPTOPELIA Bonaparte

Palaearctic, Oriental and Ethiopian genus of about 15 species, seven in Palaearctic, two breeding in Europe and the British Isles, where an Asiatic species has been recorded as a scarce vagrant.

Turtle Dove A
Streptopelia turtur (Linnaeus)

Western and central Palaearctic, marginally Ethiopian. Breeds Eurasia and northern Africa from Britain and the Canaries eastwards to Mongolia and Afghanistan, north to the Baltic (not Scandinavian peninsula), Urals and southern Siberia, south to Saharan mountains, northern Sudan, Palestine and Iran; between 58°N and 15°N. Winters in northern tropical Africa, also Turkestan and northwest India.

S.t.turtur (Linnaeus) breeds Eurasia east to west Siberia and north Iran.

MB. Fairly numerous. Breeds widely in southern and central England, and locally west to Devon, Carmarthen, Brecon, Montgomery, Denbigh, Cheshire and southwest Lancashire; on east side of Pennines extends locally north through Yorkshire to Durham and Northumberland, with a few pairs in southeast Scotland in East Lothian and, not regularly, in Berwick; also breeds occasionally in Dublin and Wicklow in southeast Ireland, and has bred recently in Down and Cork. Small numbers remain through the summer in some western districts, for example in the Isles of Scilly, Caernarvon, Wigtown, Kirkcudbright and southwest Ireland, but they are rarely suspected of breeding. Resident late April to early October.

PV. Mid-April to early June, mid-August to mid-October, mainly within breeding range, but regularly also on coasts of southwest England, western Wales and southern Ireland (often in considerable numbers in all three areas, especially in spring), and in small numbers as far north as Shetland. The origin of these birds is uncertain: most may be British although in some areas they doubtless include some from the Continent. Exceptional after October, but has recently wintered on about three occasions, with Collared Doves.

Rufous Turtle Dove   A
Streptopelia orientalis (Latham)

Central and eastern Palaearctic and north Oriental. Breeds Asia from the Urals and Afghanistan eastwards to the Kuriles and Formosa, north to southern Siberia, south to India and Thailand; between 64°N and 10°N. Partially migratory, northern populations wintering in southern parts of the breeding range and beyond it from southern Iran through India to southern China and the Ryu Kyu Islands.

    S.o.orientalis (Latham) breeds from central Siberia and northern Mongolia east to northern China and Japan.

    SV. Three: Yorkshire (October 1889), Norfolk (January 1946), Isles of Scilly (May 1960). First two referred to *S.o.orientalis*, race of the third not determined. (*S.o.meena* (Sykes), breeding from 58°N in western Siberia south through central Asia to northwest India, seems equally if not more likely than *S.o.orientalis* to occur as a vagrant.)

Collared Dove   A
Streptopelia decaocto (Frivaldszky)

Oriental and Palaearctic. Breeds Eurasia from the British Isles, southern Scandinavia, the Low Countries, France and north Italy eastwards through the Balkans and southwest Asia to Burma and Ceylon, and east from Turkestan to Korea; between 60°N and 8°N. Mainly sedentary, but has undergone a very marked range expansion northwest across Europe since about 1930.

    S.d.decaocto (Frivaldszky) breeds range of species except Burma.

    RB. Not scarce. Remarkable increase and range expansion since it first arrived and bred in Norfolk in 1955. Supported by further immigration, it now breeds locally in all except a very few counties in England, Wales and Scotland, and in at least half those in Ireland; it has become widespread and common in some, especially coastal, areas. Becomes resident in newly colonized districts, surplus birds dispersing elsewhere, mostly west and northwest, but exceptional British-ringed birds have been found in France (three), Belgium and northwest Germany.

Order CUCULIFORMES

Family CUCULIDAE

Genus CLAMATOR Kaup

Old World genus of five species, two in Palaearctic, one breeding in Europe and occasionally wandering to the British Isles.

Great Spotted Cuckoo   A
Clamator glandarius (Linnaeus)

Ethiopian and southwestern Palaearctic. Breeds Mediterranean region and parts of southwest Asia from Iberia eastwards to southwest Iran, north to southern France, Asia Minor, south to Morocco, Egypt and Palestine; also in Africa from Senegal and Somalia south to Cape Province; between 44°N and 34°S. Partially migratory, Palaearctic breeders wintering in tropical Africa.

Monotypic.

SV. Twelve: Galway (March 1842), Northumberland (August 1870), Norfolk (October 1896, July 1941, August 1958), Kerry (early spring 1918), Merioneth (April 1955), Orkney (August 1959), Anglesey (April 1960), Isle of Man (March 1963), Sussex (August 1967), Cornwall (April–June 1968).

Genus CUCULUS Linnaeus

Old World and Australasian genus of twelve species, six in Palaearctic, two breeding in Europe and one in the British Isles.

Cuckoo A
Cuculus canorus Linnaeus

Palaearctic and north Oriental. Breeds Eurasia and northwest Africa from Scandinavia, British Isles, Iberia and Morocco eastwards to northeast Siberia, Japan and Indo-China, north to the tree-line, south to Atlas range, Asia Minor, Himalayas and central Burma; between 70°N and 20°N. Winters tropical Africa and subtropical Asia (India to southern China).

C.c.canorus Linnaeus breeds Europe, except Iberia, east to Siberia, northern China and Japan.

MB. Not scarce. Widely distributed, breeding in every county in Britain and Ireland, but only irregularly in Shetland. Resident mid-April (rarely late March) to July or August, some juveniles remaining through to September; also a few records October–December.

PV. Mainly mid-April to early June, with much less noticeable passage in autumn, though small numbers occur then on the east coast in July and August. Involvement of Continental birds probably slight, but very small numbers are noted annually at Fair Isle (where not known to breed) and one ringed there in May was recovered two days later in Norway.

Genus COCCYZUS Vieillot

New World genus of seven species, two occurring as vagrants in the British Isles.

Black-billed Cuckoo A
Coccyzus erythropthalmus (Wilson)

Nearctic. Breeds North America east of the Rocky Mountains from southern Canada south to Wyoming, Arkansas and South Carolina; between 50°N and 33°N. Winters from northwest South America south to Peru.

Monotypic.

SV. Six: Antrim (September 1871), Isles of Scilly (October 1932), Argyll (November 1950), Shetland (October 1953), Cornwall (October 1965), Devon (October 1967).

Yellow-billed Cuckoo   **A**
Coccyzus americanus (Linnaeus)

Nearctic and north Neotropical. Breeds North America from British Columbia and Quebec south to central Mexico and the Gulf coast, also in the Caribbean area; between 50°N and 15°N. Winters South America from Columbia to the Argentine.

    C.a.americanus (Linnaeus) breeds range of species except northern Mexico and the mountains west of the continental divide in the United States.

    SV. About 25 (twelve 1825–1904, four 1921–40, six 1952–53, three 1960–65); one late September, two December, the remaining dated records all October–November; 13 in England (one Yorkshire, the rest in the south between the Isles of Scilly and Sussex), three Wales (Pembroke, Cardigan, Anglesey), six Scotland (Inner Hebrides, Northern Isles, Nairn, Angus), three Ireland (Cork, Wicklow, Mayo).

Order STRIGIFORMES

Family TYTONIDAE

Genus TYTO Billberg

Cosmopolitan genus of ten species, one in Palaearctic, breeding also in Europe and the British Isles.

Barn Owl   **A**
Tyto alba (Scopoli)

Cosmopolitan. Breeds from the Atlantic islands, British Isles and west Europe eastwards to western Russia, north to Denmark, south to the Sahara, Arabia and southern Iran; also from India to the southwest Pacific region and Australia; in tropical Africa and the New World;

absent from north, east and central Asia; between 58°N and 45°S. Mainly sedentary, though northern populations are partially migratory.

T.a.alba (Scopoli) breeds British Isles east to western Germany, western Yugoslavia and Greece, south through Europe to North Africa.

T.a.guttata (C. L. Brehm) breeds north and east of nominate *alba* to Denmark and the southern tip of Sweden, the Baltic and Ukraine.

RB. Not scarce. Widely distributed in Britain and Ireland, breeding in every county north to Argyll and Fife, and much more locally and scarcely north to east Sutherland; absent or very scarce in northeast Scotland, and absent from nearly all Scottish islands with the exception of Arran, Bute and Islay. Mainly sedentary; some erratic dispersal in winter mainly of juveniles, but no evidence of emigration. *T.a.alba*.

SV. About 50 or more records of *T.a.guttata*, August to April, mainly October to December, chiefly from southeast England (Sussex to Norfolk), but also north to Shetland (five) and west to Ireland (three, all in 1932, January to April). *T.a.alba* has occurred as rare vagrant in Shetland (including Fair Isle) and the Isles of Scilly; the origin of these birds is not known.

Family STRIGIDAE

Genus OTUS Pennant

Cosmopolitan genus of 36 species, four in Palaearctic, one breeding in Europe and occurring as a vagrant in the British Isles.

Scops Owl

A

Otus scops (Linnaeus)

Palaearctic and Oriental. Breeds discontinuously from France and Iberia across central and southern Europe to Turkestan mountains, north to central Russia and Mongolia, south to the Sahara, Asia Minor and Afghanistan; eastern Asia from India, Malaya and Philippines north to Amur basin and Japan; between 56°N and 8°N. Partially migratory; European and western Asian population winters in north tropical Africa, other northern breeders winter in subtropical Asia.

O.s.scops (Linnaeus) breeds north Africa, Europe (except Iberia and the Balearic Islands) east to central Russia, the Caucasus and Turkey.

SV. About 67 recorded, but only eight since 1950, and only three of these during 1956–68; noted in all months April to September, but chiefly in spring; the majority England (widely scattered, but nine in Norfolk and four or five in each of Cornwall, Hampshire, Kent and Yorkshire), two Wales (both Pembroke), one Isle of Man, 14 Scotland (including six Shetland, three Orkney), and nine Ireland (three Wexford, the rest scattered).

Genus BUBO Dumeril

Nearly cosmopolitan genus of eleven species, two in Palaearctic, one marginally, the other breeding in Europe and formerly wandering to the British Isles.

Eagle Owl A
Bubo bubo (Linnaeus)

Palaearctic, north Oriental and north Ethiopian. Breeds from Lapland, Germany, central France and Iberia eastwards across Eurasia to Sakhalin and the Kuriles, south to southern Sahara in Africa, Arabia, southern India and southern China; between 69°N and 10°N. Mainly sedentary.

B.b.bubo (Linnaeus) breeds Europe, except Iberia, east to central Russia and north Ukraine; has decreased in many parts of the range.

SV. About 20 records in the 18th and 19th centuries, mostly poorly documented and rather vague, and some at least referring to escapes from captivity; birds in Orkney (1830), Shetland (autumn 1863, March 1871) and Argyll (February 1883) seem the most likely to have been genuine vagrants, correctly identified. In the 20th century noted in the Outer Hebrides (November 1931), Devon (April 1933), Yorkshire (December 1943) and Shropshire (April 1954), but none of these records entirely satisfactory.

Genus NYCTEA Stephens

Circumpolar monospecific genus, reaching the British Isles mainly as an irregular visitor, chiefly in winter, although a pair has bred since 1967.

Snowy Owl   **A**
Nyctea scandiaca (Linnaeus)

Northern Holarctic. Breeding distribution circumpolar, on low tundra
from Novaya Zemlya, arctic islands of Canada and northwest Greenland south to the tree-line in northern Eurasia and North America;
also Iceland, mountains of Scandinavia and the Bering Sea islands; between 83°N and 58°N. Irregular or eruptive movements—related to
food supply—when reaches south to central Europe, Turkestan, northern China and the southern United States.

Monotypic.

CB. A pair bred successfully in Shetland in 1967 and 1968.

SV. Irregular visitor, chiefly in winter. In the 19th century fairly
frequent in Scotland (especially Shetland, also Orkney and Hebrides)
and Ireland (especially north and northwest), occasionally in England
and Wales, becoming less frequent this century, and very few recorded
anywhere, 1950 to 1962. From 1963 to 1966 a striking increase (but
fewer in 1967 and 1968 except in Shetland), with several noted mainly
in winter south to southern England, and others throughout the year
in east Scottish Highlands and Shetland, where a pair bred from 1967
onwards (see above). In Ireland, only two records since 1950: Antrim
(January 1956) and Roscommon (November 1968).

Genus SURNIA Dumeril

Holarctic monospecific genus, breeding in Europe and wandering to
the British Isles.

Hawk Owl   **A**
Surnia ulula (Linnaeus)

Northern Holarctic. Breeds in boreal forests of Eurasia and North
America south to southern Fenno-Scandia, central Russia, northern
Mongolia, British Columbia, Michigan and New Brunswick; between
70°N and 46°N; also in mountains of Turkestan. Partially migratory,
also irruptive, occasionally reaching as far south as central Europe,
Korea and the northern United States.

S.u.ulula (Linnaeus) breeds Eurasian range of species except central
Turkestan.

S.u.caparoch (Müller) breeds North America.

SV. Ten, but only three of these in this century, two of them since 1959. Three (off Cornwall in March 1830, Somerset in August 1867, Lanark in December 1863) were referred to the American race, *S.u. caparoch*; two (Wiltshire prior to 1876, Aberdeen in November 1898) to the Eurasian race, *S.u.ulula*; while the racial identity of the remaining five (Shetland in winter 1860–61, Renfrew in November 1868, Northampton in November 1903, Lancashire in September 1959, Cornwall in August 1966) was not determined.

Genus ATHENE Boie

Palaearctic, Oriental and north Ethiopian genus of three species, two in Palaearctic, one marginally, the other breeding in Europe and introduced to Britain (not Ireland).

Little Owl C
Athene noctua (Scopoli)

Palaearctic, and northeast Ethiopian. Breeds from western Europe and northwest Africa eastwards to northern China, north to the Baltic, Urals, Turkestan and Mongolia, south to the Sahara, northeast Africa, Somaliland, Arabia, Baluchistan and Tibet; between 57°N and 8°N. Mainly sedentary. Introduced England and New Zealand.

A.n.vidalii A. E. Brehm breeds western Europe from the Low Countries and western Germany through France to Spain and Portugal. British population is descended from introduced stock of this race.

IB. Not scarce. Introduced in the late 19th century (main releases in Kent and Northampton), and now widespread in England and Wales, breeding in every county with the possible exception of Radnor (recorded in recent years but no nest since 1946); also breeds Berwick (since 1958), Midlothian (1968), perhaps Roxburgh, East Lothian and Dumfries, and just possibly Wigtown, but not elsewhere in Scotland. Mainly sedentary, but some short-distance wandering, vagrants having reached eastern Ireland three times, and the Isle of Man once.

Genus STRIX Linnaeus

Nearly cosmopolitan (mainly northern hemisphere and not Australasia) genus of 12 species, five in Palaearctic, three breeding in Europe but only one in the British Isles.

Tawny Owl A
Strix aluco Linnaeus

Palaearctic and north Oriental. Breeds from western Europe and north-west Africa east across Eurasia to southern China and Formosa, north to Scandinavia, the Urals, mountains of Turkestan and Manchuria, south to the Middle Atlas in Morocco, the Lebanon, southern Iran and the Himalayas; between 64°N and 20°S. Sedentary.

S.a.sylvatica Shaw breeds from Britain and France (except north and east) south to Iberia.

RB. Fairly numerous. Widely distributed throughout mainland Britain, but entirely absent—even as a vagrant—from Ireland, the Isle of Man, Orkney, Shetland, and many Hebridean islands.

Genus ASIO Brisson

Nearly cosmopolitan (not Australasian) genus of about 15 species, three in Palaearctic, one marginally, the other two breeding in Europe and the British Isles.

Long-eared Owl A
Asio otus (Linnaeus)

Holarctic. Breeds Eurasia and northwest Africa from the Atlantic to the Pacific, north to 66°N in Scandinavia, 60°N in the Urals, and south Yakutia in east Siberia, south to the Canaries, Morocco, Palestine, Turkestan and Japan; also from southern Canada to the southern United States; between 66°N and 28°N. Partially migratory, wintering south to Egypt, northern India, southern China and Mexico.

A.o.otus (Linnaeus) breeds Old World range of species except Canaries.

RB. Not scarce. Distributed widely but thinly throughout Ireland and over much of Scotland (not certainly in the Outer Hebrides and on parts of northwest mainland; irregular Shetland) and northern England, south to Cheshire, Stafford, Derby, Nottingham and north Lincoln; also Isle of Man; breeds very much more locally and in decreasing numbers farther south in England and in Wales, in many counties restricted to a handful of localities at most, in others not known as a regular breeder, and in several—especially in central and southwest England and west Wales—not known to have bred at all in recent years. Sedentary; some short-distance dispersal but no evidence of emigration.

WV and **PV**. Immigrants from northern Europe (Netherlands and Norway east to Finland and the Baltic States; also one ringed bird from southeast Germany) arrive in small numbers on the east coast, especially Northern Isles, chiefly October–November, and depart mid-March to mid-May. The majority probably remain here through the winter. The irregular occurrence of autumn migrants on the south coast (formerly fairly regular in southwest England) suggests that some may continue to France, or alternatively that some immigration takes place across the English Channel.

Short-eared Owl A
Asio flammeus (Pontoppidan)

Holarctic, Neotropical and central Pacific. Breeds Eurasia and North America from the Arctic Ocean (including Baffin Island and Iceland) south to the British Isles, France, Italy, Black Sea, Turkestan, Manchuria, California and Virginia; elsewhere, in parts of Caribbean area, South America, Falklands, Galapagos, Marianas, Carolines and Hawaiian Islands; between 72°N and 53°S. Holarctic breeders are partially migratory, in winter reaching as far south as northern Africa (to Abyssinia), tropical Asia to Ceylon and Malaya, and through Mexico to Guatemala.

A.f.flammeus (Pontoppidan) breeds North America, Iceland, Eurasia.

RB and **MB**. Not scarce. Breeds regularly but in fluctuating numbers in Orkney and nearly all mainland counties of Scotland and northern England south to mid-Lancashire and mid-Yorkshire, also very locally in north Wales, Suffolk, Kent and Essex; has bred occasionally or sporadically in recent years in the Inner Hebrides, Isle of Man, south Wales, and several other counties in southern England, most often in Norfolk, also once as far south and west as Wiltshire; has bred occasionally in the past in southwest England, but the only Irish breeding record was in Galway in 1959. British birds are partially migratory, some dispersing south and west within the British Isles, while ringed birds have reached Belgium, France (two), Spain and Malta.

PV and **WV**. Immigrants from northern Europe (ringed birds from Iceland, Norway, Finland and Germany) arrive in variable numbers, September to December (chiefly October–November), some departing March to June, and others perhaps—though not certainly—remaining here to breed in some years. Migrants regularly reach Ireland and the English south coast, most of them probably continuing, but others remaining through the winter, with some evidence of return passage in spring.

Genus AEGOLIUS Kaup

Palaearctic, Nearctic and Neotropical genus of four species, one in Palaearctic, breeding in Europe and sometimes wandering to the British Isles.

Tengmalm's Owl   **A**
Aegolius funereus (Linnaeus)

Northern Holarctic. Breeds from north Scandinavia to east Siberia south to southern Sweden, central Russia and Mongolia, and again in mountains of central Europe, central Asia and western China; also in North America (where called Boreal Owl) from Alaska to Labrador and south to southern Canada; between 69°N and 42°N. Mainly sedentary; eruptively migrant, when may reach southern Europe, Japan and the northern United States.

A.f.funereus (Linnaeus) breeds Europe east to central Russia.

SV. Nearly 50 recorded, most before about 1918, and since 1950 only two, both in Orkney (December 1959–January 1960, May 1961); most have been noted October to February, some March to May; twelve or more Scotland, including six Shetland, 1897–1918 (others said to have been seen earlier in the 19th century); the remainder England, nearly all in eastern counties, including twelve Yorkshire, though none of these more recent than 1901.

Order CAPRIMULGIFORMES

Family CAPRIMULGIDAE

Genus CHORDEILES Swainson

Nearctic and Neotropical genus of five species, one of which has occurred as a vagrant in Europe, including the British Isles.

Nighthawk
A

Chordeiles minor (Forster)

Nearctic and north Neotropical. Breeds from south Mackenzie, James Bay and central Quebec south to central Mexico, Puerto Rico and Bahamas; between 62°N and 18°N. Winters South America from Colombia to Argentina.

C.m.minor (Forster) breeds northern and eastern North America south to Washington, Ohio River and north Georgia.

SV. Three, all Isles of Scilly: September 1927, two September 1955 (one remaining into October).

Genus CAPRIMULGUS Linnaeus

Cosmopolitan genus of about 39 species, ten in Palaearctic, only two breeding in Europe and one in the British Isles, where two others have each been recorded once.

Red-necked Nightjar
B

Caprimulgus ruficollis Temminck

Southwestern Palaearctic. Breeds most of Iberia, and northwest Africa south to the Great Atlas and east to Tunisia; between 43°N and 34°N. Migratory, wintering in Senegal and probably elsewhere in savannahs south of the Sahara.

SV. One, Northumberland, October 1856. The faded specimen was identified first as *C.r.ruficollis* Temminck (breeds Iberia, Morocco), later as *C.r.desertorum* Erlanger (breeds east Morocco to Tunisia); the race is probably best regarded as indeterminable.

Nightjar   A
Caprimulgus europaeus Linnaeus

Western and central Palaearctic. Breeds southern Fenno-Scandia, British Isles, Iberia and northwest Africa east to Lake Baikal and central Turkestan, north to 60°N in western Siberia, south to Morocco, Syria and northwest India; between 63°N and 25°N. Winters in Africa from the Sudan and Abyssinia to Cape Province.

C.e.europaeus Linnaeus breeds Europe south to the Pyrenees, Hungary, northern Ukraine, and southern Siberia to Lake Baikal and north Mongolia.

MB. Not scarce. Distributed widely but locally throughout England, Wales and Ireland, breeding in decreasing numbers in virtually every county, though doubtfully now in Oxford, Cambridge, Carmarthen, Brecon, Radnor, and the Isle of Man; in Scotland breeds sparsely, mainly in the southwest but also in a few localities north to east Sutherland. Resident May (rarely late April) to August or September.

PV. Very inconspicuous on passage, chiefly May and September, when scattered records from all coasts, including occasional migrants or vagrants in Orkney and Shetland. Extent of passage of Continental birds is not known, but it is certainly small and perhaps not annual.

Egyptian Nightjar   B
Caprimulgus aegyptius Lichtenstein

Southwestern and central Palaearctic. Breeds northern Sahara in Morocco, Algeria, Tunisia, Libya, Egypt; southwest Asia from Iraq to Turkestan, north to the Aral Sea and Tian Shan foothills; between 42°N and 25°N. Winters in the southern Sahara and northern Sudan.

SV. One, Nottingham (June 1883). Race not determined.

Order APODIFORMES

Family APODIDAE

Genus HIRUNDAPUS Hodgson

Cosmopolitan, mainly tropical, genus of 19 species, one in Palaearctic, occasionally straggling to Europe and the British Isles.

Needle-tailed Swift   A
Hirundapus caudacutus (Latham)

Central and eastern Palaearctic and northern Oriental. Breeds discontinuously from western Siberia east to Japan and the Kuriles, north to the middle Yenisei and Lena rivers, south to Mongolia and northern China, and also in the Himalayas and Assam Hills east to Yunnan and Formosa; between 60°N and 20°N. Winters in Australia and Tasmania.

H.c.caudacutus (Latham) breeds range of species except Himalayas, southwest China and Formosa.

SV. Three: Essex (July 1846), Hampshire (July 1879), Cork (June 1964).

Genus APUS Scopoli

Palaearctic, Oriental and Ethiopian genus of ten species, seven in Palaearctic, four breeding in Europe and one in the British Isles, where two others are scarce visitors.

Alpine Swift   A
Apus melba (Linnaeus)

Southern Palaearctic, Oriental and Ethiopian. Breeds northwest Africa

and from Iberia east through southern Europe and southwest Asia to
southern Turkestan and Ceylon, north to the Alps, Crimea and the
Caucasus, south to Sinai and Baluchistan, also eastern and southern
Africa and Madagascar; between 47°N and 35°S. Partially migratory;
European and some Asiatic breeders are known to winter in eastern
and central tropical Africa.

   A.m.melba (Linnaeus) breeds southern Europe and southwest Asia
east to the Caucasus and northern Iran.

   SV. Over 100 records of single birds (three to seven annually in
recent years), a few of small parties (none recent), and one of about 100
birds involved in the same movement in Kent, July 1915. Noted all
months March to November, rather more in autumn (July–October)
than spring (April–June), dates evenly scattered at both seasons, with
slight tendency towards late September–early October peak. Majority
of records are from England, especially coasts from the Isles of Scilly
to Norfolk, but there are several from Scotland (north to Orkney and
Shetland), Wales and Ireland.

Swift   **A**

Apus apus (Linnaeus)

Palaearctic. Breeds Eurasia and northwest Africa from the Atlantic east
to southern Manchuria and eastern China, north to Lapland, the Urals,
Baikal region, south to Morocco, the Mediterranean islands, Iran and
western Himalayas; between 69°N and 28°N. Winters in Africa from
10°S south to Cape Province.

   A.a.apus (Linnaeus) breeds northwest Africa, Eurasia east to Lake
Baikal, Turkestan and Palestine.

   MB. Numerous. Widely distributed, breeding throughout Britain
and Ireland north to Inverness, and locally farther north in eastern Ross,
eastern Sutherland and northern Caithness; absent from northwest
Scotland, the Hebrides, Orkney and Shetland. Resident late April to
mid-August. British birds winter mainly in south Congo and Malawi.

   PV. Passage and weather movements, all months, late April to
August, stragglers regularly in September, occasionally October, and
very rarely in winter; largest movements in southern England, but
occurs regularly—sometimes in numbers—north to Shetland. Weather
movements involve mainly non-breeders of Continental as well as
British origin. Extent of regular passage of Continental birds not known.

Little Swift (or House Swift) A
Apus affinis (J. E. Gray)

Southwestern Palaearctic, Ethiopian and Oriental. Breeds throughout
Africa and southern Asia east to southern China, Formosa, the Philippines and Borneo, north to Morocco, Syria, south Transcaspia and
Kashmir; between 40°N and 35°S. Mainly resident, but *galilejensis*
winters to just south of the breeding range.

A.a.galilejensis (Antinori) breeds from Morocco east to Kashmir, and
south to the central Sahara and Arabia.

SV. One, Cape Clear, Cork (June 1967). Race not determined but
unlikely to have been other than *galilejensis*.

Order CORACIIFORMES

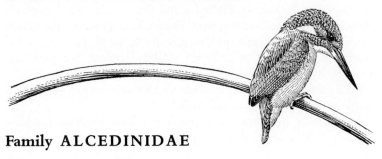

Family ALCEDINIDAE

Genus ALCEDO Linnaeus

Old World and Australasian genus of eight species, one in Palaearctic, breeding also in Europe and the British Isles.

Kingfisher   A
Alcedo atthis (Linnaeus)

Palaearctic, Oriental and Australasian. Breeds northwest Africa, Eurasia and Melanesia from the Atlantic to Japan and Formosa, north to southern Scandinavia, central Russia and southern Siberia, south and southeast to Palestine, Ceylon, through Malaysia and New Guinea to the Solomons; between 60°N and 10°S. Northern populations winter in southern parts of the breeding range and beyond it in northeast Africa, Arabia, Philippines and Indonesia.

A.a.ispida Linnaeus breeds Europe (except southern Iberia, southern Italy, Greece) east to the Baltic countries and Black Sea.

RB. Not scarce. Widely distributed in England, Wales and Ireland, breeding locally in practically every county (not certainly in Donegal, nor in the Isle of Man; irregular Anglesey), but in Scotland has decreased and now breeds only very sparsely, and chiefly irregularly, in a few counties north to Arran and southern Argyll in the west and Kincardine (perhaps southeast Aberdeen) in the east. Mainly sedentary, but some dispersal to coasts in autumn and winter, with regular autumn appearance of birds in the Isles of Scilly (where does not breed) perhaps indicating emigration on a small scale. Vagrant to north Scotland; has reached the Outer Hebrides, Orkney and Shetland (not Fair Isle) on a few occasions.

Family MEROPIDAE

Genus MEROPS Linnaeus

Old World genus of 21 species, three (one marginally) in Palaearctic, of which two (one marginally) breed in Europe and wander to the British Isles, where one has bred.

Bee-eater   A
Merops apiaster Linnaeus

Southwestern Palaearctic, Oriental and Ethiopian. Breeds northwest Africa, Iberia eastwards to the Altai and Kashmir, north to southern France, central Russia and the north Caspian area, south to Palestine and Baluchistan; between 53°N and 25°N. Winters in tropical Africa south to Cape Province (where some breed); also Arabia.

Monotypic.

CB. Bred Sussex 1955 (three pairs, two successfully); a pair attempted to breed Midlothian 1920.

SV. Over 200 recorded, usually singly but sometimes in small parties; one to six records annually in recent years, with 35 in all (involving 46 birds) during 1958–68. Noted in all months April to October, rarely November, once into December; rather more in spring than autumn. Principally in southern and eastern England, less often elsewhere, though recorded on more than twelve occasions in both Scotland and Ireland, and several times in Wales.

Blue-cheeked Bee-eater   A
Merops superciliosus (Linnaeus)

Palaearctic and Ethiopian. Breeds north Africa and southwest Asia from the Moroccan Sahara east to northern India, north to the northern

G

Caucasus, south to Egypt, Iraq; also in eastern and southern Africa, and Madagascar; between 45°N and 25°S. Partially migratory, northern breeders wintering in Africa south of Sahara.

SV. One, Isles of Scilly (June 1951). Race not determined.

Family CORACIIDAE

Genus CORACIAS Linnaeus

Old World, mainly tropical, genus of eight species, two (one marginally) in Palaearctic, one breeding in Europe and wandering to the British Isles.

Roller   A
Coracias garrulus Linnaeus

Western and central Palaearctic. Breeds from northwest Africa, Iberia, southern France, Germany and Gotland (Sweden) east to the Altai and Kashmir, north to central Russia and west Siberia, south to Palestine, Iraq and Baluchistan; western limits of range shrinking eastwards in middle Europe; between 59°N and 25°N. Winters in eastern and southern Africa, also Arabia.

C.g.garrulus Linnaeus breeds range of species except Iraq to Turkestan and Kashmir.

SV. Over 160 recorded, but relatively few in recent years (25 during 1958–68); mainly May to July, also August–November, with records in the past in April and, very rarely, in other months. Principally in southeast England—Hampshire to Norfolk—but many others widely scattered in England, Wales and Scotland, from the Isles of Scilly north to Orkney and Shetland; 14 in Ireland, where most dated occurrences have been in autumn.

Family UPUPIDAE

Genus UPUPA Linnaeus

Old World monospecific genus, breeding in Europe and occurring as an annual visitor to the British Isles, where it sometimes breeds.

Hoopoe

A

Upupa epops Linnaeus

Palaearctic, Ethiopian and Oriental. Breeds from Iberia, France, Germany and Estonia east across Eurasia to Ussuriland and eastern China, north to central Siberia, south to Ceylon and Sumatra, also over the greater part of Africa, and Madagascar; between 59°N and 35°S. Northern populations winter in Africa and southern Eurasia north to the Mediterranean basin and the Yangtse.

U.e.epops Linnaeus breeds Canaries, northwest Africa, Eurasia east to central Siberia, Turkestan and northwest India.

CB. Occasional breeding recorded in southern England, chiefly in south coast counties, also north to Hereford and Buckingham, on average once or twice each decade, but four times in the 1950s.

PV. Variable but small numbers, chiefly March to May, mid-August to mid-October, occasionally other months February to November, very rarely in winter; usually single birds, sometimes two or three together, occasionally small parties. Annual, especially in spring, nearly all coastal counties from Cornwall to Norfolk, and in Pembroke, Wexford and Cork; fairly regular (not infrequently inland) elsewhere in southern halves of England, Wales and Ireland, less often farther north and in Scotland, with tendency for northern areas to receive more in autumn (especially October) than in spring.

Order PICIFORMES

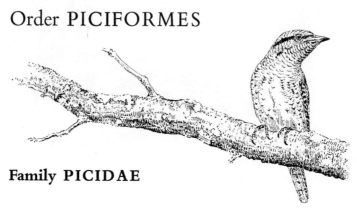

Family PICIDAE

Genus JYNX Linnaeus

Palaearctic and Ethiopian genus of two species, one in each region, that
in Palaearctic breeding in Europe and the British Isles.

Wryneck   A
Jynx torquilla Linnaeus

Palaearctic. Breeds from Scandinavia, southern England and central
Iberia east through Eurasia to northern Mongolia, north to southern
Siberia, south to the Mediterranean islands and Iran, also in eastern
Algeria, the Himalayas and western China; between 67°N and 35°N.
Most populations migratory; winters south to tropical Africa, sub-
tropical Asia from India to southern China, and southern Japan.

J.t.torquilla Linnaeus breeds Europe east to the Urals except Italy and
Sardinia.

MB. Extremely scarce. British breeding population now reduced to
a few pairs in Kent with perhaps the odd pair or two still in Surrey;
marked decrease and contraction of range in recent years—the con-
tinuation of a trend that has lasted since the early 19th century when
species bred in practically every county in England and Wales. Resident from late March to September.

PV. Mid-April to early June (scarce, regular only at Fair Isle), and
end August to mid-October, when regular in small but variable numbers on the British east coast (Shetland to Kent), less often on other
coasts of Britain and Ireland (annual Sussex, Dorset and Isles of Scilly),
and noted only infrequently inland; the birds involved belong to the

Scandinavian and, probably, northwest Russian breeding populations. Migrants occasionally remain till mid-November, and there are at least two winter records (Pembroke, January 1965; Cornwall, through winter 1967–68).

Genus PICUS Linnaeus

Palaearctic and Oriental genus of 14 species, only four in Palaearctic, two breeding in Europe and one in Britain (not Ireland).

Green Woodpecker A
Picus viridis Linnaeus

Western Palaearctic. Breeds from southern Scandinavia, Britain and Iberia across most of Europe and western Asia to the Caspian Sea, also in southwest Iran and northwest Africa; between 65°N and 30°N. Mainly sedentary.

P.v.viridis Linnaeus breeds Europe except the Pyrenees and Iberia.

RB. Not scarce. Widely distributed in England and Wales, breeding in every county, and more locally in Scotland (colonized only since 1950) north to Clackmannan and probably Perth, odd birds recorded in recent years north to Argyll and Aberdeen. Absent from Ireland (where recorded as vagrant only three times, all in 19th century) and the Isle of Man.

Genus DENDROCOPOS Koch

Nearly cosmopolitan (not Australasian) genus of 33 species, 15 in Palaearctic, five breeding in Europe but only two in Britain (not Ireland).

Great Spotted Woodpecker A
Dendrocopos major (Linnaeus)

Palaearctic and, marginally, Oriental. Breeds Eurasia and northwest Africa from the Atlantic to the Pacific, north to the tree-line in Europe and Siberia, south to the Canaries, Iran, Turkestan, northern Burma and southern China; between 67°N and 20°N. Generally resident; some northern populations migrate eruptively or, to some extent, regularly.

D.m.major (Linnaeus) breeds Scandinavia, and east Europe, intergrading with other races to the south (Denmark, Germany), southeast (Ukraine) and east (west Siberia).

D.m.anglicus Hartert breeds Britain.

RB. Fairly numerous. Widely distributed, breeding in every mainland county of Britain (except possibly Caithness), also in the Isle of
Wight and Anglesey; absent from Ireland and the Isle of Man. Endemic *D.m.anglicus* is sedentary, although a specimen from Fermanagh
(December 1959) was referred to this race.

PV and **WV**. Winter visitors and passage migrants, *D.m.major*,
from Scandinavia and perhaps farther east, arrive in small and very
variable numbers—perhaps not annually—on the east coast, especially
the Northern Isles, mainly September–October, and into November in
irruption years; in larger irruptions (e.g. 1949, 1962, 1968) birds
probably reach most parts of Britain and spill over into Ireland, where
recorded more than 80 times, September to May. Onward passage to
adjacent Continent probably also occurs. Apparently no return passage
recorded, and has occurred in spring at Fair Isle, for example, on only
three occasions.

Lesser Spotted Woodpecker   **A**
Dendrocopos minor (Linnaeus)

Western and northern Palaearctic. Breeds from Scandinavia, Britain
and Iberia east across most of northern Eurasia to the Pacific, north to
the tree-line in Europe and Siberia, south to the Mediterranean, Iran,
northern Kazakhstan, northern Korea and northern Japan; also northwest Africa; between 70°N and 35°N. Mainly sedentary.

D.m.comminutus Hartert breeds England and Wales.

RB. Not scarce. Widely but thinly distributed throughout England
and Wales, breeding in every county, though perhaps not regularly in
the Isle of Wight, Pembroke, Anglesey, Durham and south Northumberland. Not recorded in Scotland until September 1968, when two
occurred in east Stirling/south Perth; no records from Ireland or Isle
of Man.

Order PASSERIFORMES

Family ALAUDIDAE

Genus MELANOCORYPHA Boie

Palaearctic genus of six species, three breeding in Europe, two of these and a third from Asia having wandered to the British Isles.

Calandra Lark   A
Melanocorypha calandra (Linnaeus)

Southern Palaearctic. Breeds from Iberia and Morocco eastwards through the Mediterranean and Iranian regions, to northern Afghanistan and Russian Turkestan, and through the Balkans and southern Russia to the north Caspian; between 50°N and 30°N. Northern populations winter in southern parts of the breeding range and in Egypt.

    SV. One: Dorset (April 1961). Subspecies not determined.

Bimaculated Lark   A
Melanocorypha bimaculata (Ménétries)

Central Palaearctic. Breeds southwest Asia from Asia Minor and the Near East eastwards to Zaisan Nor and north to the southern Urals; between 50°N and 30°N. Winters south to the Sudan, Ethiopia, Arabia and northwest India.

    SV. One: Lundy, Devon (May 1962). Subspecies not determined.

White-winged Lark   A
Melanocorypha leucoptera (Pallas)

Central Palaearctic. Breeds from the Crimea and southeast Russia east through the Kirghiz Steppes to Lake Balkhash and Zaisan Nor; between 55°N and 43°N. Winters south to Turkey, northern Iran and Turkestan.

Monotypic.

SV. Four records involving six birds: Sussex (November 1869, three together November 1917, August 1933), Hertford (August 1955).

Genus CALANDRELLA Kaup

Southern Palaearctic and Ethiopian genus of 12 species, four in Palaearctic, two breeding in Europe and wandering to the British Isles.

Short-toed Lark   **A**
Calandrella cinerea (Gmelin)

Southern Palaearctic and Ethiopian. Breeds from northwest Africa, Iberia and southern France east through Mediterranean Europe, Asia Minor and Asian steppes to Manchuria, north to southern Russia and about 50°N in Siberia, south to eastern and southern Africa, Arabia and the Himalayas; between 50°N and 35°S. Winters in Africa, India, northern Burma and eastern China.

Subspecific status of birds recorded in British Isles is uncertain, but two types occur: (a) reddish western types as represented by *C.c. brachydactyla* (Leisler) (Iberia to southern Russia), *C.c.rubiginosa* Fromholz (northwest Africa) and *C.c.hermonensis* Tristram (Syria to Palestine), and (b) greyish eastern types as represented by *C.c.artemisiana* Banjovski (Caspian, Transcaucasia, Asia Minor, Iran) and *C.c.longipennis* (Eversmann) (Russian Altai to Manchuria) and intermediate populations in east Iran and north Afghanistan.

SV. Almost 100 recorded (currently an average of about three a year, but 12 or more in both 1967 and 1968) in all months April to December, but mostly in May, September and October; excluding 1967 and 1968, when most were in autumn, records in recent years have tended to be more common in spring. Almost half the total were identified at Fair Isle, and most of the remainder were on the Isles of Scilly and the south and southeast coasts of England and Ireland. Where determined (mainly at Fair Isle), all spring and summer (April to August) and a few autumn birds have resembled the reddish western races, but in autumn most have resembled the greyish eastern types.

Lesser Short-toed Lark   A
Calandrella rufescens (Vieillot)

Southern Palaearctic. Breeds Canaries, Iberia, south and east Mediterranean, and from southeast Russia and the Middle East eastwards to Manchuria and perhaps northeast China; between 50°N and 27°N. Winters in Egypt, the Sudan, Iranian region, India and China.

SV. Four records, involving a total of 42 birds, all in Ireland: Kerry (thirty in January 1956), Wexford (five in March 1956, five in March 1958), Mayo (two in May 1956). Subspecies not determined.

Genus GALERIDA Boie

Palaearctic, Ethiopian and Oriental genus of six species, two in Palaearctic, both breeding in Europe and one straggling to the British Isles.

Crested Lark   A
Galerida cristata (Linnaeus)

Palaearctic, marginally Oriental and Ethiopian. Breeds from southern Sweden, France and Iberia east across continental Europe and southern Asia to Korea, north to the Baltic States and southern Russia, south to the north African coastal belt, sub-Sahara and from Sierra Leone to Somaliland, Arabia and northern India; between 60°N and 5°N. Mainly sedentary.

G.c.cristata (Linnaeus) breeds Europe except Iberia, Italy and Balkans, east to the Crimea.

SV. Fifteen recorded, including two together twice; one before 1845, nine 1846-81, five 1947-65. Dates widely scattered, in March (two), April (two), June, September (two), October (three), November, and December-January (two). Six Cornwall, one Devon, four Sussex, one Kent, two (together) London, one Fair Isle. One (Cornwall, September 1846) identified as *G.c.cristata*; the races of the others not determined.

Genus LULLULA Kaup

Palaearctic monospecific genus, breeding in Europe and the British Isles.

Woodlark   A
Lullula arborea (Linnaeus)

Western Palaearctic. Breeds from northwest Africa, Iberia, southern England and southern Fenno-Scandia east through Europe to the Urals and through Asia Minor and the Near East to northern Iran; between 61°N and 32°N. Sedentary and migratory, wintering mainly within the breeding range.

L.a.arborea (Linnaeus) breeds whole of range except southern parts of Mediterranean peninsulas and northwest Africa.

RB. Scarce and decreasing. Distributed locally in Wales and southern England, chiefly in south coast counties from Sussex to Cornwall, with small numbers northwest through Wiltshire, Gloucester, Worcester and Shropshire and into Wales where it nests (or is present in the breeding season) in all counties north to Merioneth, Denbigh and Montgomery, with the possible exception of Brecon; very small, much reduced numbers are still found in Suffolk, Norfolk and Nottingham. In other counties of central and southern England it has now ceased to breed or does so only irregularly. Breeding birds are probably mainly sedentary, though there is evidently a limited dispersal in winter. The species is now recorded only infrequently in England and Wales to the north of the present breeding range, most of these records being during the periods March to May and September to November. It was formerly quite frequent at Fair Isle at these times but is now irregular there. It has been recorded only very rarely elsewhere in Scotland and in Ireland, where, however, it has bred on three occasions in the past.

Genus ALAUDA Linnaeus

Palaearctic and Oriental genus of two species, both in Palaearctic, one breeding in Europe and the British Isles.

Skylark   A
Alauda arvensis Linnaeus

Palaearctic. Breeds from northwest Africa, Iberia, the British Isles and Scandinavia eastwards across Eurasia (mainly south of 65°N) to Anadyr, Kamchatka and Ussuriland, south to northern Iran, northern China and perhaps Japan; between 70°N and 30°N. Mainly migratory; winters within or to just south of the breeding range.

A.a.arvensis Linnaeus breeds Europe south to central France and east to the Urals.

RB. Abundant. Widely distributed, breeding in all counties of Britain and Ireland. Probably mainly sedentary, but some island and upland populations migrate or disperse to unknown winter quarters, and part of the British population may winter to the south of the English Channel.

PV and **WV**. Passage mainly mid-September to November, February to April, all areas, but probably mainly on east and southeast coasts. Migration at these times includes arrival and departure of winter visitors from central and northern Europe.

Genus EREMOPHILA Boie

Holarctic genus of two species, both in Palaearctic, one breeding in Europe and occurring as a winter visitor to the British Isles.

Shore Lark   A
Eremophila alpestris (Linnaeus)

Holarctic and (locally) Neotropical. Breeds Norway and across northern Eurasia north of the Arctic Circle from Fenno-Scandia east to the Kolyma; not found over a wide area of the central Palaearctic; breeds again, discontinuously, from the Balkans, Asia Minor and the Near East eastwards across central Asia through Mongolia to the Stanovoi Mountains; also in northwest Africa, North America (where known as the Horned Lark) from the arctic south to Mexico, and again in Colombia; between 77°N and 5°N. Northern Palaearctic birds winter from the British Isles, central and southeast Europe to the Mediterranean, and in central and east Asia.

E.a.flava (Gmelin) breeds northern Eurasia.

E.a.alpestris (Linnaeus) breeds Newfoundland and eastern Canada.

WV. Regularly, October to April (rarely September and May), in small numbers on the British east coast, Lincoln to Kent, less often Northumberland to Yorkshire and in Sussex; infrequent on other coasts of England and Wales and in east Scotland (but several have been recorded at Fair Isle, mostly in autumn); rarely inland and only four records from Ireland. Wintering population is *E.a.flava*.

SV. The subspecies *E.a.alpestris* has been recorded once, in the Outer Hebrides (September 1953).

Family HIRUNDINIDAE

Genus RIPARIA Forster

Holarctic, Ethiopian and Oriental genus of four species, two in Palae-arctic, one breeding in Europe and the British Isles.

Sand Martin   A
Riparia riparia (Linnaeus)

Holarctic and Oriental. Breeds British Isles and throughout continental Eurasia (except in the extreme north and northeast) to Kamchatka, Sakhalin and Japan (Hokkaido), south into northern Africa, northern India and southeast China; also widely in North America (where known as Bank Swallow); between 70°N and 24°N. Winters in tropical Africa, northern India, Indo-China and South America.

    R.r.riparia (Linnaeus) breeds North America, northwest Africa, and Eurasia east to the Kolyma, the western Altai and western Iran.

    MB. Numerous. Widely distributed, breeding in all counties except Shetland, Orkney and the Outer Hebrides, though only locally in some western districts of Britain and Ireland, and irregularly in the Isle of Wight. Resident from late March to early October.

    PV. Mid-March to June, July to October; all areas, but most numerous in the southern half of England, and only small numbers noted as far north as Orkney and Shetland. The majority seen on passage are probably of British origin, but some are from adjacent parts of the Continent, the breeding population in the Low Countries perhaps being continuous with that in southeast England.

Genus HIRUNDO Linnaeus

Nearly cosmopolitan (not Neotropical) genus of 13 species, six in

Palaearctic, three breeding in Europe and one in the British Isles, where one other occurs as a scarce visitor.

Swallow   A
Hirundo rustica Linnaeus

Holarctic and northern Oriental. Breeds from the British Isles and across the greater part of continental Eurasia mainly south of Arctic Circle to Kamchatka and Japan, and south into northwest Africa, Egypt, east Arabia, the Iranian region, northwest India, north Burma, China and Formosa; also in North America south to Mexico; between 71°N and 20°N. Winters in tropical and southern Africa, Egypt, India, Malaya, the Philippines and South America.

H.r.rustica Linnaeus breeds northwest Africa and western Eurasia east to northwest China and the Himalayas, except on the Levant coast.

MB. Numerous. Widely distributed, breeding in all counties except the Outer Hebrides (where irregular but becoming more frequent) and Shetland (irregular), though only locally and sparsely in northwest Scotland and Orkney. Resident from late March and April to September–October; British breeders winter chiefly in South Africa.

PV. Late March into mid-June, August to mid-November, with occasional birds not infrequently to mid-December (especially in southwest England), but only erratically in winter thereafter. Passage movements observed in most parts of the British Isles probably involve mainly native birds, but Continental birds do occur, as shown by ringing recoveries as far afield as Finland and Poland. Migrants in late autumn (and appearing well after the departure of local breeding birds) may well chiefly originate from outside the British Isles.

Red-rumped Swallow   A
Hirundo daurica Linnaeus

Southern Palaearctic, Oriental and Ethiopian. Breeds northwest Africa and Iberia, spreading in recent years to southernmost France and occasionally Sardinia, Corsica and Italy; also from the Balkans, Cyprus, Asia Minor and Iran through the south Siberian steppes and Mongolia to Manchuria, south to India, Ceylon and central China; also widely in the Ethiopian region; between 54°N and 15°S. Winters in Africa and from India to southern China.

H.d.rufula Temminck breeds throughout the northwest African and Eurasian range of the species east to Russian Turkestan and Kashmir.

SV. Twenty-one recorded; three together at Fair Isle (June 1906), the rest singly (four 1949–52, fourteen 1959–68): two March, seven April, four May, two June, singly August, October and November; in the Isles of Scilly, Devon (two), Sussex, Kent (five), Hertford (two), Norfolk (two), Lancashire, Yorkshire (three) and Wexford. *H.d. rufula* obtained Fair Isle; subspecies of the remainder not determined but other races seem most unlikely to occur here.

Genus DELICHON Horsfield and Moore

Palaearctic and Oriental genus of three species, two in Palaearctic, one breeding in Europe and the British Isles.

House Martin   A
Delichon urbica (Linnaeus)

Palaearctic and Oriental. Breeds British Isles and northwest Africa, and throughout Eurasia (except in the extreme north and northeast) east to Japan, and south to the Mediterranean, Iranian region, Himalayas and Formosa; between 71°N and 23°N. Winters in Africa (chiefly in the southeast, and occasionally breeds in South West Africa and Cape Province), northern India and Malaysia.

D.u.urbica (Linnaeus) breeds northwest Africa and western Eurasia, east to the Yenisei and Kashmir.

MB. Numerous. Widely distributed, breeding in all counties in Britain and Ireland except the Outer Hebrides, only irregularly in Orkney and Shetland, and sparsely in northwest Scotland. Resident mid-April to mid-October.

PV. Late March into June, August to mid-November, a few (especially in southwest England) annually into December. All areas, including the Northern Isles; the scale and extent of passage of birds from the Continent is largely unknown, though it is probably small. One bird ringed in Northumberland in May was found two weeks later in Norway.

Family MOTACILLIDAE

Genus MOTACILLA Linnaeus

Palaearctic, Ethiopian and Oriental (also marginally Nearctic) genus of about eight species, six of these in Palaearctic, four breeding in Europe and three in the British Isles, where the fourth occurs as a scarce visitor.

Yellow Wagtail, Blue-headed Wagtail, etc.   A
Motacilla flava Linnaeus

Palaearctic and northwest Nearctic. Breeds from Fenno-Scandia, Britain and Iberia eastwards throughout the greater part of the Palaearctic mainland and east into western Alaska, south to northwest Africa, Egypt, southern Iran, the Altai and Manchuria; between 72°N and 26°N. Winters in Africa (mainly south of the Sahara), India, southeast Asia and the East Indies.

M.f.flavissima (Blyth) (Yellow Wagtail) breeds Britain and very locally on western coasts of Europe from Brittany to southern Norway.

M.f.flava Linnaeus (Blue-headed Wagtail) breeds from southernmost Fenno-Scandia to the Urals (Ufa), south to France, north Italy and Rumania.

M.f.cinereocapilla Savi (Ashy-headed Wagtail*) breeds Italy, Sicily, Sardinia, intergrades with other races in southern France, Switzerland, Austria and Yugoslavia.

M.f.beema (Sykes) (Sykes' Wagtail*) breeds southeast Russia east to the Yenisei.

M.f.leucocephala Przewalski (White-headed Wagtail*) breeds in east-central Asia.

M.f.thunbergi Billberg (Grey-headed Wagtail) breeds Fenno-Scandia and Russia (north of nominate *flava*) east to northwest Siberia.

* See footnote on page 190

M.f.simillima Hartert (Eastern Blue-headed Wagtail*) breeds in extreme eastern Siberia and the Kuriles.

M.f.feldegg Michahelles (Black-headed Wagtail) breeds from the Balkans east to the Caspian and Afghanistan.

MB. Fairly numerous. The breeding race, *M.f.flavissima*, is distributed widely but rather locally in England (breeds in all counties, but absent from the Isle of Wight and Isle of Man, and very scarce in Dorset, Devon and Cornwall) and Wales (Carmarthen and border counties only); in Scotland breeds regularly in a few parts of the Clyde region (Ayr, Renfrew, Lanark), occasionally in Stirling, and formerly also farther north; formerly bred in Ireland but is now only sporadic there, although one to three pairs have bred in the last few years in Wicklow. Resident from early April to early October; has exceptionally overwintered in England—the normal winter quarters are in tropical west Africa.

CB. Nominate *flava* breeds occasionally (perhaps just annually; numbers fluctuate), sometimes hybridizing with *M.f.flavissima*, chiefly in southern and eastern England or on the fringe of the range of *flavissima* (and sometimes beyond it—for example, Kerry in 1965). Two pairs showing characters of *M.f.cinereocapilla* bred in Northern Ireland in 1956. Birds identical with *M.f.beema* have occasionally been found breeding in southern England, but these birds may be hybrids. A bird showing the characters of *M.f.leucocephala* bred in Kent in 1908.

PV. Late March into June, August to mid-October, mainly of *M.f.flavissima* (hence mostly of British origin, see above), this subspecies occurring in all areas including west to Ireland and north to Shetland; nominate *flava* also occurs regularly in small numbers, chiefly on and near the east and south coasts from Shetland to Cornwall, also occasionally in Wales and Ireland. *M.f.thunbergi* is identified almost annually in spring and sometimes in autumn at Fair Isle, but only occasionally elsewhere, most often on the British south and east coasts in May.

SV. A specimen resembling *M.f.cinereocapilla* was collected in Cornwall in May about 1860, and there are a few recent sight-records of birds, apparently this race, in Essex, Middlesex, Norfolk and Fife, between April and June (see also under **CB** above). Specimens resem-

---

* In addition to birds resembling the races listed above, individuals matching no known race have often been reported (especially from southeast England) and it may be that most or all of the birds listed above as *cinereocapilla*, *beema*, *leucocephala* and *simillima* (but perhaps not *feldegg* as it is much more distinct) are hybrids or mutants of the regularly occurring races.

bling *M.f.beema* have been collected at Fair Isle (May 1910) and in Sussex (May 1923, April 1939), and there are several apparent sight-records, mainly from southeast England (see also under **CB** above, and footnote). Specimens identical with *M.f.simillima* were collected at Fair Isle in October 1909 and September 1912, and there is a sight-record from Suffolk (October 1967). There are the following sight-records (but no specimens) of *M.f.feldegg*: Cornwall (June 1964), Dorset (October 1958), Dumfries (June 1925), East Lothian (July 1952), Shetland (May 1936 and May 1960).

Citrine Wagtail A
Motacilla citreola Pallas

Central Palaearctic. Breeds from northeast and southeast Russia east through Siberia and Mongolia to Amurland, south to Iran and the northwest Himalayas; between 71°N and 25°N. Winters from southern Baluchistan and India east to southeast China.

SV. Thirteen, all since 1954 and all in autumn: Fair Isle (September 1954, October 1954, October 1960, September 1961, 1962, 1964), Suffolk (October–November 1964 and October 1967), Hampshire (two together, October 1966), Northumberland (September 1967), Norfolk (September 1968), Fife (September 1968). Subspecies not determined.

Grey Wagtail A
Motacilla cinerea Tunstall

Palaearctic. Breeds from southern Sweden, British Isles and Iberia east through continental Europe (except in the northeast and most of Fenno-Scandia) and from Asia Minor and the Urals east across central Asia to Kamchatka and the Kuriles, south into northwest Africa and the Atlantic Islands, the Mediterranean islands, Iranian region, Himalayas, north Korea and Japan; between 66°N and 28°N. Partially migratory, wintering in southern parts of the breeding range and beyond it as far as northern tropical Africa, Arabia, India, Ceylon and New Guinea.

M.c.cinerea Tunstall breeds range of species except the Atlantic Islands and extreme eastern Asia.

RB. Not scarce. Widely but rather locally distributed, breeding most commonly in hilly districts of the western and northern British

Isles, and most locally in eastern England, where it is absent as a regular breeder from a wide area from Essex north to east Yorkshire and west to Warwick; otherwise it breeds in all counties except Orkney, Shetland and the Outer Hebrides (where a pair or two breeds irregularly in Lewis at the present time). Mainly sedentary, but some upland and northern breeding grounds are deserted in autumn and winter, when a general southward movement occurs within the British Isles, some Grey Wagtails wintering in parts of eastern England where they do not breed. The possibility that some birds emigrate to the Continent is suggested by (a) observations of migrants departing from the English south coast in autumn, (b) the recovery in Yorkshire in April of a Grey Wagtail ringed in Portugal in October, and (c) the recovery in northern France in winter of an adult ringed in Scotland in July.

PV. Passage movements in March–April and (in greater numbers except in Shetland where the species is most common in spring) from mid-August to October probably mainly concern birds of British and Irish origin. Involvement of Continental birds is probably small, but the recovery of a Belgian-ringed nestling in Norfolk in March indicates that some do occur here, and there is the possibility (but no evidence) that small numbers may winter in Britain.

Pied Wagtail, White Wagtail   A
Motacilla alba Linnaeus

Palaearctic, Ethiopian and Oriental. Breeds southeast Greenland, Iceland, and from Fenno-Scandia, British Isles and Iberia (and Morocco) eastwards through the whole of Europe and Asia except the Malayan region; also over much of the Ethiopian region; between 75°N and 35°S. Mainly migratory, Palaearctic birds wintering in southern parts of the breeding range in Eurasia, Africa, Arabia and east to the Philippines.

M.a.yarrellii Gould (Pied Wagtail) breeds Britain and Ireland, and occasionally in adjacent parts of the Continent from southern Norway to northwest France.

M.a.alba Linnaeus (White Wagtail) breeds southeast Greenland, Iceland, and continental Europe east to the Urals, Asia Minor and Syria.

MB and **RB**. Numerous. Widespread, breeding regularly in all parts of Britain and Ireland except Shetland (where irregular) and only sparsely in the Hebrides and Orkney. Many upland breeding areas are deserted in winter, some birds moving to lower altitudes or southwards within the British Isles; many others from most parts of the country emigrate and winter chiefly in Iberia, a few birds reaching Morocco. The breeding subspecies is *M.a.yarrellii*, apart from *M.a.alba* which nests occasionally in Shetland and exceptionally elsewhere.

PV. Passage of *M.a.alba* occurs from late March to May and August to October, to some extent in all parts of the British Isles, but most numerously on Atlantic and Irish Sea coasts in late August and September when migrants from Iceland are passing through.

Genus ANTHUS Bechstein

Cosmopolitan genus of some 30 species, 13 of which occur in the Palaearctic; seven breed in Europe, two of them only in extreme northeast Russia; three breed in the British Isles, where the other four European species plus a fifth from Asia occur as scarce visitors.

Richard's Pipit A
Anthus novaeseelandiae (Gmelin)

Central and eastern Palaearctic, Oriental, Ethiopian and Australasian. Breeds from the Irtysh in western Siberia east to Amurland, south to India, China, Malaysia, Australia, New Zealand; also in Africa; between 60°N and 53°S. Palaearctic populations winter in India, Malaysia and southern China.

A.n.richardi Vieillot breeds western Siberia east to the Yenisei, south to the Russian Altai and western China.

SV. About 500 recorded, annually in recent years, including exceptional, widespread influxes in Britain in the autumns of 1966 (about 36 birds), 1967 (130-plus birds) and 1968 (130–150 birds), when small parties of up to eight together were noted as well as the more usual single birds. Noted chiefly from mid-September to mid-November with a few into December or even later, again (but many fewer) in April, and has been reported in all other months except June and July. Records are widely scattered, but come chiefly from maritime counties south from Anglesey and Yorkshire (especially southwest England) and from Fair Isle; relatively few are noted inland and there are only nine Irish records, where it is perhaps under-recorded (especially as one was noted in both 1967 and 1968).

Tawny Pipit A
Anthus campestris (Linnaeus)

Central and western Palaearctic. Breeds northwest Africa, France (not in the northwest), southern Sweden and the Baltic States east to the Yenisei in western Siberia, south to the Mediterranean islands, Palestine, north Iran and Russian Turkestan; between 60°N and 30°N. Winters south to the equator in Africa, also in Arabia, Iran and south Afghanistan.

A.c.campestris (Linnaeus) breeds range of species except in the extreme southeast.

SV. Over 250 recorded, annually in recent years (including as many as 18 in 1967 and 25 in 1968), usually singly but occasionally two or three together. The majority have been identified in September, most of the remainder being equally divided between May and October, with a few in other months, especially April, June and August. Recorded mainly on the English south coast, also in Suffolk and Norfolk, occasionally farther north as far as Fair Isle and once the Outer Hebrides, and west to Wales; also Ireland, where ten records, all but two of them on islands off Cork or Wexford. Few have been noted inland.

Tree Pipit A
Anthus trivialis (Linnaeus)

Western and central Palaearctic. Breeds Eurasia from northern Scandinavia, Britain, France and northern Spain east to the Lena in eastern Siberia, south to Italy, the Balkans, northern Iran, the northwest Himalayas and Lake Baikal; between 70°N and 30°N. Winters in northern tropical Africa and India.

A.t.trivialis (Linnaeus) breeds range of species except Russian Turkestan, the Pamirs and northwest Himalayas.

MB. Numerous. Widely distributed in Britain, breeding regularly in all counties except Shetland, Orkney, the Outer Hebrides, Caithness and probably Anglesey, and absent also from west Cornwall, west Pembroke and the Isle of Wight. Breeds in the Isle of Man but has never been recorded nesting in Ireland. Resident from early April to September.

PV. End of March to June, August to October. Spring passage generally inconspicuous, and probably few Continental birds involved except during occasional 'falls' on the British east coast, especially at

Fair Isle. Autumn passage is more widespread and noticeable; numbers are variable but this species occurs regularly even on Irish coasts, where most birds, as well as those on the British east and south coasts, are probably of north European origin.

Olive-backed Pipit A
Anthus hodgsoni Richmond

Central and eastern Palaearctic. Breeds from the Pechora in northeast Russia east across Siberia mainly south of the Arctic Circle to Kamchatka and the Kuriles, south to the Himalayas, western China, Korea and Japan; between 65°N and 26°N. Winters from India east through the Indo-Chinese countries to eastern China and Philippines.

A.h.yunnanensis Uchida and Kuroda breeds range of species except in the extreme southeast from the Himalayas to Korea.

SV. Two, both at Fair Isle (October 1964, September 1965).

Pechora Pipit A
Anthus gustavi Swinhoe

Central and eastern Palaearctic. Breeds southern tundras and forest tundras from northeast Russia east through Siberia to the Bering Straits and Commander Islands, also in southern Ussuriland; between 72°N and 45°N. Winters in northern Borneo, the Lesser Sundas, Celebes and Moluccas.

A.g.gustavi Swinhoe breeds range of species except the Commander Islands and southern Ussuriland.

SV. Seventeen. One Yorkshire (October 1966), the rest all at Fair Isle in autumn, late August to mid-November, between 1925 and 1966.

Meadow Pipit A
Anthus pratensis (Linnaeus)

Western Palaearctic. Breeds from southeast Greenland, Iceland, British Isles and northern Scandinavia east to the Ob in western Siberia, south to France, northern Italy, the Balkans and north Ukraine; between 71°N and 42°N. Mainly migratory, wintering in southern parts of the breeding range and farther south to the Mediterranean basin and Iran.

A.p.theresae Meinertzhagen reputedly breeds in western Ireland, but the type and other specimens of this form from that area were probably passage migrants, almost certainly from Iceland.

A.p.pratensis (Linnaeus) breeds range of species except probably Iceland.

MB and **RB**. Abundant. Widely distributed, breeding in every county in Britain and Ireland, though only locally and sparsely in central-southern and southeast England. Many upland and northern breeding areas are deserted from about November to March, some birds moving southwards or to lower altitudes within the British Isles, others —together with other British and probably also Irish birds—emigrating in numbers to southwest France and the western part of the Iberian peninsula, some also to Italy and probably Morocco. The breeding race is *A.p.pratensis*.

PV and **WV**. Passage mainly March to mid-May and mid-August to October; all areas, and involving birds of Icelandic and probably Continental as well as British origin. Found in winter in all counties of Britain and Ireland, though it is scarce in the north of Scotland. The proportion of birds from overseas in the wintering population is not known, but most autumn migrants are probably transient visitors. *A.p.pratensis* and *A.p.theresae*, the latter being especially prominent on passage in western districts, notably in Ireland, though it also reaches southeast England.

Red-throated Pipit A
Anthus cervinus (Pallas)

Northern Palaearctic. Breeds in the tundra zone across the whole of Eurasia from Scandinavia to the Bering Straits; between 74°N and 64°N. Winters chiefly in tropical Africa, and in northern India, Indo-China, Indonesia and Philippines.

Monotypic.

SV. About 65 recorded, about half this total during 1958–68, when identified almost annually. Recorded slightly more frequently in autumn (mid-August to November, chiefly September–October) than spring (late April to early June). Most records are from Fair Isle, the rest mainly on the east and south coasts of England and on Great Saltee, Wexford. Majority noted singly but once six together.

Rock Pipit, Water Pipit   A
Anthus spinoletta (Linnaeus)*

Holarctic. The species is divided into two distinct ecological groups, (a) the Water Pipits ('*spinoletta* group') which breed mainly in alpine regions of Europe, southwest, central and northeast Asia, northern and western North America, and west Greenland, and (b) the Rock Pipits ('*petrosus* group') which breed on coasts of northwest Europe, the Faeroes and British Isles.

A.s.rubescens (Tunstall) breeds northeast Siberia (east of the Taimyr Peninsula), North America (where known as American Pipit) and west Greenland; winters south to Russian Turkestan and eastern China, and from northern California and Delaware south to Guatemala.

A.s.spinoletta (Linnaeus) breeds in the mountains of Spain and France east to Poland, Italy, the Balkans and probably Asia Minor; descends to lower altitudes in winter, some dispersing as far as southern England.

A.s.littoralis (C. L. Brehm) breeds coasts and islands of the Baltic and from western Norway to the White Sea; winters south to northern and western France.

A.s.petrosus (Montagu) breeds coasts of northwest France and the British Isles.

RB. Fairly numerous: Widely distributed on rocky coasts around the whole of Britain and Ireland; absent from the English east coast between Kent and south Yorkshire, and breeds only very locally in northwest England. Mainly sedentary with some local or short-distance dispersal in winter, when Rock Pipits are present on coasts of eastern England and elsewhere where the species does not breed; it is doubtful whether there is any substantial or regular emigration to the Continent. The breeding race is *A.s.petrosus*.

PV and **WV**. Birds of race *A.s.littoralis* are noted fairly regularly on the British east and south coasts (and are recorded rarely north to Shetland, west to Ireland), chiefly in October–November and late March–early April. Some autumn migrants may move on to France to winter, although most probably remain on the coasts of south and east England where they are overlooked or mistaken for *petrosus*. Birds of the subspecies *A.s.spinoletta* winter locally but regularly in south and

---

* The taxonomic treatment of the populations of *Anthus spinoletta* breeding in the British Isles follows Vaurie (1959–65). K. Williamson (1965), *British Birds*, 58: 493–504, recognized *A.s.meinertzhageni* Bird (Outer Hebrides, except perhaps St. Kilda) and regarded the population in Shetland (and possibly St. Kilda) as belonging to the subspecies *A.s. kleinschmidti* Hartert (which is otherwise confined to the Faeroes).

southwest England, occasionally north to Anglesey and Lancashire, mainly beside fresh water; they occur chiefly between October and March and there is some evidence of passage in southeast England, late September to mid-November and mid-March to mid-April.

SV. Four records of *A.s.rubescens*: St. Kilda (September 1910), Wexford (October 1951), Fair Isle (September 1953), Wicklow (November 1967).

Family LANIIDAE

Genus LANIUS Linnaeus

Holarctic, Ethiopian, Oriental and marginally Australasian (New Guinea) genus of about 23 species, twelve in Palaearctic, five breeding in Europe but only one in the British Isles, where another occurs as a winter visitor and two others as vagrants.

Red-backed Shrike   A
Lanius collurio Linnaeus

Palaearctic. Breeds Eurasia from southern Sweden, England and northern Iberia east to the Yenisei, northwest Manchuria and the Altai, north to about 64°N in Russia, south to the Mediterranean, Iran and Chinese Turkestan; between 64°N and 30°N. Winters in northeast, tropical and southern Africa, southern Iran and northwest India.

L.c.collurio Linnaeus breeds Europe (except Crimea) east to the Urals and Asia Minor. (The British breeding population has been separated as *L.c.juxtus* Clancey, but a recent study shows this race to be invalid.)

L.c.phoenicuroides (Schalow) breeds from the southern Kirghiz Steppes to Chinese Turkestan, south to south Iran.

MB. Scarce. Distributed very locally and in small, decreasing numbers in southern England southeast of a line from the Wash to the Exe Estuary, Devon, with the last main stronghold in Hampshire (absent from the Isle of Wight); still breeds in all counties in this region except Oxford and Huntingdon, though only irregularly now in Dorset, Sussex, Middlesex and Berkshire; a few pairs breed regularly just north of this line—in Somerset, Worcester and, occasionally, Gloucester. Formerly much more numerous and widespread. Resident from May to September. The breeding race is *L.c.collurio*.

PV. Regular in small numbers, May to June, August to mid-October, chiefly when birds from the Continent appear on the British east and south coasts in autumn, although at Fair Isle it is more numerous in spring. Less frequent on western coasts and in Ireland. *L.c.collurio*.

SV. Five birds—Dorset (September 1959), Norfolk (September 1961), Fife (September 1950), Fair Isle (May 1960), Cork (October 1962)—belonged to one or more of four eastern races of *L.collurio* which together form the 'isabellinus group'; on geographical grounds, the most likely of the four races to occur here is *L.c.phoenicuroides*, to which form two of the birds were tentatively ascribed.

Lesser Grey Shrike   A
Lanius minor Gmelin

Western and central Palaearctic. Breeds western Eurasia from northeast Spain, France and Germany east to the Altai, north to central Russia and about 56°N in western Siberia, south to central Italy, the Balkans, Asia Minor, probably Syria, Iran and Afghanistan; between 56°N and 34°N. Winters in tropical Africa south of the equator.

L.m.minor Gmelin breeds Europe and Asia Minor.

SV. About 65 recorded, about two-thirds of the total during 1955–1968, when identified almost annually. Noted in all months from April to November, but most have been in May–June and September–October. Nearly one-third of the total have been recorded in Shetland (chiefly at Fair Isle), the rest mainly in southern and eastern counties, including some inland; it has also been recorded in western England, north Wales, western Scotland and once in Ireland.

Great Grey Shrike   A
Lanius excubitor Linnaeus

Holarctic, northwest Oriental and north Ethiopian. Breeds Eurasia from Scandinavia, Denmark, central France and Iberia east to the Pacific, north to about 70°N in Siberia, south to north Italy, Iran, India

Mongolia and Sakhalin; also across northern Africa and Arabia, and across northern North America (where known as Northern Shrike); between 70°N and 10°N. Winters within, or just south of, the breeding range.

L.e.excubitor Linnaeus breeds from Norway south to the Pyrenees and northeast Italy, east to western Siberia and western Rumania.

L.e.pallidirostris Cassin breeds from the north Caspian region to southern Mongolia south to northern Iran and Baluchistan.

WV and **PV**. Small, rather variable numbers (usually recorded singly, but sometimes up to five or more together), chiefly October–November through to March–April, and rarely or occasionally in other months also. Winters regularly in some Scottish counties and in the eastern half of England, and at least occasionally in many other parts of Britain and (more rarely) in Ireland. The species is most numerous in autumn, especially in October, on the east coast between Shetland and Norfolk; some of these birds presumably move on to winter elsewhere in Europe. *L.e.excubitor.*

SV. *L.e.pallidirostris* has been recorded twice at Fair Isle (September 1956, October 1964).

Woodchat Shrike　　　　　　　　　　　　　　　　　　A
Lanius senator Linnaeus

Southwestern Palaearctic. Breeds from northwest Africa, Iberia and France east to central Poland and the Ukraine, and through Asia Minor and the Near East to southern Iran; between 51°N and 36°N. Winters in northern tropical and northeast Africa.

L.s.senator Linnaeus breeds northwest Africa and Europe (except the Balearics, Corsica, Sardinia), perhaps also in Asia Minor.

SV. About 250 recorded, with two to 23 annually since 1957, averaging about 13 a year. Mainly May–June and August–September, but has occurred in all months from April to October. Noted principally at coastal and island sites in southwest England and in the south Irish Sea basin (most frequently in Dorset, the Isles of Scilly, Pembroke, Caernarvon and Wexford; at both seasons but with the majority in autumn) and in Shetland with Fair Isle (records about equally divided between spring and autumn); also, rather less frequently, on the British east and southeast coasts (notably in Yorkshire and Norfolk, where most occurrences are in spring) and in southwest Ireland. Records from other coasts and inland are infrequent.

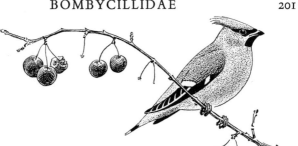

Family BOMBYCILLIDAE

Genus BOMBYCILLA Vieillot

Holarctic genus of three species, two in Palaearctic, one breeding in Europe and occurring in the British Isles as irruptive winter visitor.

Waxwing A
Bombycilla garrulus (Linnaeus)

Holarctic. Breeds from northern Fenno-Scandia east across northern Eurasia to Kamchatka, north to the tree-line, south in some years to southern Scandinavia, probably the Russian Altai, and Lake Baikal; also breeds in northwestern North America; mainly between 70°N and 55°N. Migratory (usually irruptive), in some winters reaching as far south as Algeria, the Balkans, Asia Minor, Iran, China, Japan and the southwestern United States.

B.g.garrulus (Linnaeus) breeds Norway east to west Siberia.

PV and **WV**. Very variable numbers from Fenno-Scandia and probably farther east arrive October to January (occasionally earlier or later) chiefly on the northeast coast from Shetland to Norfolk; a variable but often substantial proportion remains here through the winter and return March-April. Recorded annually in several counties in Scotland, northern England and in Norfolk, fairly regularly in others elsewhere (annually in Ireland as a whole). Flocks may be sizeable and widespread during invasions, which occur in Britain and Ireland at intervals of years or annually for up to four winters in succession (for example, 1956–57 to 1959–60).

Family CINCLIDAE

Genus CINCLUS Borkhausen

Western Nearctic and Neotropical, Palaearctic and Oriental genus of five species, two in Palaearctic, one breeding in Europe and the British Isles.

Dipper   A
Cinclus cinclus (Linnaeus)

Palaearctic. Breeds British Isles, most of Europe from Fenno-Scandia south to the Mediterranean and northwest Africa and locally east to the Urals, across southwest Asia to Iran, the Himalayas to southern Siberia, northern Mongolia and west China; between 70°N and 28°N. Mainly sedentary.

C.c.hibernicus Hartert breeds Ireland, Isle of Man (formerly), Outer Hebrides, Kintyre, Arran, Bute and west coast Scotland; intergrades with *C.c.gularis* in Ayr.

C.c.gularis (Latham) breeds Orkney, Scotland (except as above), England and Wales.

C.c.cinclus (Linnaeus) breeds Scandinavia, northern Finland, northwest Russia south to east Prussia with outpost populations in parts of France, the Pyrenees, Iberia and Turkey.

RB. Not scarce. Breeds widely, along fast-running streams and rivers, in northern and western British Isles; in all counties in Ireland, Scotland (except Shetland, doubtfully regular in Orkney) and Wales, and in north and west England east to Dorset, Wiltshire, Gloucester, Worcester, Stafford, Derby and south Yorkshire, occasionally also in Hampshire, Oxford and Warwick; formerly in the Isle of Man, but apparently not now. Sedentary, endemic races *C.c.hibernicus* and *C.c.gularis*.

SV. A few examples of nominate *cinclus* are recorded almost annually between October and April, mainly on the east coast of Britain, especially in Shetland (including Fair Isle), where most have been in spring, late March–early April; two out of about 17 records of the species at Fair Isle resembled *C.c.gularis*, or the similar *C.c.aquaticus* Bechstein of central Europe west to Belgium, which has not certainly occurred in Britain.

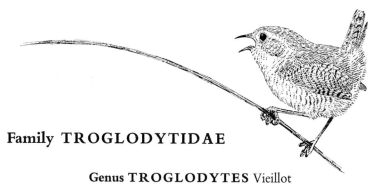

Family TROGLODYTIDAE

Genus TROGLODYTES Vieillot

Nearctic, Neotropical, Palaearctic and, marginally, Oriental genus of four or five species, of which only one occurs in the Old World, including the British Isles.

Wren   A
Troglodytes troglodytes (Linnaeus)

Holarctic and locally Oriental. Breeds Iceland, Faeroes, British Isles, northwest Africa, across Eurasia to southeast Siberia, south to Cyrenaica, the Near East, Iran, northern India, central China, Japan and Formosa; in North America (where known as the Winter Wren) from the Aleutians to Newfoundland, south to central California and the Appalachians; between 70°N and 24°N. Northernmost continental, and montane, populations are partially migratory, wintering within or just south of the breeding range.

T.t.zetlandicus Hartert breeds Shetland.

T.t.fridariensis Williamson breeds Fair Isle.

T.t.hebridensis Meinertzhagen breeds Outer Hebrides.

T.t.hirtensis Seebohm breeds St. Kilda.

T.t.indigenus Clancey breeds Ireland, Inner Hebrides, mainland Scotland, England.

T.t.troglodytes (Linnaeus) breeds continental Europe.

RB. Abundant. Very widely distributed, breeding in all parts of Britain and Ireland. Sedentary with some local post-breeding wandering (one Hampshire-ringed juvenile recovered in western France). The breeding races are *T.t.indigenus* and the four insular races named above.

WV and **PV**. Coastal passage and arrival of winter visitors, probably mainly from the Low Countries and other adjacent parts of the Continent, chiefly late September to early November, returning less numerously mid-March to mid-April. Chiefly in southeast England (but noted irregularly as far north as Shetland), where autumn (and perhaps spring) migrants include transients wintering in southern France. *T.t.troglodytes*.

Family MIMIDAE

Genus TOXOSTOMA Wagler

Nearctic and marginally Neotropical genus of ten species, one of which has strayed to the British Isles.

Brown Thrasher   A
Toxostoma rufum (Linnaeus)

Nearctic. Breeds in North America from the southern parts of Alberta, Manitoba and Maine south to the Gulf coast and southern Florida; between 50°N and 26°N. Northern populations winter south within the breeding range.

T.r.rufum (Linnaeus) breeds eastern part of range, west to Ontario, Iowa and Texas.

SV. One, Dorset (November 1966–February 1967). Subspecies not determined, but unlikely to have been other than nominate *rufum*.

Family PRUNELLIDAE

Genus PRUNELLA

Palaearctic genus of 12 species, only five (three marginally) breeding in Europe and one in the British Isles, where another occurs as a scarce visitor.

Alpine Accentor   A
Prunella collaris (Scopoli)

Palaearctic. Discontinuous montane distribution from northwest Africa, central and southern Europe east through the Caucasus, Iran, the Himalayas and central Asia to China and Japan; between 54°N and 24°N. Sedentary but some wander within and just to south of the breeding range in winter.

    P.c.collaris (Scopoli) breeds France, Iberia and Morocco east to Czechoslovakia and Rumania.

    SV. About 30 recorded, mostly August to January (18) and a few March to June (eight), nearly all in southern England, one in Wales (Caernarvon) and two as far north as Fair Isle.

Dunnock (or Hedge Sparrow)   A
Prunella modularis (Linnaeus)

Western Palaearctic. Breeds British Isles, most of continental Europe except the extreme north and south, east to Asia Minor, the Caucasus and northern Iran; between 70°N and 35°N. Partially migratory, northern populations winter south to the Mediterranean islands and north Africa.

    P.m.hebridium Meinertzhagen breeds Ireland, the Hebrides and on parts of the west Scottish mainland (Inverness to Ayr).

P.m.occidentalis (Hartert) breeds Scotland except in the west (see above), England and Wales; intergrades with nominate race in western France.

P.m.modularis (Linnaeus) breeds continental Europe south to central France, east to the Balkans, and into western Asia Minor. Variation appears to be clinal in all these forms and limits assigned to them are arbitrary.

RB. Abundant. Widely distributed, breeding in all parts of Britain and Ireland except Shetland. Essentially sedentary, movements confined to local post-breeding dispersal. *P.m.occidentalis* and *P.m.hebridium* (see above).

PV (also **WV**). *P.m.modularis* recorded regularly at Fair Isle, fairly regularly farther south on the British east coast, and at least occasionally on the English south coast, mainly end March to April and late September to October. Probably occurs elsewhere, and some winter.

Family **TURDIDAE**

Genus **CERCOTRICHAS** Boie

Ethiopian, Palaearctic and marginally Oriental genus of ten species; two breed in Palaearctic (one marginally) and one in Europe, the latter occurring in the British Isles as a rare straggler.

Rufous Bush Chat   **A**
Cercotrichas galactotes (Temminck)

Palaearctic, Ethiopian and marginally Oriental. Breeds in southern Iberia (has also bred south France), southern Balkans, Asia Minor and the Middle East through the southern Caucasus, Iraq and Iran to eastern Baluchistan and Afghanistan northwards to Lakes Aral and Balkhash;

and in Africa south to the borders of Senegal, northern Nigeria, Chad, Sudan, Ethiopia and Somaliland; between 47°N and 2°N. Winters in the southern parts of the range and in east Africa south to Uganda and Kenya.

C.g.galactotes (Temminck) breeds Iberia, north Africa south to the northern Sahara, Egypt and perhaps northern Sudan, and in the Sinai Peninsula, Israel and southern Syria.

SV. Nine: Sussex (September 1854), Devon (September 1859, October 1876, October 1959), Cork (September 1876 and April 1968), Kent/Sussex (September 1951), Wexford (September–October 1951), Lincoln (September 1963). *C.g.galactotes* in the cases of the four records 1854–76 and not determined in the other five 1951–68, though the one in Wexford was considered to be either *C.g.syriacus* (Hemprich and Ehrenberg) (breeds southeast Europe, Asia Minor, northern Syria) or *C.g.familiaris* (Ménétries) (southern Caucasus and Iraq eastwards to Baluchistan and Lake Balkhash).

Genus ERITHACUS Cuvier

Palaearctic monospecific genus breeding in Europe and the British Isles.

Robin   A
Erithacus rubecula (Linnaeus)

Western Palaearctic. Breeds Azores, Madeira, Canaries, northwest Africa, and from Iberia, France and British Isles throughout continental Europe and the Mediterranean islands, northwards to Fenno-Scandia and eastwards through most of Russia and Asia Minor to western Siberia and northern Iran; between 68°N and 28°N. Resident or migratory, wintering in central and southern parts of the range and southwards to northern Sahara, Egypt, Middle East, Iraq and southern Iran.

E.r.melophilus Hartert breeds in the British Isles.

E.r.rubecula (Linnaeus) breeds throughout the rest of the European range except the Crimea and Caucasus, and in Asia Minor, Morocco and western Algeria.

RB (also **MB**). Abundant and widely distributed throughout Britain and Ireland, breeding in all counties and most major islands except Shetland. The breeding race, *E.r.melophilus*, is essentially resident, but a small proportion of the population, mainly from southeast

H

Britain, migrates south to southwest France and Iberia, and some birds from northern Britain may winter in Ireland.

PV and **WV**. September to November and March to May, most conspicuous on the British east and south coasts when periodic large falls of Continental populations occur, usually in October and sometimes in late March, April or early May. Some autumn migrants stay to winter, while others pass on to France and Iberia. Foreign-ringed recoveries in British Isles have originated from Scandinavia, Finland, the Soviet Baltic, Poland, Germany and the Netherlands, while British-ringed ones recovered in Fenno-Scandia, Low Countries, Germany, France, Iberia and even Algeria have included a number ringed on passage during Continental influxes.

Genus LUSCINIA Forster

Palaearctic and marginally Oriental and Nearctic genus of eleven species; three breed in Europe and one in the British Isles, the other two occurring here as a scarce passage visitor and a rare straggler.

Thrush Nightingale A
Luscinia luscinia (Linnaeus)

Central Palaearctic. Breeds from southern Sweden and Finland, eastern Denmark, Baltic Germany, Poland, eastern Czechoslovakia, Hungary and northeast Yugoslavia through Rumania and Russia south to the northern Caucasus, thence across western Siberia north of the Kirghiz Steppes to the Altai; between 62°N and 43°N. Winters in east Africa from Kenya and Uganda south to the Zambezi.

Monotypic.

SV. Nine, six in May and three in autumn: Fair Isle (May 1911, May 1957, May 1958, two May 1965), Northumberland (September 1965, October 1965), Yorkshire (May 1967), Kent (August 1968).

Nightingale A
Luscinia megarhynchos Brehm

Southwestern Palaearctic. Breeds northwest Africa and from Iberia, France and England east to Denmark (occasionally), Germany, Poland, the Balkans and southwest Russia and then from the Crimea, Caucasus, Asia Minor, Syria and Iraq to the borders of Sinkiang, northern Afghanistan and eastern Iran; between 55°N and 30°N. Winters in tropical Africa from Nigeria to Kenya and Tanzania.

L.m.megarhynchos Brehm breeds northwest Africa and Europe east to southwest Russia, Asia Minor and the Caucasus.

MB. Not scarce. Distributed widely in southeast England to a line from Dorset to the Wash, and rather more locally farther west and north to Devon, Monmouth, Hereford, southeast Shropshire, Warwick, extreme south Yorkshire, and Lincoln. Formerly bred more widely in Yorkshire and sporadically in, for example, Derby and parts of southeast Wales. Resident from April to September. Recorded in very small numbers in spring and autumn on the east and south coasts, these presumably being mostly the English population. Very scarce vagrant outside the breeding range, in central and northern Wales, northern England and Scotland north to Shetland; twelve records in Ireland, one in Cork (April 1968), the rest all in May 1953–63 and all but one of these on Great Saltee, Wexford.

Bluethroat   **A**
Luscinia svecica (Linnaeus)

Palaearctic and marginally Nearctic. Breeds across northern Eurasia from Scandinavia to the Chukotski Peninsula and into western Alaska, south to central Spain (local), France, Germany, northern Yugoslavia, southern Russia, the Caucasus, Iran, northern Afghanistan and northern Kashmir, northwest China, Mongolia and the Sea of Okhotsk; between 76°N and 33°N. Winters in the Mediterranean region and northern Africa south to Nigeria and Sudan, and in the Middle East, Iran, India and southeast Asia.

L.s.svecica (Linnaeus) breeds right across the northern part of the range from Scandinavia to Alaska, mainly north of about 60°N.

L.s.cyanecula (Meisner) breeds throughout the European range east to western Russia, except Fenno-Scandia.

CB. One record: a pair bred unsuccessfully in Scotland in June 1968; only the female was seen and the race was not determined.

PV. Late March to mid-June (rare) and late August to mid-October (regular in small numbers). In autumn chiefly on the British east coast from Shetland to Kent, and also in smaller numbers on the English south coast; very seldom elsewhere; eleven records in Ireland, all August–October since 1954. In spring on both south and east coasts, but far less frequently recorded. Chiefly *L.s.svecica*, but very small numbers of *L.s.cyanecula*, perhaps particularly in March–May.

Genus TARSIGER Hodgson

Palaearctic and Oriental genus of five species; four breed in Palaearctic and one in northeast Europe, this occurring in the British Isles as a rare straggler.

Red-flanked Bluetail
Tarsiger cyanurus (Pallas)

A

Palaearctic and marginally Oriental. Breeds from northern Russia eastwards through Siberia to Kamchatka, the Commander Islands, Kuriles and Japan, south to Omsk, Semipalatinsk, northern Mongolia and central Manchuria; and also from northern Afghanistan eastwards through the Himalayas to central China, south to Assam; has also bred Kola Peninsula, and summered Finland since 1949; mainly between 63°N and 25°N. Mainly migratory, the northern populations moving south and wintering in southeast Asia from Assam through southern China to Formosa.

T.c.cyanurus (Pallas) breeds throughout the northern section of the range from northeast Europe to Kamchatka and Japan.

SV. Four, all September–October: Lincoln (September 1903), Shetland (October 1947), Kent (October 1956), Northumberland (October 1960). Race determined only in the Shetland case, but presumably all *T.c.cyanurus*.

Genus PHOENICURUS Forster

Palaearctic and marginally Oriental genus of eleven species; two breed in Europe and the British Isles (one only locally).

Black Redstart
Phoenicurus ochruros (Gmelin)

A

Palaearctic and marginally Oriental. Breeds northwest Africa and from Iberia, France, southern England and southern Scandinavia eastwards throughout continental Europe, thence through the Caucasus, Asia Minor, northern Middle East, Iran and northern Afghanistan to northern Baluchistan, Kashmir and the Himalayas east to the mountains of western China and north to those of central Asia to western Mongolia; between 58°N and 25°N. Winters mainly in the southern parts of the breeding range and in Africa north of the Sahara to Somaliland, Arabia, Iraq and southern Iran to India and Burma.

P.o.gibraltariensis (Gmelin) breeds Morocco and throughout the European range except Portugal, central and southern Spain.

MB. Very scarce. Apart from isolated earlier attempts, first recorded nesting in 1923 and regularly since 1939, particularly on bombed sites and latterly on industrial power stations. Confined mainly to the London area and the coasts of Sussex, Kent, and, rather less often, near the coasts of East Anglia; has also bred sporadically west to Cornwall, Shropshire and Lancashire, north to Nottingham and Yorkshire. Up to 40 pairs (1950) proved to have bred, and up to 64 males present (1964). The breeding population is resident at the breeding sites from about April to September; most of these birds presumably winter south of the English Channel.

PV. Late August to late November, chiefly October, and March to May. Most commonly on the British east and south coasts north to Yorkshire, less frequent north to Shetland and on the west coast, but regular also on the east and south coasts of Ireland; relatively seldom recorded inland. Ringing evidence suggests that most passage visitors are birds en route between breeding quarters in Germany (and perhaps neighbouring countries) and winter quarters in France and especially Iberia.

WV. Small numbers winter in south and southwest England, south Wales and eastern Ireland, chiefly in coastal areas.

Redstart A
Phoenicurus phoenicurus (Linnaeus)

Western and central Palaearctic. Breeds northwest Africa and from Britain, France and Iberia eastwards through most of continental Europe (except the extreme north, and parts of the Mediterranean area and southeast Russia), thence across Siberia to Lake Baikal, south to the Kirghiz Steppes and Altai, and through Asia Minor and northern Middle East to Iran and probably northwest Afghanistan; between 71°N and 30°N. Winters in southern Arabia and from Ethiopia and Kenya to west Africa.

P.p.phoenicurus (Linnaeus) breeds throughout the greater part of the

range, except the area from the Crimea, Caucasus, eastern Asia Minor
and Israel through to Iran and probably Afghanistan.

MB. Fairly numerous. Widely distributed, breeding regularly (but
not necessarily commonly) in all mainland counties of Britain except
Cornwall (where has bred in some recent years), Cambridge and
Caithness. Most numerous in the west and north of Britain, but absent
from the Isle of Man and erratic in Ireland where the few breeding
records are mainly for the periods 1885–95 and 1955–60. Resident from
April to September.

PV. Late March to mid-June and July to October or early November. Passage most conspicuous on the British east and south coasts,
particularly during falls of Continental birds in late August and early
September or arrivals of the British population in April; scarcer on west
coast and in Ireland where, however, there is an annual small-scale passage in both spring and autumn. Redstarts ringed in Germany, Denmark
and Sweden have been recovered in Britain, while British-ringed ones
have been found in Norway and Germany, as well as in France, Iberia,
Italy, Morocco, Algeria, Libya and Senegal; many of these had been
marked during influxes of Continental origin.

Genus **SAXICOLA** Bechstein

Palaearctic, Oriental and Ethiopian genus of ten species; seven in
Palaearctic, but only two breeding in Europe and the British Isles.

Whinchat   **A**
Saxicola rubetra (Linnaeus)

Western Palaearctic. Breeds from British Isles, France and northern
Iberia east through Europe, north to Fenno-Scandia and northern
Russia, and south to Corsica, northern Italy and northern Greece, thence
east to the upper reaches of the Ob and Yenisei, south to the Kirghiz
Steppes and Altai, and through Asia Minor to northern Iran; between
69°N and 34°N. Winters in tropical Africa south to Cameroon, Congo
and Rhodesia.

Monotypic.

MB. Fairly numerous. Widely distributed in western and northern
Britain (though not Shetland and scarce in Orkney and the Outer
Hebrides), but much declined in the English Midlands and sparse and
very local south of a line from the Severn to the Wash and in Ireland.

Now very scarce in such counties as Worcester, Warwick, Leicester and Nottingham, and almost extinct in Sussex, Surrey and other counties south of the Thames where, however, it was never common. On the other hand, there is no evidence of a decrease in most upland populations, while the species has actually increased in parts of southwest and northeast England, Wales and southwest Scotland; it also now appears to be spreading in Ireland where it has always been very local and where it breeds at all numerously only in Kildare. Resident from April to September.

PV. April–May (early June) and mid-July to early October; individuals have occasionally wintered. Passage most conspicuous on British east and south coasts, particularly during falls of Continental birds in late August and early September or arrivals and departures of the British population in spring and autumn, and at these times occurs in many inland and coastal areas in both Britain and Ireland where not normally found breeding. The only two foreign-ringed Whinchats recovered in Britain had been marked in Sweden and Heligoland; one British-ringed bird has been recovered in Sweden, as well as others in France (seven), Spain (14), Portugal (15) and Algeria (one), thus indicating the directions taken to and from Africa.

Stonechat   A
Saxicola torquata (Linnaeus)

Palaearctic, Ethiopian and marginally Oriental. Breeds most of Eurasia from the British Isles, France and Iberia east through Europe north to Denmark, southern Poland and southern Russia, south to include the larger Mediterranean islands, through Asia Minor, the Caucasus, Iraq and Iran, and thence (after a gap over a sizeable area of northern and eastern Europe and western Asia) from northern and eastern Russia, eastern Kirghiz Steppes and eastern Turkestan right across Asia to Japan, north to the lower reaches of the Ob, Yenisei and Lena, and south to northern Baluchistan, the Himalayas and Burma; also in northwest Africa, in much of Africa south of the Sahara, and in Madagascar and the Comoro Islands; between 70°N and 35°S. Western populations resident or partially migratory, eastern populations highly migratory, wintering in northeast Africa, Arabia, India and southeast Asia.

S.t.hibernans (Hartert) breeds British Isles, northwest France and coastal Portugal.

S.t.maura (Pallas) breeds from north and east Russia and northeast Iran east to northwest Mongolia, south to northern Baluchistan and the Punjab.

RB (also **MB**). Not scarce. Breeds most maritime counties of Britain and Ireland from Orkney southwards (has bred Shetland), except on the east coast of England where confined to a few pairs in Northumberland and East Anglia; most numerous in Ireland, west and northeast Scotland, west Wales, Cornwall and Hampshire. Very much more local and sporadic inland where now known to nest regularly only in Surrey, Shropshire and Montgomery; formerly nested in most English counties, but ceased to do so over a wide area following the hard winters of the 1940s. The breeding population is *S.t.hibernans* and is largely resident, but many northern, island and inland birds move out in autumn and return in spring. At these times the species occurs in, for example, parts of eastern and inland England where it no longer breeds and some individuals winter in such areas. That others emigrate is shown by recoveries (chiefly ringed on passage and often in their first winter) in France and Belgium south to Spain (nine), Majorca (two) and even Algeria (one). There is no evidence, from ringing or observation, of influxes of Continental Stonechats and the Continental race *S.t.rubicola* (Linnaeus) has not been identified in the British Isles.

SV. There are three records of the northeast Russian and western Asiatic race *S.t.maura*: Norfolk (September 1904), Fife (October 1913), Fair Isle (November 1964).

Genus OENANTHE Vieillot

Palaearctic, Oriental, Ethiopian and marginally Nearctic genus of some 20 species; 14 breed in Palaearctic and six in Europe, but only one in the British Isles where, however, five more have occurred as stragglers.

Isabelline Wheatear   B
Oenanthe isabellina (Temminck)

Palaearctic and marginally Oriental. Breeds from southern Greece (very local), southeast Russia, Asia Minor, the Middle East and northern Arabia eastwards through central Asia and Iran to southern Lake Baikal, northwest Manchuria, Mongolia, Tibet, the Himalayas and possibly northwest India; between 54°N and 26°N. Winters in and beyond the southern parts of the range from northwest India, southern Afghanistan, southern Iran and Iraq, Arabia and Africa south to the Congo and west to Mali.

Monotypic.

SV. One: Cumberland (November 1887).

Wheatear   **A**

Oenanthe oenanthe (Linnaeus)

Holarctic and marginally Ethiopian. Breeds throughout Europe; in most of Asia except the east and south (north to the Arctic Ocean, south to Asia Minor, Iran and Afghanistan, east to Mongolia, northern Manchuria and the Chukotski Peninsula); in northwest Africa and in Somaliland; in northern Alaska and Yukon; and in northeast Canada from northern Quebec and Labrador north to Baffin Land, Ellesmere Island and Greenland; between 78°N and 26°N. Winters largely in African savannahs from Senegal to Nigeria, Congo and Zambia, but also east to northwest India and in eastern North America.

O.o.oenanthe (Linnaeus) breeds throughout Eurasia except Iceland, Faeroes and Jan Mayen, and in Alaska and Yukon.

O.o.leucorrhoa (Gmelin) breeds in northeastern Canada, Greenland, Jan Mayen, Iceland and Faeroes (though the populations in the last three are intermediate between this form and nominate *oenanthe*).

MB. Fairly numerous. Widely distributed over much of Britain and Ireland, except in the southern half of England where now very local and scarce. Found commonly in western England and much of Wales, and from Lancashire and Yorkshire northwards, though local in parts of southern Scotland; in Ireland commonest in mountainous and maritime regions, and rather local in the central counties. *O.o. oenanthe*.

PV. March to early June and late July to October or early November. Wheatears from Greenland and Iceland pass regularly through Britain and Ireland, particularly in northern and western coastal areas, and Continental birds sometimes occur in heavy falls on the east coast. The only foreign-ringed ones recovered in Britain have been two each from Greenland and Iceland. Passage through, for example, central southern England is probably largely made up of the British population, but may sometimes include Continental and Greenland birds. *O.o. oenanthe* and *O.o.leucorrhoa*.

Desert Wheatear A
Oenanthe deserti (Temminck)

Palaearctic and marginally Ethiopian. Breeds north Africa north of a line from southern Rio de Oro to northern Sudan eastwards through northwest Arabia, the Middle East, southern Caucasus and Iran to northern Afghanistan, Himalayas, Tibet, Kirghiz Steppes, Sinkiang, Mongolia and Gobi; between 50°N and 17°N. Sedentary and migratory, Asiatic populations moving south to winter in northwest India through Iran and Arabia to northeast Africa south to Darfur and Somaliland.

O.d.deserti (Temminck) breeds from Egypt east of the Nile through northwest Arabia and the Middle East.

O.d.homochroa (Tristram) breeds in north Africa west of the Nile, including the whole of the Saharan range.

O.d.atrogularis (Blyth) breeds from the southern Caucasus through Iran, northern Afghanistan and Turkestan north to the Kirghiz Steppes, Mongolia and Gobi.

SV. Sixteen (three 1880–87, two 1906–07, two 1928–29, one 1940, eight 1949–66): one August, four October, one October–November, three November, one November–January, two December, one January–February, two April, one June; in Cornwall, Hampshire, Sussex (two), Essex, Norfolk, Yorkshire (three), Durham, Clackmannan, Angus, Orkney and Shetland (three). *O.d.deserti* (one), *O.d.homochroa* (three), *O.d.atrogularis* (one); races of the other eleven not determined.

Black-eared Wheatear A
Oenanthe hispanica (Linnaeus)

Southwestern Palaearctic. Breeds northwest Africa and from Iberia, southern France, Italy and the Balkans through Asia Minor and the Middle East to Iran; between 46°N and 27°N. Winters in Africa in the savannahs and southern Sahara from Senegal to Ethiopia.

O.h.hispanica (Linnaeus) breeds northwest Africa, Iberia, southern France, Italy (except the far south) and northwest Yugoslavia.

O.h.melanoleuca (Güldenstädt) breeds from southernmost Italy, south Yugoslavia and the rest of the Balkans eastwards to Iran.

SV. Nineteen (two 1878–92, five 1907–16, eight 1940–54, four 1964–68): one March, five April, five May, one June, one August–September, five September, one November; in Devon, Hampshire,

Middlesex, Berkshire, Norfolk, Yorkshire (two), Lancashire (five), Isle of Man, Shetland (four), Outer Hebrides and Wexford. Two (one Lancashire, one Yorkshire) *O.h.melanoleuca* and another sight-record (Lancashire) considered to be of this race; of the others, at least five have been *O.h.hispanica* and five more probably this race; the rest indeterminate.

Pied Wheatear A
Oenanthe pleschanka (Lepechin)

Palaearctic. Breeds from Cyprus, Bulgaria, Rumania and southern Russia eastwards through southern Siberia, central Asia, Iran and north-west Afghanistan to Lake Baikal, Mongolia, northern China and the Himalayas; between 54°N and 27°N. Winters in southern Arabia, northeast and east Africa south to northern Tanganyika.

O.*p.pleschanka* (Lepechin) breeds throughout the range except Cyprus.

SV. Four, all October–November: Fife (October 1909), Orkney (November 1916), Dorset (October 1954) and Pembroke (October 1968). Race not determined in the last two cases, but probably O.*p. pleschanka* like the first two.

Black Wheatear A
Oenanthe leucura (Gmelin)

Palaearctic. Breeds in Iberia, southeast France, extreme northwest Italy, and northwest Africa from northern Rio de Oro and Morocco east to Libya; between 44°N and 28°N. Largely resident, but some wander eastwards in the Mediterranean area in winter.

SV. Five, all August–October except one in Ireland in June: Shetland (September 1912, October 1953), Cheshire (August 1943), Kent (October 1954), Donegal (June 1964). Race not determined in any case.

Genus MONTICOLA Boie

Palaearctic, Oriental and Ethiopian genus of nine species; five breed in Palaearctic and two in Europe, one straggling to the British Isles.

Rock Thrush   A
Monticola saxatilis (Linnaeus)

Palaearctic. Breeds northwest Africa and from Iberia through southern
Europe north to Switzerland, southern Poland and southern Russia,
east through Asia Minor, the Caucasus and Iran to Afghanistan and
Baluchistan, thence north to the Altai, Mongolia and Lake Baikal; also
in China; between 56°N and 28°N. Winters in Africa from west Africa
to the Sudan and Somaliland south to southern Tanzania.

Monotypic.

SV. Eight, six May–June and two October–November: Hertford
(May 1843), Orkney (two, May 1910), Shetland (November 1931,
October 1936), Kent (June 1933), Outer Hebrides (June 1962), Devon
(May 1963).

Genus ZOOTHERA Vigors

Oriental, Ethiopian, Australasian and Palaearctic genus of 29 species;
three species in Palaearctic (two only in the very south), one breeding
sporadically in extreme eastern Europe and occurring as a straggler
west to the British Isles.

White's Thrush   A
Zoothera dauma (Latham)

Palaearctic, Oriental and Australasian. Breeds sporadically as far west as
western Siberia (and even into eastern Russia) but mainly from the
Yenisei north to the middle Tunguska and south to Lake Baikal, thence
eastwards to Manchuria, Korea and Japan; also from Himalayas to
Burma, northern Thailand and north Indo-China; and in India, Ceylon
and Malay peninsula through Indonesia to Australia and Tasmania;
between 64°N and 43°S. Palaearctic populations winter in northern
India and Burma, southern China, Thailand, Indo-China, Formosa and
the Philippines.

Z.d.aurea (Holandre) breeds throughout the main Palaearctic
range except Japan, Ussuriland and Korea.

SV. About 33, mainly October–January, but one in 'spring', one
in May and one in September: Cornwall, Devon (two), Somerset,
Gloucester (two), Hampshire, Sussex, Suffolk (two), Norfolk, Warwick,
Shropshire, Cheshire, Yorkshire (five), Durham (three), Berwick,
Perth, Aberdeen, Fair Isle (four), Cork, Longford, Mayo. Only eight

since 1940: Fair Isle 1944, 1948, 1958, Devon 1952, Perth 1956, Durham 1959, Cheshire 1964 (May), Gloucester 1966. Presumably all *Z.d.aurea*, though race not determined in many cases.

Genus CATHARUS Bonaparte

Neotropical, Nearctic and marginally Palaearctic genus of some twelve species; one breeds in northeast Palaearctic and this and one other have straggled to the British Isles.

Grey-cheeked Thrush   A
Catharus minimus (Lafresnaye)

Holarctic. Breeds northeast Siberia from the lower Kolyma to Anadyr and the Chukotski Peninsula, and in northern North America from Alaska and northern British Columbia to Labrador, Newfoundland, Nova Scotia and the northeastern United States; between 68°N and 42°N. Winters from Nicaragua through Venezuela and Colombia to northern Brazil and northern Peru.

    C.m.bicknelli (Ridgway) is confined to southern Quebec, Nova Scotia and the mountains of the northeastern United States.

    C.m.minimus (Lafresnaye) breeds throughout the rest of the range in Canada and northeast Siberia.

    SV. Seven, all October–November, and all since 1953: Shetland (October 1953, October 1958), Caernarvon (October 1961, October 1968), Outer Hebrides (October 1965), Moray (November 1965), Durham (October 1968). *C.m.bicknelli* (Caernarvon, 1961) and *C.m. minimus* (Moray and probably Outer Hebrides); races not determined for the other records.

Olive-backed Thrush (or Swainson's Thrush)   A
Catharus ustulatus (Nuttall)

Nearctic. Breeds North America from Alaska, Yukon, Mackenzie and Labrador south to California, Colorado, Minnesota, Michigan and Pennsylvania; between 67°N and 33°N. Winters from central Mexico south to Peru, northwest Brazil, Bolivia and northwest Argentine.

    C.u.swainsoni (Tschudi) breeds throughout the northern and eastern part of the range south to British Columbia and the northeastern United States.

SV. Three: Mayo (May 1956), Pembroke (October 1967), Cork (October 1968). *C.u.swainsoni* in the first case, but race not determined in the other two.

Genus TURDUS Linnaeus

Nearly cosmopolitan genus of some 63 species, of which 21 are in the Palaearctic; seven breed in Europe; five now breed regularly in the British Isles and a sixth has done so; the two scarcest of these six are regular winter visitors here and five others have occurred as stragglers, including one from the Nearctic.

Ring Ouzel   A
Turdus torquatus Linnaeus

Palaearctic. Breeds Europe and southwest Asia with a very broken distribution in three areas: Fenno-Scandia and the British Isles; mountainous regions of southern Europe, from northern Iberia eastwards to southern Poland, southwest Russia and the Balkans; and from eastern Turkey and the Caucasus to Transcaspia and northern Iran; between 71°N and 36°N. Migratory and sedentary, wintering at lower levels in the southern parts of the range, in the Mediterranean region from Iberia and northwest Africa through the Balkans and Egypt to Asia Minor and southern Iran.

T.t.torquatus Linnaeus breeds in Fenno-Scandia and the British Isles.

MB. Not scarce. Decreased in some areas, but still widely distributed on upland moors in northern and western Britain and in Ireland (though not now apparently in the Isle of Man). Breeds in most counties of northern and western England west of a line from Yorkshire to Devon, in all counties of Scotland except Shetland and the Outer Hebrides (but only occasionally in Orkney), in all but two counties (Pembroke and Anglesey) of Wales, and locally on hill ranges in about twelve counties of Ireland. Resident from April to September. Ringing recoveries indicate that British birds winter in southern France, northeast Spain and northwest Africa.

PV (and **WV**). Late August to November and March to May, individuals occasionally or rarely staying through the winter. Passage is recorded in many English counties and appears to be augmented by Scandinavian migrants, particularly on the east coast in autumn, although there have been no recoveries in Britain of foreign-ringed Ring Ouzels.

Blackbird A
Turdus merula Linnaeus

Western and southern Palaearctic and marginally Oriental. Breeds from the Azores, Canaries and northwest Africa throughout Europe (except Iceland, northern Fenno-Scandia and northern Russia) and eastwards through Asia Minor to Iran, Russian Turkestan, Sinkiang, northern Afghanistan and Baluchistan, the Himalayas, Tibet and southern China; between 63°N and 23°N. Largely resident, but migration from Scandinavia and partial migration from other populations result in wintering as far south as Egypt, southern Iraq, southern Afghanistan and various parts of southeast Asia.

T.m.merula Linnaeus breeds in most of the European range from the British Isles and Iberia to the Urals in Russia (but not southern Russia and the Balkans).

RB (also **MB**). Abundant and widely distributed in all parts of Britain and Ireland, including many outlying islands; still increasing and spreading to the more marginal habitats, such as small islands, open hills and city centres. The breeding population is largely sedentary, although ringing shows that many birds from Scotland and northern England winter in Ireland, smaller numbers from Great Britain winter south of the English Channel, and many others move considerable distances within the country.

PV and **WV**. Late September to November and February to April. Large numbers of Continental Blackbirds arrive in the British Isles in autumn, many remaining for the winter, as is amply shown by numerous recoveries here of birds ringed in Fenno-Scandia, Germany, the Netherlands and Belgium, and vice versa. Other ringing recoveries show that some of these immigrants move on south, particularly to France and Spain.

Eye-browed Thrush A
Turdus obscurus Gmelin

Central and eastern Palaearctic. Breeds Siberia and eastern Asia from the Yenisei, Lake Baikal and northern Mongolia to Yakutsk and the shores of the Sea of Okhotsk south to Amurland, with isolated populations in Kamchatka, the Kuriles (possibly), Sakhalin and Japan; mainly between 69°N and 45°N (with some south to 35°N). Migratory, wintering in Burma, southern China and Formosa south through the Malay peninsula and the Philippines to Indonesia.

Monotypic.

SV. Three, all in one autumn: Northampton (October 1964), Outer Hebrides (October 1964), Isles of Scilly (December 1964).

Black-throated Thrush A
Turdus ruficollis Pallas

Central Palaearctic. Breeds in central Asia from the upper Kama in eastern Russia to the Yenisei, the Tunguska and Lake Baikal south to Tarbagatai, Altai and northern Mongolia; between 65°N and 47°N. Winters from Iraq (occasionally) and Iran through Afghanistan, Baluchistan and northern India to Assam, Burma and Yunnan.

T.r.atrogularis Jarocki breeds in the western and northern part of the range from eastern Russia to the Yenisei, the Tunguska and northern Altai. (Only this form is correctly known as the Black-throated Thrush, the distinctive *T.r.ruficollis* being known as the Red-throated Thrush.)

SV. Three: Sussex (December 1868), Perth (February 1879), Fair Isle (December 1957–January 1958).

Dusky Thrush A
Turdus naumanni Temminck

Central and eastern Palaearctic. Breeds northern and central Siberia from the Taz, Yenisei and Lake Baikal eastwards to Anadyr, Kamchatka and the coasts of the Sea of Okhotsk; between 71°N and 52°N. Winters from Manchuria south through China to Burma and Assam.

T.n.eunomus Temminck breeds across the northern half of the range from the Taz and Yenisei to Anadyr and Kamchatka. (Only this form is correctly known as the Dusky Thrush, the distinctive *T.n.naumanni* being known as Naumann's Thrush.)

SV. Four: Nottingham (October 1905), Durham (December 1959–February 1960), Fair Isle (October 1961), Shetland (September 1968).

Siberian Thrush A
Turdus sibiricus Pallas

Central and eastern Palaearctic. Breeds Siberia and eastern Asia from the Yenisei and Lake Baikal to the Sea of Okhotsk, Amurland, northern Manchuria, Sakhalin and Japan; between 69°N and 35°N. Winters in eastern India and Burma south through Thailand, Indo-China and the Malay peninsula to Indonesia.

SV. One: adult male, Fife (October 1954). Race not determined.

Fieldfare   A
Turdus pilaris Linnaeus

Palaearctic. Breeds northern Eurasia from Fenno-Scandia, Germany and Switzerland east through Poland, Russia and Siberia to the upper Lena, Lake Baikal and the Altai; also in southern Greenland; between 70°N and 47°N. Resident and migratory, northern populations moving well south in winter, extending to most parts of Europe (including Iceland) and much of southwest Asia, south to Iberia (scarce), Asia Minor and Iran and occasionally farther south.

Monotypic.

CB. Nested Orkney in 1967 and Shetland in 1968.

WV and **PV**. September (occasionally August, July or even June) to April (occasionally May or even June). Common and widespread throughout Britain and Ireland from November to March. Fieldfares ringed here on passage have been recovered farther south in winter in Belgium, France, Spain, Portugal, Italy, Austria, Yugoslavia, Greece, Bulgaria, the Ukraine and Turkey, while recoveries on the breeding grounds and of foreign-ringed ones in Britain show Norway, Sweden, Finland and even Russia as areas of origin.

Redwing   A
Turdus iliacus Linnaeus

Palaearctic. Breeds from Iceland, Faeroes, Scotland, Fenno-Scandia and Poland eastwards across Russia and Siberia to Lake Baikal, the Lena and the lower Kolyma; between 70°N and 50°N. Mainly migratory, wintering in the British Isles, central and southern Europe, Asia Minor, Iran and Turkestan, south occasionally to the Canaries, Mediterranean islands, north Africa, Egypt and apparently even northwest India.

T.i.coburni Sharpe is confined as a breeding form to Iceland and Faeroes.

T.i.iliacus Linnaeus breeds throughout the rest of the range.

MB (perhaps **RB**). Very scarce. Until recently breeding was apparently only sporadic, but since 1953 the species has probably nested every year, chiefly in Sutherland and Ross and less regularly in

Inverness, Moray and Shetland; about 25 pairs were known to nest in Scotland in 1968; attempted to nest in Kerry in 1951. Mainly and perhaps entirely *T.i.iliacus*.

WV and **PV**. September to April. Common and widespread throughout Britain and Ireland from October or November to March. Redwings ringed here on passage have been recovered in winter south to Iberia, Sardinia, Italy, Greece and Lebanon, while recoveries on the breeding grounds and of foreign-ringed ones in Britain show Iceland, Fenno-Scandia, the Baltic States and Russia as the areas of origin. *T.i.coburni* and *T.i.iliacus*.

Song Thrush   A
Turdus philomelos Brehm

Western and central Palaearctic. Breeds from Fenno-Scandia, British Isles, France and northern Spain eastwards across most of the rest of Europe (except the extreme south), thence through western Siberia to Lake Baikal and Asia Minor to parts of Iran; between 69°N and 35°N. Resident and migratory, northern populations moving southwards, wintering south to the Mediterranean and north Africa, Egypt, the Middle East and Iraq.

T.p.hebridensis Clarke is confined to the Outer Hebrides and the Isle of Skye; populations in the Inner Hebrides, other parts of western Scotland and Kerry are intermediate between this and the next race.

T.p.clarkei Hartert is typically found in the rest of the British Isles and in northern and western France and the south Netherlands; populations in the rest of France and central and southern Europe north to Denmark and Germany, south to northern Iberia and Italy and east to Czechoslovakia, northern Greece, Bulgaria and Rumania are intermediate between this and the next race.

T.p.philomelos Brehm breeds in almost all the rest of the range from Fenno-Scandia and eastern Europe across Siberia to Lake Baikal and across Asia Minor to Iran.

RB (also **MB**). Abundant and widespread, breeding in all parts of Britain and Ireland, except Shetland where nesting is now only occasional. *T.p.hebridensis* and *T.p.clarkei* (see above). Both subspecies are essentially sedentary, but *T.p.hebridensis* has been recorded in winter in England and once in Algeria, while some British-ringed *T.p.clarkei* have been recovered south to France, Portugal, Spain and the Balearic Islands.

PV and **WV**. September to April or May. Passage of Continental birds is recorded on many parts of the east and southeast coasts, and observation and ringing suggest that some winter. Most recoveries of foreign-ringed Song Thrushes in Britain are from the Netherlands, Belgium and Germany, but include some from Sweden and Norway. *T.p.clarkei* and *T.p.philomelos*.

Mistle Thrush A
Turdus viscivorus Linnaeus

Western and central Palaearctic. Breeds from Fenno-Scandia, British Isles, France and Iberia east throughout Europe, Russia and Asia Minor to central Siberia east of the Yenisei, Altai, western Sinkiang, Afghanistan, northern Baluchistan and Iran; also in northwest Africa; between 69°N and 28°N. Sedentary and partially migratory, the northern populations moving south and there being some extension beyond the southern breeding limit in north Africa, the Middle East and Iran.

T.v.viscivorus Linnaeus breeds throughout most of the range east to the Ob in western Siberia and thence south to Iran; the populations of Corsica, Sardinia, northwest Africa and the southern Crimea are distinct.

RB (also **MB**). Numerous. Greatly increased since about 1800 and now widespread, breeding in every county of Britain and Ireland except Shetland and the Outer Hebrides (where a pair bred in 1968), but only irregularly in Orkney and sparsely in the extreme northwest and north of the Scottish mainland. The British population is essentially sedentary, but some emigration occurs as indicated by the recoveries in France (17) and Belgium (one) of British-ringed birds.

PV and **WV**. There is observational evidence of immigration from the Continent in September–November with a return in February–April, though it should be added that no foreign-ringed Mistle Thrush has been recovered in Britain or Ireland.

American Robin A
Turdus migratorius Linnaeus

Nearctic. Breeds most of North America from Alaska, Mackenzie, Quebec and Labrador south to southern Mexico; between 69°N and 17°N. Resident and partially migratory, northern populations moving southwards, wintering mainly from southern British Columbia, Illinois and Virginia south to Mexico and Guatemala.

T.m.migratorius Linnaeus breeds from Alaska to Nova Scotia and Georgia.

SV. Twelve records (involving 13 birds) during 1952–67, all October–February (especially November–January) except two in May: Devon (October–November 1952, October 1955, November 1962), Wexford (December 1954), Kerry (January 1955, January 1965), Orkney (May 1961), Isles of Scilly (two, December 1963), Dorset (January–March 1966), Surrey (February–March 1966), Kirkcudbright (May 1966), Shetland (November 1967). Seven older records during 1876–94 (five) and 1927–37 (two) have less general acceptance, but they form a similar pattern, all September–December except two in April–May: Kent (April or May 1876), Dublin (May 1891), Sligo (December 1892), Leicester (October 1893), Leitrim (December 1894), Shropshire (September 1927), Kent (December 1937). Race not determined in most cases, but some of the earlier specimens were recorded as *T.m.migratorius*.

Family SYLVIIDAE

Genus CETTIA Bonaparte

Palaearctic and Oriental genus of ten species, eight in Palaearctic, only one breeding in Europe and straggling to the British Isles.

Cetti's Warbler   A
Cettia cetti (Temminck)

Southern Palaearctic. Breeds from northwest Africa and Iberia east to Russian Turkestan, north to central France (lately expanding northwards), north Italy, Rumania, the Ukraine and Kirghiz Steppes, south to the Mediterranean islands and Persian Gulf; between 51°N and 30°N. Mainly sedentary, but eastern populations winter south to eastern Iran and northwest India.

C.c.cetti (Temminck) breeds northwest Africa, Iberia and France east to Crete and the Crimea.

SV. Seven, all since 1961: Hampshire (March–April 1961), Sussex (October 1962, September 1968), Buckingham (July–September 1967), Kent (March 1968), Somerset (April 1968), Cork (August 1968).

Genus LOCUSTELLA Kaup

Palaearctic genus of six or seven species, four breeding in Europe and two (one marginally) in the British Isles, three others occurring here as rare stragglers.

Savi's Warbler   A
Locustella luscinioides (Savi)

Western Palaearctic. Breeds northwest Africa and from Iberia, Netherlands and Germany across southern Europe and southwest Asia to Russian Turkestan; between 55°N and 33°N. Winters probably in tropical and northeast Africa.

L.l.luscinioides (Savi) breeds northwest Africa and Europe east to the Volga.

MB. Extremely scarce. Bred in small numbers in the fens (Norfolk, Cambridge, Huntingdon) until the middle of the 19th century, but then no records of birds summering until 1960 when a small population was discovered at Stodmarsh, Kent. Since then small, fluctuating numbers have been noted annually, breeding has been proved, and a maximum of twelve singing males noted, in 1965. Resident from mid-April to July.

SV. Fifteen records (apart from those above), two 1908, one 1954, the remainder since 1960, including six in five counties in 1968. One October (Pembroke), the rest all April to August, chiefly April–May, in Somerset, Wiltshire, Sussex (two), Berkshire, Suffolk (three), Norfolk, Cambridge, Lincoln, Warwick, Fair Isle (two).

River Warbler   A
Locustella fluviatilis (Wolf)

Western central Palaearctic. Breeds from the Baltic States, east Germany and the Balkans eastwards across central and southern Russia to the region of Tyumen in western Siberia; between 62°N and 45°N. Winters in east Africa, south occasionally to the Transvaal.

Monotypic.

SV. One, Fair Isle (September 1961).

Pallas's Grasshopper Warbler A
Locustella certhiola (Pallas)

Central and eastern Palaearctic. Breeds from western Siberia and Russian Turkestan east to Kamchatka, south to Manchuria and Japan; between 62°N and 35°N. Winters from India and southeast China south to the Philippines.

L.c.rubescens Blyth breeds across the northern part of the range, from western Siberia to the Amur basin.

SV. Three: Dublin (September 1908), Fair Isle (October 1949, October 1956). Race not certainly determined but all three resembled *L.c.rubescens.*

Grasshopper Warbler A
Locustella naevia (Boddaert)

Palaearctic. Breeds Eurasia from southern Fenno-Scandia, British Isles, France and northern Iberia east across Europe, south to northern Italy and the Balkans, thence across Russia and southern Siberia to northwest Mongolia; also in the Caucasus and probably north Afghanistan; between 61°N and 40°N. Winters in Africa (precise range uncertain—probably mainly in the northern tropical region), also Iran and India.

L.n.naevia (Boddaert) breeds Europe east to central Russia and the Crimea.

MB. Not scarce. Widely distributed throughout Britain and Ireland (recently spreading in Ireland to several western districts), north to Argyll, Stirling and probably Inverness; breeds at least occasionally in the Isle of Man and northeast Scotland, and recorded increasingly in summer in recent years in the northern part of the Scottish mainland. Resident mid-April to September.

PV. Passage early April to May, end July to late October; nowhere conspicuous, except during periodic heavy 'falls' of migrants which occur most often in the Irish Sea area (especially at lighthouses), where they undoubtedly comprise mainly birds of British and Irish origin.

Passage migrants occur regularly as far north as Fair Isle, and these birds at least, as well as stragglers in late October on the English south coast, are likely to be of Continental origin.

Lanceolated Warbler   A
Locustella lanceolata (Temminck)

Central and eastern Palaearctic. Breeds from eastern-central Russia and across Siberia to Kamchatka, south to the Russian Altai, Manchuria, northern Korea and north Japan; between 63°N and 39°N. Winters in southern Asia from India to Indo-China.

Monotypic.

SV. Twelve (six 1908–28, one 1938, five 1953–61); once in May, the remainder September to early November. All at Fair Isle apart from one Lincoln (November 1909) and one Orkney (October 1910).

Genus ACROCEPHALUS Naumann

Palaearctic and Ethiopian (also Oriental and Australasian) genus of about 17 species, seven breeding in Europe and three in the British Isles, where six others occur as scarce visitors, one of them having bred on one occasion.

Aquatic Warbler   A
Acrocephalus paludicola (Vieillot)

Western Palaearctic. Breeds locally from the Netherlands, southern Finland and central Russia, south through Denmark and central Europe to Italy, Hungary and the northern Caspian; between 60°N and 44°N. Winters probably in tropical Africa.

Monotypic.

SV. Over 150 recorded, annually in recent years, with about two-thirds the total since 1958. Nearly all in autumn, August to early October, with one record for each month from April to July and two in November. Noted chiefly on the English south coast, occasionally elsewhere (most often in Norfolk and at Fair Isle; also inland in southern England), but only rarely in Ireland.

Moustached Warbler   A
*Acrocephalus melanopogon** (Temminck)

Southwestern Palaearctic. Breeds from Tunisia and southern Spain across southern Europe including the Balearic Islands and Sicily, north to Austria, and east to the Iranian region, Russian Turkestan and northwest India; between 48°N and 30°N. Partially migratory; winters in the southern part of the breeding range, some birds occasionally reaching areas south of the Sahara, and also eastern Arabia.

    A.m.melanopogon (Temminck) breeds Tunisia and southern Spain eastwards to Austria and Rumania.

    CB. A pair bred Cambridge, 1946.

    SV. Three other records involving four birds: Hampshire (two August 1951), Kent (April 1952), Buckingham (July 1965). Race not determined but presumed to be nominate *melanopogon*.

Sedge Warbler   A
Acrocephalus schoenobaenus (Linnaeus)

Western and central Palaearctic. Breeds British Isles and throughout continental Europe except Iberia and some other Mediterranean coasts, thence eastwards across Siberia to the Yenisei, south to the Caucasus and northwest Iran and the Russian Altai; also locally in northwest Africa; between 71°N and 30°N. Winters in tropical and southern Africa, north to eastern Nigeria and Kenya.

    Monotypic.

    MB. Numerous. Widely distributed, breeding in every county except Shetland, though rather sparsely in parts of northwest Scotland; it has colonized and markedly increased in the Outer Hebrides during the present century. Resident mid-April to September.

    PV. Passage mainly mid-April to mid-May, late July to mid-October, most numerous in southern England and on Irish Sea coasts, where, however, nearly all migrants must be of British or Irish origin. Relatively few migrants occur on the British east coast (though they are noted regularly in small numbers at Fair Isle, mainly in spring) and it seems unlikely that there is any substantial regular passage of Continental birds through Britain.

---

    * Vaurie (1959), *The birds of the Palearctic fauna*, and other authors place this species in a monospecific genus, *Lusciniola* Gray.

Paddyfield Warbler A
Acrocephalus agricola (Jerdon)

Central and southeastern Palaearctic. Breeds southern Russia, and Asia from the Caspian east to central Mongolia, south to eastern Iran, northern Afghanistan and probably to India; also in Manchuria; between 60°N and 25°N. Winters in the southern Iranian region and from India east to China.

A.a.brevipennis (Severtzov) breeds range of species except Manchuria and (probably) India.

SV. Two, both at Fair Isle (September–October 1925, September 1953). Race not determined but unlikely to have been other than *A.a.brevipennis*.

Blyth's Reed Warbler A
Acrocephalus dumetorum (Blyth)

Central Palaearctic. Breeds from southern Finland and the Baltic States across Russia and Siberia to the Upper Lena, south to the Aral-Caspian region, eastern Iran, northern Afghanistan and northwest Mongolia; between 63°N and 35°N. Winters in India south to Ceylon.

Monotypic.

SV. Nine or ten recorded, all except two of which were in the autumn of 1912: Fair Isle (September 1910; four or five September–October 1912; September 1928), Yorkshire (September 1912), Northumberland (September 1912), Norfolk (October 1912).

Marsh Warbler A
Acrocephalus palustris (Bechstein)

Western Palaearctic. Breeds Europe and southwest Asia from southern England, Low Countries and eastern France east to the southern Urals, north to southernmost Sweden and Finland, south to northern Italy and Iran; between 61°N and 38°N. Winters in east Africa from Kenya to Natal.

Monotypic.

MB. Very scarce. Has decreased and is now confined to a few localities in Somerset, Gloucester, Worcester, and perhaps Dorset, with occasional pairs sometimes breeding elsewhere in southern England. Resident late May to August.

SV. Away from the breeding haunts occurs only as a vagrant, late May to June, August to October, most frequently at Fair Isle (chiefly in spring)—although only once elsewhere in Scotland (at St. Kilda)—occasionally on the English south coast west to Isles of Scilly, and only extremely rarely elsewhere. There are no certain records for Ireland.

Reed Warbler   A
Acrocephalus scirpaceus (Hermann)

Western and central Palaearctic. Breeds northwest Africa, and Eurasia from Iberia, Britain and the Low Countries east to Russian Turkestan, north to southern Fenno-Scandia, the Baltic States and southern Russia, south to the Mediterranean and Caspian Seas and Iran; between 62°N and 30°N. Winters across tropical Africa.

A.s.scirpaceus (Hermann) breeds northwest Africa and Europe east to western Russia.

MB. Fairly numerous. Distributed widely in central and southern England and East Anglia, west locally to west Cornwall, Glamorgan, Brecon, Shropshire, Denbigh and probably Anglesey (breeding proved 1968), and north locally to Westmorland (irregular Cumberland) and south Northumberland (not Durham); has bred Ireland (Down) but not Scotland. Resident mid-April to September.

PV. Mid-April to May, August to October. Most numerous in southern England, but also fairly regularly in autumn as far north as Shetland, and as far west as southwest Ireland. Proportion of Continental birds among migrants is not known, but is probably small in most areas.

Great Reed Warbler   A
Acrocephalus arundinaceus (Linnaeus)

Palaearctic. Breeds northwest Africa, and Eurasia from Iberia, France and the Netherlands east to the Russian Altai, north to southern Sweden and the Baltic States, south to the Mediterranean islands, Palestine, the Caspian Sea and Kashmir; thence from eastern Mongolia to Japan and east China; between 60°N and 26°N. Winters in tropical and southern Africa and southern Asia.

A.a.arundinaceus (Linnaeus) breeds northwest Africa and Europe east to west Siberia and Kirghiz Steppes.

SV. Over 60, including sight-records (see below), annually in recent years, and more than half the total since 1958. Most in May–June (some staying into July) with a few from July through to September. Chiefly in south and southeast England, very occasionally elsewhere, but four have reached as far north and west as Scotland (Shetland, two Fair Isle, Inverness), one Wales and two Ireland (both Cork). Some, and probably all, nominate *arundinaceus*. Note that sight-records, included above, do not normally exclude the Clamorous Reed Warbler *Acrocephalus stentoreus* (Hemprich and Ehrenberg) of southern Asia and Egypt.

Thick-billed Warbler   A
Acrocephalus aedon (Pallas)

Central and eastern Palaearctic. Breeds southern Siberia from the Ob eastwards to the area of Lake Baikal, south to northern Mongolia; and again farther east to Manchuria, Ussuriland and northeast China; between 55°N and 30°N. Winters from India to southeast China.

    A.a.aedon (Pallas) breeds east to Baikal region.

    SV. One, Fair Isle (October 1955). Race not determined but most likely to have been *A.a.aedon*.

Genus HIPPOLAIS Baldenstein

Palaearctic (also marginally Ethiopian and Oriental) genus of six species, five breeding in Europe, but none in the British Isles, where two occur as annual visitors in very small numbers (and one is reputed to have bred) and another two as rare vagrants.

Icterine Warbler   A
Hippolais icterina (Vieillot)

Western Palaearctic. Breeds from the Arctic Circle in Europe south to northern and eastern France and northern Italy, east to the Urals and the Russian Altai; between 67°N and 45°N; also in northern Iran. Winters in eastern tropical and southern Africa.

    Monotypic.

    CB. Said to have bred once, Wiltshire, 1907.

    PV. Passage May to June (irregular, the great majority recorded at Fair Isle, with only scattered records from other parts of Britain and Ireland), and late August to mid-October, when noted regularly in very small numbers at bird observatories and similar sites on the east and south coasts of Britain (chiefly in Shetland, Fife, Northumberland, Yorkshire, Lincoln, Norfolk, Kent, Dorset and the Isles of Scilly) and in southwest Ireland (Cork), less often in the Irish Sea basin, and only rarely on other coasts and inland.

Melodious Warbler   A
Hippolais polyglotta (Vieillot)

Southwestern Palaearctic. Breeds northwest Africa, and southwest Europe from Iberia, Sicily, Italy and northwest Yugoslavia north to France (not in the extreme north and east); between 50°N and 31°N. Winters in tropical west Africa.

Monotypic.

SV. Only three recorded prior to 1951, but identified annually since 1953, with as many as 50 in some years. Nearly all in autumn, August to mid-October, with a few May to July. Principally at recently established coastal and island bird observatories in southwest England (chiefly Isles of Scilly and Dorset), southwest Ireland (Cork), and the south Irish Sea basin (chiefly Wexford, Pembroke, Caernarvon), but also fairly often in southeast England. Rarely inland or farther north, only three having been known to reach Scotland.

Olivaceous Warbler   A
Hippolais pallida (Hemprich and Ehrenberg)

Southwestern Palaearctic and northern Ethiopian. Breeds from southern Spain and northwest Africa locally across the Sahara to Lake Chad; also in Egypt and from the Balkans through Asia Minor, Cyprus, the Near East and southwest Asia to northern Afghanistan and the western Tian Shan; between 46°N and 13°N. Winters chiefly in eastern tropical Africa or, in the case of the western Mediterranean population, in west Africa from Senegal to north Nigeria.

H.p.opaca (Cabanis) breeds southeast Spain, Morocco, north Algeria and north Tunisia.

H.p.elaeica (Lindermayer) breeds southeast Europe and southwest Asia.

SV. Ten, all in autumn and all since 1951: Pembroke (September–October 1951), Dorset (August 1956, September 1962, August 1967), Donegal (September 1959), Isles of Scilly (October 1961, September–October 1962), Fife (September 1967), Kent (September 1967), Cornwall (September 1968). That in 1951 was identified as *H.p.opaca*, those in 1956, 1959 and Fife in 1967 as *H.p.elaeica*, while the subspecies of the other four was not determined.

Booted Warbler   A
Hippolais caligata (Lichtenstein)

Central Palaearctic. Breeds from northwest Russia east across southern Siberia to the Yenisei valley, northwest Mongolia and western Sinkiang, south to southern Iran; between 61°N and 25°N. Winters in India and southern Arabia.

    H.c.caligata (Lichtenstein) breeds range of species south as far as the Kirghiz Steppes.

    SV. Five: Fair Isle (September 1936, August 1959, August–September 1966, September 1968), Isles of Scilly (October 1966). The first of these recorded as *H.c.caligata*, the rest indeterminate, but probably this race.

Genus SYLVIA Scopoli

Palaearctic and Ethiopian genus of 18 species, all but one in Palaearctic, 13 breeding in Europe and five in the British Isles, one other occurring here as a scarce passage visitor and a further four as rare stragglers.

Barred Warbler   A
Sylvia nisoria (Bechstein)

Central Palaearctic. Breeds from southern Sweden and Finland, eastern Denmark, Germany, northeast France and northern Italy eastwards through eastern Europe (north to central Russia, south to the Balkans) and Asia Minor, thence across western Asia to northwest Mongolia and northern Afghanistan; between 61°N and 37°N. Winters from southern Arabia to eastern tropical Africa.

    S.n.nisoria (Bechstein) breeds from central Europe east to western Siberia and Asia Minor.

    SV. Regular in small numbers (almost invariably immatures), August to mid-October, chiefly in Shetland and Orkney and on the British east coast south to Suffolk, also not infrequently on the English south coast and on islands in the Irish Sea area. Seldom inland, and only twice in spring: Shetland (June 1914), Suffolk (May 1960).

Orphean Warbler A
Sylvia hortensis (Gmelin)

Southwestern Palaearctic. Breeds from northwest Africa, Spain, southern and eastern France and Switzerland through southern Europe, including the Mediterranean islands, and the Balkans, Asia Minor, the Near East, Transcaspia and Iran to northwest India; between 46°N and 25°N. Winters in northern tropical and northeast Africa, Arabia and India.

SV. Three: Yorkshire (July 1948), Dorset (September 1955), Cornwall (October 1967). Subspecies not determined.

Garden Warbler A
Sylvia borin (Boddaert)

Western and central Palaearctic. Breeds Eurasia from northern Scandinavia, the British Isles and Iberia east to the upper Yenisei, north to the White Sea and about 63°N in the Urals, south to northern Italy, Bulgaria, the Crimea, perhaps northern Iran, and the Russian Altai; between 70°N and 40°N. Winters across tropical Africa.

S.b.borin (Boddaert) breeds Europe east to the Urals.

MB. Numerous. Widely distributed in England and Wales (but absent from the Isle of Man, and scarce in some western areas such as western Cornwall and Anglesey) and in southern Scotland, becoming more local in central Scotland, and breeding only exceptionally north of Angus: in recent years there have been one or two breeding records from each of Moray, Inverness, Ross and Orkney. In Ireland it is very local and is known as a breeder only in Westmeath, Roscommon, Cavan and Fermanagh, although it possibly also breeds regularly in Limerick and Tipperary, and sporadically elsewhere. Resident from late April to early September.

PV. Mid-April into June, late July to October; occasionally November, exceptionally in winter. Passage most conspicuous on the British east and south coasts, particularly during periodic falls of migrants from northern continental Europe in September and early October; scarcer on the west coast and in Ireland. Garden Warblers ringed in Germany, Belgium, Netherlands and France (almost certainly as migrants) have been recovered in Britain.

Blackcap A
Sylvia atricapilla (Linnaeus)

Western Palaearctic. Breeds northwest Africa (and Atlantic Isles), and throughout Europe, except in the extreme north, eastwards through western Asia to the Irtysh and northern Iran; between 69°N and 30°N, excluding the Canary and Cape Verde Islands populations. Winters mainly from the Mediterranean basin south in Africa to Upper Guinea and Tanzania, also in limited numbers in western Europe north to the British Isles.

S.a.atricapilla (Linnaeus) breeds Europe and northwest Africa east to Asia Minor and the Urals.

MB. Numerous. Widely distributed in England and Wales, breeding in every county though not in the Isle of Man; breeds locally in Scotland north to the Firths of Forth and Clyde, also in Perth and Inverness, and irregularly in northeast Scotland and south Argyll. In Ireland it is extremely local and is known to breed in only a few localities, mainly in the east of the country, and in recent years especially in the northeast where numbers are evidently increasing. Resident April to September.

PV. End March into June, mid-August to October and even into November. Passage migrants occur in small numbers in all areas and regularly include some to the north and west of the breeding range. Most migrants are of British origin, but birds from the Continent are in the majority at Fair Isle in late spring, on the British east coast in autumn, and on the British east and south coasts from October onwards.

WV. Small numbers of individuals overwinter, even in Scotland but mainly in southwest England and Ireland. These birds may largely be of Continental rather than British origin, as indicated by December–January recoveries here of birds ringed in autumn in Norway and Austria.

Whitethroat A
Sylvia communis Latham

Western Palaearctic. Breeds northwest Africa and Eurasia from central Scandinavia, British Isles and Iberia east to northern Mongolia, north to central Finland and northern Russia, south to Mediterranean islands, northern Iran and northern Afghanistan; between 65°N and 32°N. Winters tropical Africa.

S.c.communis Latham breeds northwest Africa and Europe east to the Pechora Basin and Crimea.

MB. Abundant. Widely distributed over the whole of Britain and Ireland (with the exception of Orkney and Shetland) but breeds somewhat locally in northwest Scotland and only very locally in the Outer Hebrides. Resident mid-April to September.

PV. Passage April to May, late July to October (exceptional in winter). Noted in all areas, most conspicuously on coasts, including small numbers north to Fair Isle (mainly in spring); the greatest numbers occur on the coasts of southern England and the Irish Sea, and at both seasons the majority of these are undoubtedly of British and Irish origin. Any passage of Continental birds through Britain appears to be slight, though some certainly occur on the British east coast.

Lesser Whitethroat   A
Sylvia curruca (Linnaeus)

Central and western Palaearctic. Breeds Eurasia from northern Fenno-Scandia, Britain and central France east to Transbaicalia and probably Manchuria, north to the Arctic Circle, south to northern Italy, the Balkans, southwest Iran and Mongolia; between 67°N and 30°N. Winters chiefly east of the Nile in northeast Africa (also west to Nigeria), in the southern Iranian region and northwest India.

S.c.curruca (Linnaeus) breeds Eurasia east to the Yenisei.

S.c.blythi Ticehurst and Whistler breeds western Siberia east to Transbaicalia and south to the Kirghiz Steppes and Mongolia.

MB. Fairly numerous. Generally distributed in England south of a line from the Cheshire Dee to the Wash, but becomes more local towards southwest England and is absent from Cornwall and much of Devon (though it has bred recently in the Isles of Scilly); the species also breeds locally north to Cumberland and Northumberland, and very locally in Wales mainly in the east and north, but apparently not in west Glamorgan, Carmarthen, Pembroke, Cardigan, Merioneth and Anglesey. Absent from Scotland (summering birds are occasionally noted, and pairs bred on at least nine occasions prior to 1949, chiefly in the south but also north to Ross); also absent as a breeder from Ireland and the Isle of Man. Resident late April to September. *S.c. curruca.*

PV. Passage mid-April into June, mid-August to October, occasionally November. Chiefly in southeast England, where migrants are mainly of British origin (oriented, unlike most other British summer visitors, on a southeast–northwest axis), but those in late spring and late autumn, especially at Fair Isle, are most probably birds from northwest continental Europe; migrants are scarce on the west coast and in Ireland. *S.c.curruca.*

SV. Autumn (September–October) migrants resembling *S.c. blythi* are recorded more or less regularly at Fair Isle, and occasionally on the coast of northeast England; also once in Ireland.

Sardinian Warbler **A**
Sylvia melanocephala (Gmelin)

Southwestern Palaearctic. Breeds Canaries and the Mediterranean basin from Morocco and Iberia east to Asia Minor, the Near East and Egypt; between 45°N and 28°N. Mainly sedentary, but some birds winter south to the Sahara, north Iraq and Arabia.

S.m.melanocephala (Gmelin) breeds range of species except for the eastern Mediterranean islands and the Near East.

SV. Three: Lundy, Devon (May 1955), Fair Isle (May 1967), Pembroke (October 1968). Subspecies not determined but unlikely to have been other than nominate *melanocephala.*

Subalpine Warbler **A**
Sylvia cantillans (Pallas)

Southwestern Palaearctic. Breeds in the Mediterranean basin from Morocco, Iberia and southern France east to Asia Minor and Syria, though not in Palestine and Egypt; between 44°N and 30°N. European populations winter in west Africa just south of the Sahara; some birds reach Arabia and the Sudan.

S.c.cantillans (Pallas) breeds Iberia, France, Corsica, Sardinia, Italy and Sicily.

S.c.albistriata (C. L. Brehm) breeds from Yugoslavia east to Asia Minor and Syria.

SV. Thirty-seven recorded, all but six of these since 1951. Mainly May–June (22) and September–October (eight), also four April, and one in each of July, August and November. Recorded most frequently at Fair Isle and in Norfolk, the remainder chiefly on the British east and south coasts from Shetland to the Isles of Scilly, also one Pembroke, one Lancashire, one Isle of Man, one St. Kilda and five Ireland. None has been noted inland. Two (St. Kilda, June 1894; Fair Isle, May 1966) were identified as nominate *cantillans*; two (Fair Isle, May 1951 and

I

April 1964) and perhaps a third (Northumberland, October 1963) resembled *S.c.albistriata*; the rest not racially identified.

Spectacled Warbler   A
Sylvia conspicillata Temminck

Southwestern Palaearctic. Breeds Cape Verde Islands, Canaries, Madeira, northwest Africa and from southern Iberia east to Italy and Sicily, also in the Near East and probably Egypt; between 44°N and 15°N. Mediterranean population is partially migratory, probably wintering mainly just south of the breeding range.

  S.c.conspicillata Temminck breeds range of species, except for the Atlantic islands.

  SV. One, Yorkshire (October 1968). Subspecies not determined but highly unlikely to have been other than *S.c.conspicillata*.

Dartford Warbler   A
Sylvia undata (Boddaert)

Southwestern Palaearctic. Breeds from southern England, western France, Iberia and Morocco east to Italy, Sicily and Tunisia; between 51°N and 35°N. Mainly sedentary.

  S.u.dartfordiensis Latham breeds southern England, Channel Islands and northwest France.

  RB. Very scarce and local. Numbers fluctuate but have generally decreased during this century. As a regular breeder it is now largely confined to a few localities in Dorset and Hampshire, spreading very locally when the population is high (after a series of mild winters) into Devon, the Isle of Wight, Sussex and Surrey. Formerly bred west to Cornwall, east to Kent, north to Berkshire and Middlesex, and occasionally or erratically farther north still (e.g. bred in Essex in 1948). The origin of individuals recorded occasionally in autumn elsewhere in southern England (in recent years in the Isles of Scilly, Somerset, and on Lundy and the south coast from Devon to Kent) is not known, but some, especially those in western districts, may include wanderers from northwest France. There are two Irish records: Wexford (October 1912) and Cork (October 1968).

Genus PHYLLOSCOPUS Boie

Palaearctic, Oriental and Ethiopian (also marginally Australasian and

Nearctic) genus of about 35 species: six breed in Europe and three in the British Isles, where the other three European species plus four from Asia have been recorded as scarce visitors.

Willow Warbler A
Phylloscopus trochilus (Linnaeus)

Palaearctic. Breeds from Fenno-Scandia, the British Isles and northern France eastwards across northern Eurasia to Anadyrland, north as far as the North Cape and the southern limit of arctic tundra, south to northern Italy, northern Rumania, and about 50°N in Russia and Siberia; extreme limits 72°N and 45°N. Winters in tropical and southern Africa.

P.t.trochilus (Linnaeus) breeds Europe from Denmark, the British Isles and northern France east to Poland and Rumania.

P.t.acredula (Linnaeus) breeds mainly from Scandinavia east to western Siberia, and south to the Ukraine and Kirghiz Steppes.

MB. Abundant. Very widely distributed, breeding in all parts of Britain and Ireland except Shetland, though only locally in Orkney and the Outer Hebrides. Resident from April to September. *P.t.trochilus* breeds throughout the British Isles, but some individuals breeding in Scotland and northern England resemble *P.t.acredula*.

PV. Passage end March into June, mid-July to October (exceptional in winter). In both spring and autumn the earlier movements comprise mainly British birds, the later ones, especially those in autumn, usually Continental migrants. Mainly *P.t.trochilus*, which is noted most numerously in April and late July–August on the coasts of southern England and the southern Irish Sea area. *P.t.acredula*, from Scandinavia eastwards, is recorded regularly on the British east coast (especially Fair Isle) in spring and autumn, and birds resembling this race are surprisingly frequent at both seasons on southern and western coasts; at least some of these may breed in the British Isles (see above).

Chiffchaff A
Phylloscopus collybita (Vieillot)

Western and central Palaearctic. Breeds Canaries, northwest Africa and Eurasia from Iberia, the British Isles and Scandinavia east to the Kolyma in northeast Siberia, north to the Arctic Circle and beyond in Russia and Siberia, south to the Balkans, northern Iran and the northwest Himalayas; between 71°N and 28°N. Most populations are migratory, wintering mainly from the Mediterranean region and northern tropical Africa east to northern and central India, also in small numbers in western Europe as far north as England.

P.c.collybita (Vieillot) breeds western Europe north to Denmark, east to Poland and Bulgaria.

P.c.abietinus (Nilsson) breeds from Scandinavia and west Russia south to Iran.

P.c.fulvescens (Severtzov) breeds from the Urals east to the Yenisei, south to Semipalatinsk; also in Iran.

P.c.tristis Blyth breeds in northern Siberia from the Yenisei to the Kolyma, south to Lake Baikal.

MB. Numerous. Widely distributed in southern Britain north to Ayr and, locally, Argyll in the west, but in the east becoming rather sparse and local north of south Yorkshire, though breeding regularly to south Fife; occasionally breeds elsewhere in Scotland, in recent years in Perth, the Inner Hebrides, Ross (where perhaps regular in the east) and Sutherland; a few individuals are recorded regularly in summer in various parts of Scotland to the north of the normal breeding range. Widespread in Ireland, though scarce in west Galway and west Mayo. Resident from mid-March to October (a few overwinter, mainly in southwest England, but these birds are not necessarily of British origin). *P.c.collybita.*

PV, also **WV**. Passage March to May, late August to early November. All areas; most conspicuous on coasts of southern England and the Irish Sea, where migrants are mainly *P.c.collybita* of British origin, though 'falls' there in late October and November seem more likely to concern Continental birds, some of which remain in winter. *P.c. abietinus* is also regular, especially on the British east coast in autumn, sometimes in some numbers. Birds resembling *P.c.fulvescens* (and perhaps including some examples of the similarly plumaged *P.c.tristis*) are recorded annually in late autumn at Fair Isle, occasionally elsewhere in Scotland, and also, less frequently, in England and Ireland, where some individuals resembling this subspecies have wintered.

Bonelli's Warbler A
Phylloscopus bonelli (Vieillot)

Southwestern Palaearctic. Breeds from northwest Africa, Iberia and France (not extreme north) east through southern Europe and Asia

Minor to the Near East (Syria), north to southern Germany; between 51°N and 30°N. Winters across tropical Africa.

P.b.bonelli (Vieillot) breeds northwest Africa and Europe east to Czechoslovakia and Italy.

SV. Twenty-two recorded (three 1948–55, the remainder since); one April, two May–June, six August, ten September, two October, one November. Once inland (Cheshire, May–June), the rest coastal or insular: Isles of Scilly, Cornwall, Devon, Dorset (two), Kent (two), Suffolk, Glamorgan, Pembroke, Caernarvon (five), Northumberland, Fair Isle, Cork (three), Wexford. Probably *P.b.bonelli*, though none racially identified.

Wood Warbler   A
Phylloscopus sibilatrix (Bechstein)

Western Palaearctic. Breeds Eurasia from central Scandinavia, British Isles and France east to the Irtysh in western Siberia, north to northwest Russia, south to the Pyrenees, Italy, the Balkans, Crimea and Caucasus; between 64°N and 30°N. Winters in tropical Africa south to the equator.

Monotypic.

MB. Fairly numerous. Widely distributed from southern England north to Ross and perhaps Sutherland, most numerous and widespread in the west (especially in Wales) and breeding only locally in eastern England and Scotland, being especially scarce and local from Kent to southeast Yorkshire (absent from many counties in this region) and in east Scotland north of the Tay; breeds irregularly in the Inner Hebrides; absent from west Cornwall, the Isle of Wight, probably the Isle of Man, the Outer Hebrides, Northern Isles, and Ireland (where bred sporadically prior to 1938; also in Wicklow in 1968). Resident mid-April to August.

PV. Noted in coastal areas, mid-April into late June, late July to September, but irregularly at most places and rarely more than two or three together; very few reach Ireland. Some on the British east and south coasts, including a few more or less regularly at Fair Isle, are presumably of Continental origin.

Dusky Warbler A
Phylloscopus fuscatus (Blyth)

Central and eastern Palaearctic. Breeds Siberia from the Ob east to Anadyr, north to about 60°N on the Yenisei, south to the Russian Altai, eastern Himalayas, central China and Manchuria; between 65°N and 30°N. Winters from northern India east to southern China.

P.f.fuscatus (Blyth) breeds range of species southeast to west China.

SV. Eleven, all in late autumn, and all except one since 1961: Orkney (October 1913), Fair Isle (October 1961), Isles of Scilly (October 1964, October 1968), Lincoln (November 1964), Yorkshire (October 1965), Kent (November 1967), Norfolk (four in October–November 1968). *P.f.fuscatus* in the first case and probably also in the other ten.

Radde's Warbler A
Phylloscopus schwarzi (Radde)

Southeastern Palaearctic. Breeds Siberia from the Russian Altai east to Amurland and Sakhalin, north to Lake Baikal, south to Manchuria and Korea; between 58°N and 38°N. Winters from Burma to Indochina.

Monotypic.

SV. Ten, all in October, and all except one since 1961: Lincoln (1898), Norfolk (1961 and 1968), Fife (1962 and 1968), Kent (1962), Suffolk (1964, and two in 1966), Pembroke (1968).

Yellow-browed Warbler A
Phylloscopus inornatus (Blyth)

Central Palaearctic. Breeds across northern Siberia from the northern Urals east to Anadyr, south to Afghanistan, the northwest Himalayas and northern Mongolia; between 70°N and 30°N. Winters from Afghanistan and India to Malaysia and south China.

P.i.inornatus (Blyth) breeds over the greater part of the species' range but not in the extreme southeast.

SV. Together with the Richard's Pipit *Anthus novaeseelandiae*, this is the most regular of all Siberian vagrants, up to 20 or more having been recorded annually in recent years, from late August to November, but chiefly from late September to mid-October. Annual at Fair Isle; nearly annual on the Isle of May (Fife), the coast of northeast England and north Norfolk, and at the Isles of Scilly and Cape Clear (Cork);

less frequent elsewhere, though it has occurred in most coastal regions and particularly on the remoter offshore islands. Rarely noted inland and almost unknown in spring: several are said to have been seen—Fair Isle, Norfolk, Essex, Devon, and probably elsewhere—in March, April or May, but these records lack proper documentation. There is at least one winter record—Norfolk, December 1967 to January 1968.

Pallas's Warbler A
Phylloscopus proregulus (Pallas)

Central and eastern Palaearctic. Breeds Asia from the Russian Altai eastwards to Sakhalin, south to the Afghan border, Himalayas, northern Mongolia and central China; between 60°N and 28°N. Winters from northern India east to southern China.

P.p.proregulus (Pallas) breeds range of species except in the extreme southeast.

SV. Thirty-nine recorded (one 1896, one 1951, nineteen 1957–66, eighteen in 1968), all in October and November, and all coastal or insular: Isles of Scilly (six), Dorset, Isle of Wight, Sussex (three), Kent (six), Essex, Suffolk (two), Norfolk (four), Lincoln (two), Yorkshire (eight), Durham, Northumberland, Aberdeen, Fair Isle, Cork.

Arctic Warbler A
Phylloscopus borealis (Blasius)

Palaearctic and northwest Nearctic. Breeds across northern Eurasia from arctic Scandinavia to the Bering Straits and into Alaska, north to 75°N on the Taimyr Peninsula, south to about 60°N in Russia, and in Asia to Mongolia, Korea and Japan. Winters in the Oriental region east of India.

P.b.talovka Portenko breeds in the western part of the species' range east to central Siberia and northwest Mongolia.

SV. About 53 recorded, two-thirds of these during 1958–68, when noted in all years except one. Chiefly August–September, with a few in October and one in late July. Principally at Fair Isle and on the east coast from Shetland south to Norfolk, the remainder widely scattered on coasts south and west to the Isles of Scilly, Caernarvon, Cork and Donegal. Subspecies not identified, but unlikely to be other than *P.b.talovka*.

Greenish Warbler A
Phylloscopus trochiloides (Sundevall)

Central and eastern Palaearctic. Breeds from southern Finland, the Baltic States and northeast Germany eastwards across central Russia and Siberia to the Sea of Okhotsk, south to the Ukraine, northern Afghanistan, Mongolia and Manchuria; also through the Himalayas to central China; between 63°N and 27°N. Winters in India and the Indo-Chinese region.

P.t.viridanus Blyth breeds from the Baltic east to the Yenisei, southeast to the northwest Himalayas.

SV. Seventy-one recorded: one 1896, ten 1945–56, the rest 1957–68 (when noted annually). Recorded in all months from June to November, mainly September–October; also five in winter, December to March. Only three inland (including one of those in winter), the remainder widely scattered on the east and south coasts of Britain and Ireland from Shetland to Cork, with a few on islands in the Irish Sea basin and one in Donegal. Some identified as, and probably all, *P.t.viridanus*.

Genus CISTICOLA Kaup

Southern Palaearctic, Ethiopian, Oriental and Australian genus of some 40 species, one breeding in Europe and recorded once as a straggler in the British Isles.

Fan-tailed Warbler A
Cisticola juncidis (Rafinesque)

Palaearctic, Ethiopian, Oriental and Australian. Breeds in Africa (excluding equatorial forest), southern Europe and Mediterranean region, east to China and Japan, Indo-Malaya and northern Australia; between 45°N and 35°S. Mainly sedentary.

SV. Recorded once, Co. Cork, April 1962. Subspecies not determined.

Genus REGULUS Cuvier

Holarctic genus of five species, two in Palaearctic, both breeding in
Europe and both (one marginally) in the British Isles.

Goldcrest   A
Regulus regulus (Linnaeus)

Palaearctic. Breeds Azores and Eurasia from northern Spain, the
British Isles and Scandinavia eastwards (discontinuously in Asia) to
Amurland and Japan, north to Lapland, central Russia and the upper
Irtysh, south to Italy, the Balkans, northern Iran and the Himalayas;
between 70°N and 25°N. Winters in southern parts of the breeding
range and beyond to the Mediterranean region, Iran and south China.

    R.r.regulus (Linnaeus) breeds Europe east to western Siberia and
Asia Minor.

    RB. Widely distributed, breeding throughout Britain and Ire-
land, except in Shetland and only irregularly in Orkney; breeds less
widely in parts of eastern England than elsewhere in Britain, while the
local distribution in northwest Scotland and the Outer Hebrides (where
restricted to only a few localities) is due to the absence of suitably
wooded areas. Apparently mainly sedentary, though there is some
evidence of dispersal in early autumn (especially in the area of the Irish
Sea), when some may emigrate.

    PV and **WV**. Passage and immigration of Continental winter
visitors, late September to November, returning March–April, most
numerous on the British east and south coasts during periodic 'falls' of
migrants in October and, less often, mainly on south coasts, in spring.
An unknown—but perhaps relatively small and variable—proportion
of autumn migrants remains in winter. The area of origin of these
immigrants probably includes central Europe in some years as well as
Scandinavia.

Firecrest   A
Regulus ignicapillus (Temminck)

Western Palaearctic. Breeds Europe from Denmark and northwest
Russia southeast to the Balkans and into Asia Minor, south to the
Mediterranean islands, and southwest to France and Spain, and to
northwest Africa, Madeira and the Canaries; between 55°N and 28°N.

Partially migratory, wintering in southern parts of the breeding range.

R.i.ignicapillus (Temminck) breeds throughout the Eurasian range of the species.

MB or **RB**. Extremely rare. Small breeding population discovered in Hampshire in 1961, where several pairs have been noted annually since, with breeding proved in 1962 and 1965. The migratory status of these birds is uncertain.

PV. Mainly mid-March to April, mid-September to early November, annually in small numbers at both seasons on the English south coast and in still smaller numbers in East Anglia, also less frequently inland in southern England and on the coasts of Wales and southwest Ireland; found only as a rare vagrant in northern England, Scotland and the rest of Ireland.

WV. Small numbers winter regularly in southwest England (Isles of Scilly to Dorset) and occasionally elsewhere along the south coast and inland as far as the English Midlands.

Family MUSCICAPIDAE

Genus FICEDULA Brisson

Palaearctic and Oriental genus of 26 species, ten in Palaearctic; only three breed in Europe and one in the British Isles, where the other two occur as vagrants, one of them annually.

Pied Flycatcher   A
Ficedula hypoleuca (Pallas)

Western Palaearctic. Breeds northern Eurasia from north Scandinavia, Britain and Germany east to the upper Yenisei, south locally to France, Iberia, northern Italy, the Balkans and Crimea, also in northwest

Africa; between 70°N and 35°N. Winters in tropical Africa south to Tanzania.

F.h.hypoleuca (Pallas) breeds Europe east to the Urals and Crimea.

MB. Breeds widely in Wales (all counties except Pembroke and Anglesey) and extends eastwards more locally to Gloucester, Worcester, Shropshire and Cheshire; also breeds widely in northern England from the southern Pennines (mainly Derby), mid-Yorkshire and Westmorland north to the Scottish border, extending more locally north into Dumfries, Kirkcudbright, Selkirk and Midlothian; small, isolated populations exist in south Devon, west Somerset (Exmoor), and, in Scotland, in Clackmannan, and, perhaps not permanently, in Perth and Inverness. Absent as regular breeder elsewhere, though has nested occasionally in several counties, most recently in Cornwall, Lancashire, Roxburgh, Berwick, Ayr, Stirling, Banff and Ross. Resident from mid-April to August.

PV. April into June, mid-August to mid-October. Few in spring, but more widespread in autumn when birds from northern and eastern continental Europe appear in numbers, especially in late August and September on the east and south coasts of Britain, and also regularly in smaller numbers in many other coastal and insular localities elsewhere in Britain and around Ireland.

Collared Flycatcher A
Ficedula albicollis (Temminck)

Western Palaearctic. Breeds chiefly in central and southeast Europe, from the Baltic region (Gotland and the Runo Islands) east to Moscow, south locally to eastern France, northern Italy, Sicily, Greece and the Ukraine, also from Asia Minor east to Transcaspia and northern Iran; between 57°N and 37°N. Winters in tropical Africa, from Ghana and Uganda south to Nyasaland.

F.a.albicollis (Temminck) breeds European range of species (except Greece) east to Moscow and the Ukraine.

SV. Five, all except one in spring: Shetland (May 1947), Caernarvon (May 1957), Essex (September 1962), Orkney (May 1963), Cumberland (June 1964). Subspecies not determined but unlikely to have been other than *F.a.albicollis*.

Red-breasted Flycatcher   A
Ficedula parva (Bechstein)

Palaearctic. Breeds northern Eurasia from Germany east to Anadyr and Kamchatka, north to southern Finland and about 65°N in Siberia, south to Austria, the Balkans, Caucasus, Iran, the Russian Altai and northern Mongolia; between 65°N and 35°N. Winters in southern and southeast Asia, south to Ceylon and Borneo.

F.p.parva (Bechstein) breeds Europe east to eastern Russia.

SV. Formerly scarce and irregular, but in recent years between 30 and 100 individuals have been recorded in every autumn between late August and November, chiefly from mid-September to mid-October. Small numbers, usually in ones and twos but sometimes up to five or more at once, are now recorded fairly regularly in many coastal areas, and annually or nearly so at several bird observatories from Fair Isle to Norfolk, in the Isles of Scilly and the southern Irish Sea basin, and in southwest Ireland. Inland records are infrequent, as are those in spring, when the species has been noted in a number of widely scattered localities between late April and June. Very few have been identified racially, and it is possible that birds of the Siberian subspecies *F.p. albicilla* (Pallas) have occurred in the British Isles as well as nominate *parva*.

Genus MUSCICAPA Brisson

Palaearctic, Oriental and Ethiopian genus of 21 species, six in Palaearctic, only one breeding in Europe and the British Isles.

Spotted Flycatcher   A
Muscicapa striata (Pallas)

Western and central Palaearctic. Breeds Eurasia from northern Scandinavia, the British Isles and Iberia east to northern Mongolia, north to northern Russia and about 60°N in western Siberia, south into northwest Africa, the Mediterranean region, Persian Gulf and west Himalayas; between 70°N and 28°N. Winters in tropical and southern Africa, also in Arabia and northwest India.

M.s.striata (Pallas) breeds across Europe east to the Irtysh in west Siberia, south into northwest Africa, the Mediterranean (not the Balearics, nor Corsica and Sardinia) and to the Black Sea (not Crimea).

MB. Fairly numerous. Widely distributed, breeding in all counties

in Britain and Ireland except Shetland, though only locally in the Hebrides, Caithness and Orkney. Resident from late April to September.
PV. Passage end April into June, August to mid-October. All areas, but at both seasons recorded most numerously on coasts of southern England and the Irish Sea basin, where migrants must be predominantly of British or Irish origin. Smaller numbers occur regularly on the east, especially northeast, coast—north to Fair Isle and Shetland—perhaps mainly northern Continental birds, as some certainly are.

Family **TIMALIIDAE**

Genus **PANURUS** Koch

Palaearctic monospecific genus breeding locally in Europe and the British Isles.

Bearded Tit   A
Panurus biarmicus (Linnaeus)

Palaearctic. Breeds locally from the Netherlands, England, southern France and Spain east across middle and southern Europe and western and central Asia to Manchuria and Ussuriland, north to Lithuania and southwest Siberia, south to Sicily, Greece, Syria and Persian Baluchistan; between 55°N and 30°N. Mainly sedentary, with some dispersal within or to just south of the breeding range.

P.b.biarmicus (Linnaeus) breeds western Europe and east to Lithuania, Yugoslavia, Albania and Greece.

RB (also irruptive visitor). Scarce. Marked recovery of resident population from near extinction in 1947 (when only two to four known pairs) to 200–300 breeding pairs in the 1960s (except in 1963, when reduced to about 140 pairs after hard winter). Until 1960 the species was confined to Norfolk and Suffolk (still its strongholds) but in recent years small colonies have been established (perhaps not permanently) in Essex and Kent and breeding has also taken place in at least four other counties in England, and in Anglesey in 1967. Generally sedentary, but eruptive migration in autumn has occurred annually since 1959. In this period, small numbers of Bearded Tits have been noted in many parts of England and Wales, including some counties in which the species had not previously been recorded. Dispersal was greatest in autumn 1965 (parties and small flocks north to Northumberland and Lancashire, west to Flint, Anglesey and the Isles of Scilly), when immigration from the Netherlands also occurred (seven recoveries of Dutch-ringed birds, plus one ringed in southern England returning to the Netherlands). Immigration of Dutch-ringed birds (two) occurred also in autumn 1966.

Family AEGITHALIDAE

Genus AEGITHALOS Hermann

Palaearctic (also marginally Oriental) genus of five species, only one breeding in Europe and the British Isles.

Long-tailed Tit   A
Aegithalos caudatus (Linnaeus)

Palaearctic. Breeds from Scandinavia (north Norway, central Sweden), the British Isles and Iberia east across Europe and Siberia to Kamchatka, south to Sicily, southern Iran, northern Mongolia and, in the far east, to the Yangtse in China, and Japan; between 70°N (61°N in Asia) and 27°N. Northern populations are irregularly migratory, reaching southern parts of the breeding range in winter.

A.c.caudatus (Linnaeus) breeds from Scandinavia east to the Urals, south to Poland and the Ukraine.

A.c.europaeus (Hermann) breeds continental Europe south of nominate *caudatus* as far as central and eastern France, the Alps and the Balkans.

A.c.rosaceus Mathews breeds British Isles.

RB. Fairly numerous. Widely distributed, breeding in all counties of Britain and Ireland except the Northern Isles, Outer Hebrides (bred 1939) and Caithness (has bred), though perhaps not regularly in extreme southwest Ireland. Sedentary, but with some local post-breeding and winter wandering. *A.c.rosaceus*.

SV. One *A.c.caudatus*, Northumberland, November 1852. One *A.c.europaeus*, Kent, 1882. *A.c.caudatus* is said to have been seen on a few occasions on the east side of Britain, and the only record of the species in Shetland (four birds in April 1860) perhaps refers to this form. Occasional vagrants on the Isles of Scilly (where the species does not breed), and the irregular appearance of apparent migrants at Dungeness, Kent, and elsewhere on the English south coast are of unknown origin.

Family REMIZIDAE

Genus REMIZ Jarocki

Palaearctic monospecific genus, breeding in Europe and recorded once to the British Isles.

Penduline Tit   A
Remiz pendulinus (Linnaeus)

Palaearctic. Breeds locally in eastern Spain, southern France and Italy, and from eastern France, Denmark and Balkans across Russia and southern Siberia to Manchuria, south to Iran, Afghanistan, and in the far east probably to the Yangtse; between 55°N and 30°N. Sedentary or partially migratory, wintering south to Iraq and northwest India.

R.p.pendulinus (Linnaeus) breeds Europe (where recently spreading north and west) east to the Volga and into western Asia Minor.

SV. One, Yorkshire (October 1966). Presumed *R.p. pendulinus*.

Family PARIDAE

Genus PARUS Linnaeus

Palaearctic, Nearctic, Ethiopian and Oriental genus of 41 species, 18 in Palaearctic of which only nine breed in Europe and six in the British Isles.

Marsh Tit   A
Parus palustris Linnaeus

Palaearctic and marginally Oriental. Breeds discontinuously in the west from southern Scandinavia, Britain and the Pyrenees across Europe to the Urals, south to southern Italy and into Turkey, in the east from the Altai east to Sakhalin and south to the Yangtse in China, also in Burma; between 61°N and 25°N. Sedentary.

P.p.dresseri Stejneger breeds Britain and northwest France.

RB. Not scarce. Breeds widely in England and Wales, nowhere numerously, but probably in every county except perhaps Anglesey. In Scotland it is restricted to the extreme southeast: has bred in Roxburgh since 1966, otherwise it is confined to a few pairs in Berwick. Absent from the Isle of Man and (even as a vagrant) Ireland.

Willow Tit   A
Parus montanus von Baldenstein

Palaearctic. Breeds from Scandinavia, Britain and northern France east across northern Eurasia to Kamchatka, north to the tree-line, south to the Alps, central Balkans, Kirghiz Steppes, Mongolia and Japan; between 70°N and 34°N. Essentially sedentary.

P.m.borealis Selys-Longchamps breeds from Scandinavia east to northwest Siberia.

P.m.kleinschmidti Hellmayr breeds Britain.

RB. Not scarce. Widely though rather sparsely distributed in England and Wales (breeding in every county except Anglesey) and in the southwest and central Scottish Lowlands (Wigtown, Kirkcudbright, Dumfries, Lanark, Renfrew, West Lothian, Stirling; perhaps still in Ayr); formerly also in several parts of the Scottish Highlands north to Inverness and Ross, but since about 1950 breeding apparently not recorded in the Highlands. Absent, even as a vagrant, from the Isle of Man and Ireland. Resident, endemic subspecies, *P.m.kleinschmidti*.

SV. One *P.m.borealis*, Gloucester, March 1907. A party of four or five birds seen in Hertford in January 1908 were said to belong to this race; the only record of the species from Fair Isle, in November 1935, was perhaps this race.

Coal Tit   **A**
Parus ater Linnaeus

Palaearctic and marginally Oriental. Breeds from northern Scandinavia, the British Isles and Iberia (also northwest Africa) east across Eurasia to Kamchatka, south to Greece, the Lebanon, Iran, the Himalayas, southeast China and Formosa; between 67°N and 24°N. Northern-most populations are partially migratory, some birds reaching southern parts of the breeding range and just beyond.

P.a.hibernicus Ogilvie-Grant breeds Ireland, except in the northeast where the population tends towards *britannicus*.

P.a.britannicus Sharpe and Dresser breeds Britain, also in northeast Ireland.

P.a.ater Linnaeus breeds continental Europe and northern Asia, except Iberia and parts of China.

RB. Numerous. Widely distributed, breeding in all parts of Britain and Ireland except Shetland, Orkney and until recently the Outer Hebrides (where a few pairs have become established at Stornoway since 1966). Sedentary. *P.a.britannicus* in Britain and northeast Ireland; *P.a.hibernicus* over the rest of Ireland.

SV. Until recently only four specimens and four sight-records of

P.a.ater, but in 1957, and to a lesser extent in 1959, large-scale irruptions from adjacent parts of the Continent (northern France, the Low Countries and northern Germany) occurred in autumn, chiefly October, and affected particularly the coasts of southern and eastern England and the southern Irish Sea. Many of these birds wintered in Britain and there was some evidence of a return passage in the following springs; a few have been recorded in other recent years, mainly in southern England, but also west to Cork.

Crested Tit   A
Parus cristatus Linnaeus

Western Palaearctic. Breeds Scotland and from central Fenno-Scandia east across central Russia to the Urals and south across the greater part of continental Europe to southern Iberia, northern Italy and Greece; between 67°N and 37°N. Mainly sedentary.

    P.c.scoticus (Prazák) breeds Scotland.

    P.c.cristatus Linnaeus breeds Scandinavia. Russia and the eastern Balkans.

    P.c.mitratus C. L. Brehm breeds continental Europe west of nominate *cristatus* except in Brittany and parts of Iberia where replaced by other races.

    RB. Scarce. Distribution restricted to mature pine woods in the east Scottish Highlands, where the species breeds in east Ross, east Inverness, Nairn, Moray and Banff, recently spreading as far as, if not actually into, southeast Sutherland and north Aberdeen. Resident, endemic subspecies, *P.c.scoticus*.

    SV. One example of *P.c.cristatus* (Yorkshire, March 1872) and one of *P.c.mitratus* (Isle of Wight, prior to 1844). Four other specimens of nominate *cristatus* are said to have been collected in the 19th century in Yorkshire, Suffolk (two) and Hampshire. A few sight-records of the species in southern England (mostly in the 19th century) presumably refer to one or the other of these two races.

Great Tit   A
Parus major Linnaeus

Palaearctic and Oriental. Breeds across the greater part of Eurasia from the British Isles to Japan, north to northern Fenno-Scandia and 61°N in east Siberia, south into northwest Africa, Palestine, Iran, Ceylon and

Indonesia; between 68°N and 10°S. Northern populations are partially migratory in varying numbers to more southerly parts of the breeding range.

P.m.major Linnaeus breeds continental Europe (except parts of Greece), also in Sicily, parts of southwest Asia, and in Siberia eastwards to the Transbaikal region.

P.m.newtoni Prazák breeds British Isles, grading into nominate *major* in southeast England.

RB. Abundant. Widely distributed, breeding throughout Britain and Ireland except in Orkney and Shetland; in the Outer Hebrides it is confined to a single locality, Stornoway, where first established 1966. Sedentary, with some movement in autumn and winter by a variable but always small part of the population over distances of up to about 100 miles. *P.m.newtoni*, grading into *P.m.major* in southeast England.

WV. Immigrants from adjacent parts of the Continent (Low Countries, north Germany, probably rarely Scandinavia) arrive irregularly in varying numbers, late September to November, in southern and eastern England (rarely north to Shetland, occasionally west to southern Ireland), returning mid-March to mid-April, chiefly from southeast England. Marked irruptions in some years (in recent years, notably 1957, also 1954, 1959) but in others very few arrivals noted. *P.m.major*.

Blue Tit   A
Parus caeruleus Linnaeus

Western Palaearctic. Breeds from the British Isles, Scandinavia and central Russia south across almost the whole of Europe and to north-west Africa, the Canaries, Asia Minor, southern Iran and southwest Transcaspia; between 65°N and 27°N. Northern populations are partially or erratically migratory, moving south within the breeding range.

P.c.obscurus Prazák breeds British Isles and Channel Islands.

P.c.caeruleus Linnaeus breeds continental Europe and Sicily except in southern Iberia, the Crimea and southeast Russia.

RB. Abundant. Widely distributed, breeding in all counties in Britain and Ireland except Orkney and Shetland; in the Outer Hebrides it is confined to a single locality, Stornoway, where first established in 1963. Essentially sedentary, but movements within the British Isles of up to 100 miles and more have been recorded. *P.c.obscurus*.

WV. Immigrants from adjacent parts of the Continent (chiefly the

Low Countries and Germany, perhaps occasionally Scandinavia) arrive in very variable numbers, chiefly in southern and eastern England (very rare as far north as Orkney and Shetland), late September to November, returning in smaller numbers (or less conspicuously) mainly late March to mid-April. Marked irruptions in some years, notably in autumn 1957, while in others practically no arrivals noticed. Immigrants must belong to subspecies *P.c.caeruleus* (from which the endemic *obscurus* is poorly differentiated) though relatively few British specimens have been assigned to this race.

Family SITTIDAE

Genus SITTA Linnaeus

Palaearctic, Nearctic, Oriental and northern Neotropical genus of 17 species, nine in Palaearctic, three breeding in Europe and one in the British Isles.

Nuthatch   A
Sitta europaea Linnaeus

Palaearctic and Oriental. Breeds from southern Scandinavia (not Finland), England and Iberia east across Eurasia to Anadyr and Kamchatka, south into Morocco, Sicily, Palestine, southern Iran, and in the far east through Japan, China, and Indo-China to India; between 66°N and 10°N. Essentially sedentary, but large-scale irruptive movements to the west or south sometimes occur among Siberian populations.

S.e.caesia Wolf breeds Europe south of the Baltic and west of Russia except in parts of Iberia and Mediterranean Europe; exact limits of the range are uncertain.

RB. Not scarce. Widely distributed in England and Wales south of a line from the Mersey to the Wash, and much more locally north of this line as far as Westmorland and south Northumberland. Sedentary;

occasionally wanders to southern Scotland: autumn/winter records in Perth in 1963–64, and Kirkcudbright in 1966, were the first since 1945. Absent, even as a vagrant, from the Isle of Man and Ireland.

Genus TICHODROMA Illiger

Palaearctic, also marginally Oriental, monospecific genus, occurring in the British Isles as a rare vagrant.

Wallcreeper   A
Tichodroma muraria (Linnaeus)

Southern Palaearctic and northern Oriental. Breeds mountains of southern Europe, southwest and south-central Asia, from Iberia, the Pyrenees, Alps and Carpathians east to Turkestan, southern Mongolia, Himalayas and China; between 49°N and 28°N. Sedentary, movements limited to altitudinal shifts to lower levels in winter.

T.m.muraria (Linnaeus) breeds southern Europe and southwest Asia east as far as western Iran.

SV. Six (including some records which lack convincing documentation): Norfolk (October 1792), Lancashire (May 1872), Sussex (about 1886, and June 1938), Somerset (September 1901), Dorset (April 1920). Presumed *T.m. muraria*.

Family CERTHIIDAE

Genus CERTHIA Linnaeus

Palaearctic, Nearctic and marginally Oriental genus of five species, all in Palaearctic; two breed in Europe and one in the British Isles (where the other has not been recorded although it nests throughout France, including the Channel Islands).

Treecreeper   **A**
Certhia familiaris Linnaeus

Holarctic. Breeds from southern Scandinavia, the British Isles, central France and the Pyrenees east across Eurasia to Sakhalin, south to Italy, the Caucasus, northern Iran, the Himalayas, central China and Japan; also in North and Central America (where known as Brown Creeper) from southeast Alaska to Newfoundland, south to Nicaragua and North Carolina; between 70°N and 15°N. Northernmost and highest montane populations are partially migratory.

    C.f.familiaris Linnaeus breeds from Fenno-Scandia and north Russia through eastern Europe to central Greece, and in western Siberia to the Yenisei.

    C.f.britannica Ridgway breeds in the British Isles.

    RB. Widely distributed, breeding in every county in Britain and Ireland except Orkney and Shetland, though only locally in northwest Scotland, and in the Outer Hebrides confined to Stornoway Woods, Lewis. Sedentary, endemic race, *C.f.britannica*.

    SV. Of seven recorded in Shetland and at Fair Isle (September to December, one April), four have been referred to nominate *familiaris*, and the other three probably also belonged to this race, which has otherwise been recorded in Britain only in the Outer Hebrides (October 1949), Fife (September 1965), Berwick (September 1899), Suffolk (March 1941) and Lincoln (March 1947). The origin of vagrants which have occurred on various other small islands around the British and Irish coasts is not known.

Family EMBERIZIDAE

Genus EMBERIZA Linnaeus

Palaearctic, Oriental and Ethiopian genus of 38 species, 31 in Palaearctic; 13 breed in Europe but only four in the British Isles, where the other eight have been recorded, one as a regular migrant and seven as vagrants.

Corn Bunting
Emberiza calandra Linnaeus

A

Western Palaearctic. Breeds Europe and western Asia north to Scotland, southern Sweden, the Baltic States and southern Russia, eastwards to Turkestan, south to the Mediterranean islands, into North Africa (to the northern Sahara, also the Canaries), Palestine and Iraq; between 61°N and 28°N. Partially migratory, wintering in southern parts of the breeding range, and noted south of it in Egypt, southwest Asia and northwest India.

E.c.calandra Linnaeus breeds Europe, the Canaries and North Africa.

RB. Not scarce. Breeds widely in England and Scotland from the English Channel coast north to the Outer Hebrides and Shetland, but it is extremely local in several counties and is absent from wide areas of southwest England (though it breeds in parts of Cornwall), the west Midlands, and northwest and central Scotland. Once widespread in Wales, it has now virtually disappeared, being currently confined to part of Flint; it has also greatly decreased in Ireland, where it is now restricted to a few coastal districts in Kerry, Mayo, Donegal, Antrim, Wexford and Waterford, with perhaps the odd pair or two still in Cork and Galway. The population is essentially sedentary; some birds may migrate but there is no adequate ringing evidence.

PV and **WV**. Status obscure. Migrants of unknown origin are recorded fairly regularly in very small numbers in spring and autumn on parts of the British east coast north to Shetland, also in western England and parts of Wales; the only foreign ringing recovery concerns a bird ringed in Kent in February and recovered in the Pas-de-Calais, France, three months later.

Yellowhammer
Emberiza citrinella Linnaeus

A

Western Palaearctic. Breeds Europe and west Asia, from northern Fenno-Scandia, the British Isles and northern Spain, eastwards to central Siberia, north to northern Russia, south to the Mediterranean and Black Seas, also in the Caucasus and Iranian regions; between 70°N and 28°N. Northern populations are migratory, wintering in southern parts of the breeding range and beyond it into North Africa, and in southwest and central Asia.

E.c.caliginosa Clancey breeds Britain and Ireland except southeast England (see below).

E.c.citrinella Linnaeus breeds western, northern and parts of eastern Europe, and southeast England.

RB. Abundant. Widely distributed, breeding in every county in Britain and Ireland except the Outer Hebrides and Shetland. Mainly sedentary, and no evidence of emigration. The subspecies breeding in Ireland and most of northern and western Britain is *E.c.caliginosa*, probably grading into nominate *citrinella* farther south and east, and replaced by this subspecies in southeast England; but differences between the two forms are slight.

PV and **WV**. Status obscure. Migrants of unknown origin—but some of them probably from northern Europe—are recorded from late September to November and from March to May on the English east coast, at Fair Isle and in Shetland (where the species also occurs as a winter visitor), also less frequently in other areas (e.g. the Outer Hebrides and Isles of Scilly) where there is no resident population.

Pine Bunting   A
Emberiza leucocephala S. G. Gmelin

Central and eastern Palaearctic. Breeds from eastern Russia eastwards across Siberia to the Pacific coast and Sakhalin, north to the tree-line, south to the mountain rim of central Asia; between 67°N and 47°N; also farther south in the mountains of Turkestan and western China. Migratory, wintering south of the breeding range from northern Iraq eastwards through India to China; also noted in winter in central Asia.

E.l.leucocephala S. G. Gmelin breeds whole range of species except western China.

SV. Three, all males in autumn: Fair Isle (October 1911), Orkney (October 1943 and August 1967). The possibility that the 1967 bird (and perhaps the other two) was an escape from captivity cannot be excluded.

Rock Bunting   A
Emberiza cia Linnaeus

Southern Palaearctic. Breeds in mountain regions from Iberia, southern France and southern Germany east through southern Europe, southwest and central Asia to China, south to the Himalayas; also in northwest Africa; between 53°N and 27°N. Essentially sedentary but wanders to some extent.

E.c.cia Linnaeus breeds Europe (except southern Spain) and the Levant.

SV. Six: Sussex (two in October 1902), Kent (May 1905), Pembroke (August 1958), Yorkshire (February–March 1965), Caernarvon (June 1967). Subspecies not determined, but wild vagrants are unlikely to be other than *E.c.cia*. The species is imported into this country as a cagebird, so the possibility that the recent records refer to escapes from captivity cannot be entirely excluded.

Ortolan Bunting   A
Emberiza hortulana Linnaeus

Western Palaearctic. Breeds Eurasia from Fenno-Scandia, Germany (not Denmark), France (except in the northwest) and Iberia east across the Urals and through Asia Minor to the Altai and Afghanistan, south to Italy, Crete, Palestine and southern Iran; between 69°N and 32°N. Winters in parts of the Mediterranean region, eastern tropical Africa (Sudan to Somalia) and south Arabia.
Monotypic.
PV. Small numbers occur annually in autumn, August to November (mainly September), on the British east coast (chiefly Fair Isle and Norfolk) and in the Isles of Scilly, and fairly regularly along the English south coast and on islands of the southern Irish Sea and southwest Ireland. In spring, small numbers are recorded almost annually from late April to June at Fair Isle, but much less often elsewhere. Rarely more than twelve together, but once (in September 1956) as many as 100 in the Isles of Scilly. Rarely noted inland.

Cretzschmar's Bunting   A
Emberiza caesia Cretzschmar

Southwestern Palaearctic. Breeds Yugoslavia, Greece, Asia Minor, Cyprus and the Near East south to northern Palestine; between 45°N and 33°N. Winters chiefly in the Sudan.
Monotypic.
SV. One, Fair Isle (June 1967).

Cirl Bunting   A
Emberiza cirlus Linnaeus

Western Palaearctic. Breeds northwest Africa, and from Mediterranean Europe north through France to southern England and southwest

Germany, and east into Asia Minor; between 52°N and 30°N. Resident, movements being limited to post-breeding wandering.

E.c.cirlus Linnaeus breeds range of species except in Corsica and Sardinia.

RB. Scarce. Very locally distributed, decreasing, and now virtually confined to those English counties lying south and southwest of the River Thames, with a few pairs north to south Worcester and west Hertford. Was formerly more widespread, breeding in various parts of Wales and occasionally north to Cumberland (where a pair bred as recently as 1955). Sedentary, but vagrants of unknown origin have reached southern Scotland (especially the Isle of May, Fife) on a few occasions, and Ireland once (Donegal, August 1902).

Little Bunting   A
Emberiza pusilla Pallas

Northern Palaearctic. Breeds from east Lapland eastwards to northeast Siberia and south to 60°N in Russia and the middle Yenisei valley and southern Yakutia in Siberia; between 72°N and 57°N. Winters in northern tropical Asia from northeast India eastwards to southern China.

Monotypic.

SV. Over 150 recorded, usually singly but occasionally two or three together. Noted annually in recent years, with about 60 in all during 1958–68. Mainly September–October, also March–May and November, with single records in February and December (both Dublin). Well over half the records are from Fair Isle (where almost annual in autumn) and the remainder are widely scattered, chiefly on coasts and marine islands, with a few inland especially in spring.

Rustic Bunting   A
Emberiza rustica Pallas

Northern Palaearctic. Breeds from northern Fenno-Scandia through Russia and Siberia to Kamchatka, north to the tree-line, and south to 59°N in Russia and the mountains of southern Siberia; between 69°N and 48°N. Winters in northern and central China and Japan.

E.r.rustica Pallas breeds range of species except the Anadyr region and Kamchatka.

SV. Almost 70 recorded, over half of these during 1958–68 when noted annually (except 1961); usually singly, rarely two together. Mainly September–October, occasionally May–June, rarely March, April and November. Recorded chiefly on the British, especially Scottish, east coast (almost annually at Fair Isle); other records are from the Isles of Scilly (six), Hertford, Yorkshire, Pembroke, Sutherland and Outer Hebrides; there is only one Irish record, from Cork. A female ringed at Fair Isle in June 1963 was recovered in October 1963 in Greece.

Yellow-breasted Bunting A
Emberiza aureola Pallas

Northern Palaearctic. Breeds from Finland through Russia and Siberia to Kamchatka and the Kurile Islands, north to 65°N in Russia, the Arctic Circle and tree-line in Siberia, south to central Russia, Mongolia and Manchuria; between 68°N and 42°N. Winters in tropical Asia from northeast India and southern China south to the Malay Peninsula.

E.a. aureola Pallas breeds range of species except in the extreme east.

SV. Twenty-seven recorded (six 1905–13, three 1936–51, eighteen 1957–68); once two, the rest singly; all September except one July, two August and two October. Noted Fair Isle (13), Fife (six, all on the Isle of May) and Norfolk (three), with one in each of Cork, Donegal, Orkney, Shetland and St. Kilda. With the exception of the three in Norfolk (all on the north coast), all of the records are from islands.

Black-headed Bunting A
Emberiza melanocephala Scopoli

Southwestern Palaearctic. Breeds from eastern Italy eastwards to Iran, north to the valleys of the lower Danube and lower Volga, south to the Balkan Peninsula, Asia Minor and the Levant coast; between 48°N and 32°N. Winters in northern and central India.

Monotypic.

SV. About 25 recorded, 16 of these since 1958, some (and perhaps the majority) of which are likely to have escaped from captivity. Including believed escapes, the records are mostly for May–June, with fewer July–November, and one in April. Five have been noted at Fair Isle, and one or two in each of the Isles of Scilly, Sussex, Pembroke, Caernarvon, Leicester, Nottingham, Fife, Argyll, Orkney, Shetland and Wexford.

Reed Bunting A
Emberiza schoeniclus (Linnaeus)

Palaearctic (except northeast). Breeds through most of Europe and northern Asia from the Atlantic to Pacific, north to the tree-line in Europe and Siberia, south to Mediterranean Europe, Turkestan and northern Japan; also locally in northwest Morocco; between 71°N and 34°N. Northern populations are migratory, wintering in southern parts of the breeding range and beyond it in Asia from Iraq to northwest India, and in northeast China and southern Japan.

E.s.schoeniclus (Linnaeus) breeds northern Europe, south to France, western Austria and central Russia; intergrades with other races in the south and east.

RB. Fairly numerous. Widely distributed, breeding in every county in Britain and Ireland, including, since about 1949, one or two pairs in Shetland. Mainly sedentary, but some upland and northern breeding areas are deserted in winter; short-distance movements occur within the British Isles (notably in October, March–April, and in hard weather) and some birds may emigrate, though there is no evidence of this from ringing.

PV and **WV**. Passage mainly late September to October and late March to May, chiefly on and near the British east and southeast coasts, including small numbers regularly at Fair Isle (where the species does not breed). Migration at these times includes the arrival and departure of winter visitors from the adjacent Continent, as well as transients from farther afield, as suggested by a winter recovery in the Landes, France, of a migrant ringed at Fair Isle in the previous October, and the recoveries in Sweden in April–May of birds ringed earlier in the spring in Gloucester and Suffolk.

Genus CALCARIUS Bechstein

Holarctic genus of three species, two confined to Nearctic, the other circumpolar and occurring in the British Isles as a scarce migrant and rare winter visitor.

Lapland Bunting A
Calcarius lapponicus (Linnaeus)

Holarctic. Breeding distribution circumpolar in arctic and subarctic areas north of the tree-line, from Scandinavia east to Kamchatka, the

Bering Sea islands, Alaska east to Labrador and Greenland; also in the alpine zone in Scandinavian mountains and southern Alaska; between 78°N and 63°N. Winters south as far as central North America, central Asia and northern China; in western Europe is known on coasts of North Sea but the main winter range of European breeding birds is not established.

C.l.lapponicus (Linnaeus) breeds range of species except the Bering Sea area, Alaska and northwest Canada.

PV. Regular in variable but generally small numbers on autumn passage, late August to early November, chiefly on northern and western islands in the northwest of the British Isles (Donegal to Shetland) but regularly also on the British east coast and in Sussex, Dorset and the Isles of Scilly; recorded quite frequently on other coasts, but only rarely inland. Much scarcer and largely irregular in spring, but small numbers occur almost annually at Fair Isle between mid-April and mid-May. The majority of migrants noted in Britain and Ireland almost certainly originate from Greenland rather than Scandinavia.

WV. Very small, variable numbers overwinter on parts of the English east coast, occasionally on the south coast, and there are a few winter records from other parts of Britain and Ireland.

Genus PLECTROPHENAX Stejneger

Holarctic (circumpolar) monospecific genus, breeding only marginally in the British Isles but occurring more commonly as a migrant and winter visitor.

Snow Bunting   A
Plectrophenax nivalis (Linnaeus)

Holarctic. Breeding distribution circumpolar in arctic and subarctic areas of the Eurasian and American continents and adjacent islands in the North Atlantic and Bering Sea, north to the summer limit of ice in Greenland, south to the continental coasts of the Arctic Ocean, the Faeroes, Scotland and Scandinavia; between 83°N and 52°N. High-arctic and continental populations winter south to central Europe and Asia and the northern United States; low-arctic and insular populations are mainly resident.

P.n.nivalis (Linnaeus) breeds range of species except Iceland, Siberia and the Bering Sea area.

P.n.insulae Salomonsen breeds Iceland.

RB. Extremely scarce. Very small and variable numbers breed in Scotland, where the species is now virtually confined to a few localities in the highest Cairngorms; it formerly bred at least occasionally on other high Scottish hills, and it may still do so in west Ross and on Ben Nevis; it has bred in the past on St. Kilda and in Shetland. The Cairngorms population is comprised of birds showing the characters of both *P.n.nivalis* and *P.n.insulae*.

PV and **WV.** Passage and arrival of winter visitors, mid-September to November, returning March to mid-April (occasionally into May and early June in Scotland and the Northern Isles). Passage noted from the Northern Isles southwards along both eastern and western coasts, and includes birds originating from Greenland as well as Scandinavia. Winters on coasts in many parts of the British Isles (though only rarely in west Wales and southwest England), also on mountains and hills inland, especially in Scotland. Usually *P.n.nivalis*, but *P.n.insulae* (which is believed to be mainly sedentary) is said to have occurred in the Outer Hebrides and at Fair Isle.

Genus ZONOTRICHIA Swainson

Nearctic and Neotropical genus of nine species, three of which have wandered to the British Isles.

Fox Sparrow A
Zonotrichia iliaca (Merrem)

Nearctic. Breeds from northern Alaska and Canada, south to California, the United States/Canadian border, and Newfoundland; between 70°N and 35°N. Winters as far south as north Mexico and the southern United States.

SV. One: Down (June 1961). Subspecific identification not attempted.

Song Sparrow A
Zonotrichia melodia (Wilson)

Nearctic. Breeds from the Aleutians, south Alaska and northern Canada southwards to central Mexico and the southeastern United

States; between 62°N and 35°N. Partially migratory, northern populations wintering south to Mexico and Florida.

SV. Two: Fair Isle (April–May 1959) and Yorkshire (May 1964). Subspecific identifications not attempted.

White-throated Sparrow A
Zonotrichia albicollis (Gmelin)

Northern Nearctic. Breeds from south Yukon, central Mackenzie and Labrador south to southwest and south-central Canada and the northeastern United States; between 65°N and 38°N. Winters south of the breeding range as far as north Mexico and the Gulf coast of the United States.

Monotypic.

SV. Eight, all except one since 1961: Outer Hebrides (May 1909), Hampshire (May 1961), Lancashire (June 1965), Fair Isle (May 1966), Cork (April 1967), Caernarvon (October–November 1967), Sussex (October 1968), Suffolk (November 1968–January 1969). The species has been imported into this country as a cage-bird in recent years, but numbers have been small and most if not all of the above records probably refer to birds of wild origin.

Genus JUNCO Wagler

Nearctic and very marginally Neotropical genus of three species, one of which has wandered to the British Isles.

Slate-coloured Junco A
Junco hyemalis (Linnaeus)

Nearctic. Breeds from north Alaska, north British Columbia and north Canada, south to the Prairie provinces and Appalachian Mountains; between 70°N and 33°N. (Replaced by close allies—perhaps races—from the United States/Mexico border south to Guatemala.) Winters in the United States south to the Gulf and Atlantic coastlands.

J.h.hyemalis (Linnaeus) breeds range of species except British Columbia and the Appalachians.

SV. Four: Clare (May 1905), Kent (May 1960) and Shetland (May 1966, May 1967). The possibility that the three recorded most recently had escaped from captivity cannot be entirely excluded.

EMBERIZIDAE

Genus PIPILO Vieillot

New World, essentially Nearctic, genus of seven species, one of which has wandered to the British Isles.

Rufous-sided Towhee A
Pipilo erythrophthalmus (Linnaeus)

Nearctic and northern Neotropical. Breeds from British Columbia, south Manitoba and Maine south to Guatemala and Florida; between 51°N and 25°N. Winters within the breeding range south of British Columbia and Massachusetts.

P.e.erythrophthalmus (Linnaeus) breeds in the northeastern part of the range, west to south Manitoba, south to Oklahoma and Georgia.

SV. One, Lundy, Devon (June 1966). Subspecies not determined, but unlikely to have been other than nominate *erythrophthalmus*.

Genus PHEUCTICUS Reichenbach

Nearctic and Neotropical genus of four species, two in Nearctic, one of which has wandered to Europe and the British Isles.

Rose-breasted Grosbeak A
Pheucticus ludovicianus (Linnaeus)

Central and eastern Nearctic. Breeds from British Columbia, south-central Canada and Nova Scotia south to Missouri and the Appalachian Mountains; between 62°N and 33°N. Winters from south Mexico to northwestern South America.

Monotypic. (Replaced by close allies, perhaps races, in the western North America and Mexico.)

SV. Four, all since 1957: Antrim (November 1957), Cork (October 1962), Isles of Scilly (October 1966), Pembroke (October 1967).

Genus PIRANGA Vieillot

Neotropical and Nearctic genus of nine species, four in Nearctic, at least one of which has wandered to the British Isles.

Summer Tanager A
Piranga rubra (Linnaeus)

Southern Nearctic. Breeds from California, south Nebraska, Ohio and Delaware south to central Mexico; between 42°N and 25°N. Winters from south Mexico to northern South America.

P.r.rubra (Linnaeus) breeds range of species except in Mexico and the arid parts of the western United States.

SV. One, Caernarvon (September 1957). No subspecific identification attempted, but probably nominate *rubra*. A tanager recorded in Down (October 1963) was either this species or Scarlet Tanager *P.olivacea*.

Family PARULIDAE

Genus MNIOTILTA Vieillot

Nearctic monospecific genus, recorded once in the British Isles.

Black-and-white Warbler A
Mniotilta varia (Linnaeus)

Nearctic. Breeds from south Mackenzie, central Manitoba and Newfoundland south to Texas and South Carolina; between 65°N and 30°N. Winters from the southern United States south to Colombia and Venezuela.

Monotypic.
SV. One, Shetland (October 1936).

Genus PARULA Bonaparte

Nearctic genus of three species, one of which has wandered to the British Isles.

K

Parula Warbler A
Parula americana (Linnaeus)

Nearctic. Breeds eastern North America from southeast Manitoba and Nova Scotia south to Texas and Florida; between 49°N and 27°N. Winters from Mexico and Florida south to Nicaragua and the Antilles. Monotypic.

SV. Three, all since 1966: Isles of Scilly (October 1966), Cornwall (November 1967), Dorset (October 1968).

Genus DENDROICA Gray

Nearctic and northern Neotropical genus of 26 species, three of which have wandered to the British Isles.

Yellow Warbler A
Dendroica petechia (Linnaeus)

Nearctic and northwestern Neotropical. Breeds from Alaska and Labrador south through North, Central and South America to Peru and Venezuela; between 70°N and 15°S. Winters mainly in Central and South America.

SV. One, Caernarvon (August 1964). Specimen preserved but subspecies not determinable.

Myrtle Warbler A
Dendroica coronata (Linnaeus)

Nearctic. Breeds from the tree-limit in northern Alaska and Canada east to Labrador and south to the northeast United States; between 70°N and 41°N. Winters from the southern part of the breeding range south to Panama and the West Indies.

SV. Three: two in Devon, on the mainland (January–February 1955) and Lundy (November 1960), and one on the Isles of Scilly (October 1968). Specimen preserved in first case, but subspecific identification not known to have been attempted. On geographical grounds, *D.c. coronata* (Linnaeus), which breeds over the whole range of the species except in extreme northwest Canada and Alaska, is the subspecies most likely to have been involved.

Blackpoll Warbler A
Dendroica striata (Forster)

Nearctic. Breeds across northern North America from northern Alaska to northern Labrador and Newfoundland, southwards to central British Columbia, central Ontario and Massachusetts; between 68°N and 43°N. Winters in South America from Venezuela south to Chile and Brazil.
Monotypic.
SV. Two, both in October 1968; one on the Isles of Scilly, the other in Caernarvon.

Genus SETOPHAGA Swainson

Nearctic and Neotropical monospecific genus, which has wandered to Europe and the British Isles.

American Redstart A
Setophaga ruticilla (Linnaeus)

Nearctic. Breeds from southeast Alaska, Mackenzie, northern Ontario and Newfoundland south to Oregon, Oklahoma and Georgia; between 66°N and 34°N. Winters from southern Baja California and Cuba south to Ecuador and northern Brazil.
SV. Two: Cornwall (October 1967), Cork (October 1968).

Genus SEIURUS Swainson

Nearctic genus of three species, one of which has wandered to Europe and the British Isles.

Northern Waterthrush A
Seiurus noveboracensis (Gmelin)

Nearctic. Breeds from Alaska, north Mackenzie, Labrador and Newfoundland south to the northern United States; between 70°N and 42°N. Winters mainly in Central and northeastern South America.
Monotypic.
SV. Two, both on the Isles of Scilly (September–October 1958, October 1968).

Genus GEOTHLYPIS Cabanis

Neotropical and Nearctic genus of 14 species, of which one species, the only one found widely in North America, has wandered to the British Isles.

Yellowthroat A
Geothlypis trichas (Linnaeus)

Nearctic. Breeds from southeast Alaska across Canada to Newfoundland, and south to Mexico and Florida; between 62°N and 18°N. Winters from the southern United States to Panama and the Antilles.

    SV. One: Lundy, Devon (November 1954). Race not determined.

Family VIREONIDAE

Genus VIREO Vieillot

New World, predominantly Nearctic, genus of 25 species, one of which has wandered to the British Isles.

Red-eyed Vireo A
Vireo olivaceus (Linnaeus)

Nearctic. Breeds from British Columbia, south Mackenzie and Nova Scotia south to the Gulf coast of North America and Florida; between 65°N and 27°N. Winters in South America in the Amazon basin.

    Monotypic.

    SV. Six records involving seven birds, all in October and all since 1951: Wexford (1951), Isles of Scilly (two in 1962; 1966, 1968), Cork (1967), Pembroke (1967).

Family ICTERIDAE

Genus ICTERUS Brisson

New World, predominantly Neotropical, genus of 24 species, one of which has wandered to the British Isles.

Baltimore Oriole A
Icterus galbula (Linnaeus)

Nearctic. Breeds from central Alberta, southern Ontario and Nova Scotia south to Oklahoma, Louisiana and Georgia; between 57°N and 30°N. Winters from Mexico through Central America to Colombia and Venezuela.

Monotypic.

SV. Ten, all since 1958, one in May, the rest all in late September or October: Devon (October 1958, two in October 1967), Sussex (October 1962), Isle of Man (October 1963), Cornwall (October 1966, May 1968), Pembroke (October 1967), Isles of Scilly (October 1967, September–October 1968).

Genus DOLICHONYX Swainson

Nearctic monospecific genus, recorded twice in the British Isles.

Bobolink A
Dolichonyx oryzivorus (Linnaeus)

Nearctic. Breeds across southern Canada and the northern United States from British Columbia and north California in the west to Nova Scotia and New Jersey in the east; between 55°N and 37°N. Winters in South America in Bolivia, Brazil, Paraguay and the northern Argentine.

Monotypic.

SV. Two, both on the Isles of Scilly (September 1962, October 1968).

Family FRINGILLIDAE

Genus FRINGILLA Linnaeus

Western and northern Palaearctic genus of three species, two breeding in Europe and one in the British Isles, the other also having bred but occurring mainly as a winter visitor.

Chaffinch   **A**
Fringilla coelebs Linnaeus

Western and central Palaearctic. Breeds in almost the whole of Europe and western Asia east to central Siberia and Transcaspia, north to the tree-line in Russia and western Siberia, south to the Canaries, northwest Africa, the Lebanon and Iran; between 70°N and 28°N. Northern populations are migratory, wintering in southern parts of the breeding range and beyond it into Egypt, Iraq and Afghanistan.

    F.c. gengleri Kleinschmidt breeds Britain and Ireland.

    F.c.coelebs Linnaeus breeds Eurasian range except British Isles, Crete, Crimea and southwest Asia.

    RB. Abundant. Widely distributed, breeding in all counties in Britain and Ireland except Shetland. Resident, endemic subspecies, *F.c. gengleri*.

    WV (also **PV**). Winter visitors, belonging to the subspecies *F.c. coelebs*, from northwest Europe (especially, as shown by ringing recoveries, from the Low Countries, northern Germany, Denmark, Norway, Sweden and Finland) are widespread in southern Britain and Ireland, arriving on the British east and south coasts from late September to mid-November, and returning mainly from the east coast in March–

April and into May. Diurnal autumn passage movements are often conspicuous inland as well as on coasts owing to concentrated migration streams, notably from Cap Gris Nez (France) into and across southeast England; spring passage tends to be less conspicuous as migrants pass over higher and are less concentrated. Passage movements at both seasons may include a small number of transient migrants.

Brambling A
Fringilla montifringilla Linnaeus

Northern Palaearctic. Breeds across northern Eurasia from Norway east to Kamchatka, north to the tree-line, south to central Sweden, the northern Baltic States, northwest Mongolia and the Amur basin; between 70°N and 50°N. Winters south of the breeding range as far as northwest Africa, the Mediterranean islands, Iraq, northwest India and southern China.

Monotypic.

CB. Bred in Sutherland in 1920, and reported to have bred in Perth, Ross and Inverness. No recent proved breeding records but birds are occasionally seen holding territory in northern Scotland in summer.

WV and **PV**. Winter visitors (presumably mainly from northern Europe, especially Scandinavia, as shown by ringing recoveries, rather than from farther east) are distributed widely and in rather variable numbers, in Britain and Ireland, except in northern Scotland and western Ireland where the species is recorded only irregularly. Arrives on the British east and south coasts, mainly from late September to mid-November; returns mainly from March to early May. Passage movements at both seasons probably include transient visitors, perhaps wintering in southern France or Iberia, as indicated by a migrant ringed in Yorkshire in October and recovered in southern France three months later. Individuals may winter in areas several hundred miles apart in different years and there may also be extensive movements within a winter. During cold weather, westward and southward movements occur within the British Isles, and include emigration across the English Channel.

Genus SERINUS Koch

Southern Palaearctic and Ethiopian genus of 32 species, six in Palaearctic; two breed in Europe and wander to the British Isles, where one of them is becoming increasingly more frequent and has bred in at least one recent year.

Serin   A
Serinus serinus (Linnaeus)

Southwestern Palaearctic. Breeds in western and central Europe (where it is gradually extending its range northwards) from Iberia east to the Ukraine, north (through France and the eastern Netherlands) to southern Sweden and the Baltic States, south to the Mediterranean islands, also in northwest Africa and Asia Minor; between 60°N and 30°N. Partially migratory, wintering in southern parts of the breeding range and beyond it to Egypt.

Monotypic.

CB. A pair bred successfully in southern England in May 1967 and there is also circumstantial evidence that a pair nested at a different locality in the same year. Breeding followed a small influx of the species in the previous October to December.

SV. About 105 records (156 birds), more than 50 of these during 1966–68. During 1959–68 it was recorded almost annually, most often in May, but also from March to August and in October–November. Earlier records were mostly November to May, and since 1966 winter records have again predominated. Noted chiefly in English south coast counties (lately especially in southwest England), with a few in eastern England north to Durham; only five Wales (Carmarthen, Pembroke), five Scotland (including one Shetland in November, and three Fair Isle, all May), and four Ireland (two Dublin, two Cork).

Citril Finch   B
Serinus citrinella (Pallas)

Southwestern Palaearctic. Breeds in montane forests of southern Europe from Spain east to Austria and north to southern Germany, also in the Balearic Islands, Corsica and Sardinia; between 49°N and 39°N. Resident, wandering to lower levels in winter.

S.c.citrinella (Pallas) breeds range of species except in Corsica and Sardinia.

SV. One, Norfolk (January 1904).

Genus CARDUELIS Brisson

Palaearctic, Nearctic, Ethiopian, Oriental and Neotropical genus of 24 species, only seven in Palaearctic, three breeding in Europe and the British Isles.

Greenfinch A
Carduelis chloris (Linnaeus)

Western Palaearctic. Breeds from central Fenno-Scandia, British Isles and Iberia eastwards across Europe to the Urals and through Asia Minor, northern Iran and southern Transcaspia to Russian Turkestan, south into northwest Africa, Mediterranean Europe and Jordan; between 65°N and 30°N. Replaced by close ally (perhaps race) in eastern Asia. Generally resident, but in winter some birds reach south as far as Cyrenaica and Afghanistan. Introduced Australia and New Zealand.

C.c.chloris (Linnaeus) breeds Scandinavia east to the Urals, south to the British Isles, northern France, Switzerland and Hungary; also in Corsica and Sardinia.

RB. Numerous. Widely distributed, breeding in all counties in Britain and Ireland except Shetland. Mainly resident but some individuals undertake long-distance movements within the British Isles, especially in winter during hard weather, when some emigrate across the English Channel, reaching as far south as Spain.

WV. Immigration of winter visitors on an unknown but probably small scale takes place in October–November, returning probably in March–April, mainly on the coasts of southeast England. A few transient migrants may also occur at these times and small numbers of Greenfinches are recorded regularly as far north as Fair Isle. The origin of immigrants is largely unknown; a limited amount of ringing evidence suggests that most come from adjacent parts of continental Europe.

Goldfinch A
Carduelis carduelis (Linnaeus)

Western and central Palaearctic. Breeds from southern Fenno-Scandia, British Isles and Iberia east through Europe and western Asia to northwest Mongolia, Turkestan and the western Himalayas, north to northern Russia and 58°N in western Siberia, south into northwest Africa and the Canaries, the Mediterranean islands, Near East, southern Iran and northwest India; between 64°N and 27°N. Partially migratory, the northern populations wintering in southern parts of the breeding range and beyond it to Egypt, northern Arabia and Baluchistan. Introduced North America, Bermuda, Argentine, Australia and New Zealand.

C.c.britannica (Hartert) breeds Britain, Ireland and the Channel Islands.

MB and **RB**. Fairly numerous. Widely distributed in Britain and Ireland, breeding north to southern Scotland, and much more locally farther north through central Scotland to Perth, Inverness (including, probably, Skye), formerly east Ross, and occasionally Aberdeen. The species occurs only infrequently in the extreme north of Scotland, the Hebrides and Northern Isles. While some birds are resident throughout the breeding range, a substantial proportion of the population emigrates across the southern North Sea and English Channel to winter in southern France, Iberia and northwest Africa. Passage movements occur on the British east and south coasts mainly from mid-September to early November, and from mid-April to mid-May, and these presumably concern birds of British origin. (Some Continental birds of the race *C.c.carduelis* (Linnaeus) may also be involved or may even winter here in small numbers; but there is no evidence of this from ringing and no specimens of this subspecies have been recorded in Britain or Ireland.)

Siskin   A
Carduelis spinus (Linnaeus)

Palaearctic. Breeds western Eurasia from the British Isles and central Scandinavia east to western Siberia, and discontinuously south to the Pyrenees, Alps, Caucasus and north Iran; also breeds in eastern Siberia, Amurland and Japan; between 67°N and 37°N; breeds irregularly beyond 'normal' range after eruptions. Partly to wholly migratory, in winter reaching the Mediterranean basin, southwest Asia and southern China; the extent of dispersal is much greater in eruption years.

Monotypic.

RB. Not scarce. Breeds widely in the eastern and central Scottish Highlands, and more locally in fluctuating numbers elsewhere on the Scottish mainland and over much of Ireland; in recent years it has begun to breed regularly or fairly regularly in northern England (especially Northumberland), East Anglia, Hampshire and Devon, and in North Wales (Caernarvon, Merioneth, Montgomery) and Radnor. British and Irish birds are probably resident; some northern birds move south within the British Isles in winter, but there is no evidence that any emigrate.

WV and **PV.** Winter visitors and passage migrants, from northern and eastern Europe, arrive in very variable numbers on the British east coast, mainly from mid-September to early November, though in irruption years immigration may continue into December. Many immigrants move inland to winter over a wide area of Britain; others move south through eastern England and depart again for the Continent from East Anglia and southeast England. Return movements are noticed on a very much smaller scale: the departure of winter visitors is probably mainly in April and there is some evidence of a small passage through Britain in May.

Genus ACANTHIS Borkhausen

Holarctic and, marginally, Ethiopian genus of six species, four in Palaearctic, all breeding in Europe; three breed in the British Isles, where the fourth occurs as a scarce visitor.

Redpoll A
Acanthis flammea (Linnaeus)

Northern Holarctic. Breeds across the whole of northern Eurasia and North America from the Arctic Ocean south to southern Greenland, Iceland, British Isles, Fenno-Scandia, northern Russia, southern Siberia, Kamchatka, southern Canada and Newfoundland, also in the Alps, between 75°N and 45°N. Winters in southern parts of the breeding range, and beyond it as far as south-central Europe, Turkestan, Japan and the northern United States.

A.f.cabaret (P. L. S. Müller) breeds British Isles and the Alps.

A.f.flammea (Linnaeus) breeds northern continental Eurasia and North America.

A.f.rostrata (Coues) breeds Baffin Island and Greenland.

RB and **MB.** Fairly numerous. Widely distributed in Scotland, Ireland, northern and eastern England and Wales, probably breeding in all counties except Shetland, Orkney, the Outer Hebrides, Isle of Man and Pembroke; breeds only locally or irregularly in much of south-central and southwestern England. Partially migratory; in some years a substantial part of the British population emigrates across the southern North Sea, and perhaps also the English Channel, to winter in adjacent parts of the Continent, southeast to south Germany. The breeding race is *A.f.cabaret*, but a pair closely resembling *A.f.rostrata* bred in Inverness in 1959.

WV and **PV**. Winter visitors and passage migrants from the Continent arrive on the British east coast from Shetland southwards in very variable (at intervals, large) numbers, mainly October–November, and depart, less conspicuously, mainly April to mid-May; these autumn immigrants, subspecies *A.f.flammea*, spread locally to probably most parts of Britain (though the species does not usually winter in the outermost Scottish isles, Pembroke and Cornwall) and the race has been identified in Ireland. Passage migrants from Greenland, *A.f.rostrata*, are recorded in small but widely fluctuating numbers, chiefly September to early October, many fewer April–May, most often in the Northern Isles (especially Fair Isle) and Hebrides, occasionally in north and west Ireland, but apparently only twice in England (Norfolk, December 1947; Isles of Scilly, October 1966); the winter quarters of this subspecies are not known, but probably include parts of Scotland and Ireland. (The Icelandic race *A.f.islandica* (Hantzsch) has probably occurred in northern Britain and Ireland, but no examples have been certainly identified.)

Arctic Redpoll A
Acanthis hornemanni (Holboell)

Northern Holarctic. Breeds generally farther north than *A.flammea* (with which it is regarded as conspecific by some authors) in circumpolar tundras of Eurasia and North America, south to the arctic fringes of Lapland, Siberia, Alaska and mainland Canada, also in northern Greenland; between 80°N and 57°N. Irregular movements occur in winter south to the Baltic area, northern Mongolia and the northern United States.

A.h.hornemanni (Holboell) breeds Ellesmere and Baffin Islands and northern Greenland.

A.h.exilipes (Coues) breeds range of species except in the part occupied by the nominate form (see above).

SV. Over 50 recorded (including as many as six together), chiefly at Fair Isle between mid-September and mid-November, but also elsewhere in Shetland, and in the Hebrides, Inverness, Argyll, Ayr, northeast England and Norfolk, late September to February, and once each in March, April and July. About 15 recorded as *A.h.hornemanni*, 14 as *A.h.exilipes*, the rest not determined.

Twite A
Acanthis flavirostris (Linnaeus)

Central and northwestern Palaearctic. Breeds discontinuously in southwest and central Asia from Turkey east to west China, north to the Kirghiz Steppes, south to the Tibetan slopes of the Himalayas; isolated populations occur in northwest Europe in the British Isles and on the coasts of Norway and the Kola Peninsula; between 71°N and 27°N. European birds are partially to wholly migratory but in Asia movements are chiefly restricted to altitudinal shifts with seasons.

A.f.flavirostris (Linnaeus) breeds Norway and the Murman coast of Kola Peninsula.

A.f.pipilans (Latham) breeds Britain and Ireland.

RB. (also **M.B.**) Not scarce. Breeds locally in Scotland (where formerly much more widespread), chiefly in the western half of the country from Shetland, Orkney and the Hebrides south to Arran, Renfrew and Stirling; also very locally in England on upland moors south as far as east Lancashire, east Cheshire, southwest Yorkshire, north Derby and north Stafford; a pair bred on the coast of North Wales in 1967; the species also breeds locally in several maritime counties in Ireland, mainly in the north and west, also in some mountainous districts inland. Some populations are resident, other birds winter on coasts of the Irish Sea and eastern England (ringing recoveries in Lincoln, Essex and Kent), while some emigrate (British-ringed nestlings have been found in Belgium and Italy; a bird ringed in the Netherlands in October was found in Yorkshire in May). *A.f.pipilans.*

WV. Winters regularly in variable numbers on coasts between Lincoln and Sussex, arriving in October–November and departing in March–April. Ringing evidence (see above) suggests that some, perhaps all, are native *A.f.pipilans.* Occasional birds noted in autumn and winter elsewhere on the east and south coasts and inland in England may belong to either race.

Linnet A
Acanthis cannabina (Linnaeus)

Western and central Palaearctic. Breeds from southern Fenno-Scandia, British Isles and Iberia east across Europe into western Siberia and through Asia Minor and Iran to Turkestan, north to northern Russia, south to northwest Africa, including the Canaries and Madeira, Cyrenaica, the Mediterranean islands, Near East and Persian Gulf; between 64°N and 26°N. Partially migratory, the northern populations wintering in southern parts of the breeding range and beyond it to Egypt and northwest India.

A.c.cannabina (Linnaeus) breeds Europe, except Scotland, northwest Africa and west Siberia.

A.c.autochthona Clancey is restricted to Scotland.

MB and **RB**. Numerous. Widely distributed; absent from Shetland and the Outer Hebrides, but otherwise breeding in all counties in Britain and Ireland, though only locally in parts of west and north Scotland, including Orkney. The species may be seen throughout the year over the greater part of this range, but locally within it may occur only as a summer visitor. In most years a substantial proportion, of the English population at least, emigrates from southern coasts in September–October, returning mainly in April; these birds winter chiefly in Spain and southern France. The breeding race is *A.c.cannabina*, except in Scotland where it is replaced by the poorly distinguished subspecies, *A.c.autochthona*.

WV and **PV**. Winter visitors, presumably from northern Europe (one nestling ringed in Norway has been recovered in Yorkshire), arrive in unknown but probably small numbers on the British east and southeast coasts from mid-September to end October, perhaps returning between mid-March and mid-April. There may also be some passage of Continental birds at these times but there are no ringing recoveries in confirmation and the position is complicated by movements of British birds. *A.c.cannabina*.

Genus CARPODACUS Kaup

Holarctic genus of 20 species, 17 in Palaearctic, only one breeding in Europe and wandering to the British Isles.

Scarlet Grosbeak or Common Rosefinch   A
Carpodacus erythrinus (Pallas)

Palaearctic. Breeds Eurasia from eastern Germany and southern Finland east to Kamchatka, north to northern Russia and the Arctic Circle in Siberia, south to central Russia, northern Mongolia and northern

China; also in mountain regions from eastern Turkey east to western China; between 68°N and 25°N. Winters in northern subtropical Asia from northern India to Vietnam.

C.e.erythrinus (Pallas) breeds from eastern Europe east to the Altai and Baikal region.

SV. Annual in autumn at Fair Isle in very small numbers (up to four at once; never adult males), late August to November, but mostly in September; also recorded there once in January (three birds) and February, twice in early April and seven times in late May–early June. Also noted fairly frequently elsewhere in Shetland and in Orkney. Elsewhere irregular (though several records in each year, 1966–68, suggest it may be becoming more frequent), nearly always singly in September (also mid-August to end October), chiefly on the British east coast (Fife to Yorkshire), occasionally on coasts of southern England and Wales, but only rarely inland and only three in Ireland (Wexford, two Donegal). Apart from Fair Isle (above) noted only seven times in spring, all since 1963: Pembroke (June 1963), Yorkshire (May 1964), Kent (May 1966), Shetland (June 1967 and 1968), Isles of Scilly (June 1968), Orkney (June 1968).

Genus PINICOLA Vieillot

Holarctic monospecific genus, breeding in Europe and wandering occasionally to the British Isles.

Pine Grosbeak   A
Pinicola enucleator (Linnaeus)

Northern Holarctic and western Nearctic. Breeds across northern Eurasia from Scandinavia east to Kamchatka, from the tree-line south to central Russia and Mongolia, and from Alaska to Newfoundland, south to central Canada and the northeastern United States, also in the mountains of western North America south to Arizona; between 70°N and 35°N. Boreal forest populations appear to be partially migratory, reaching beyond the breeding range in winter in Scandinavia, Russia, the Amur basin, and the Great Plains in the United States.

P.e.enucleator (Linnaeus) breeds from Scandinavia east to the Yenisei.

SV. At least seven: Durham (before 1831), Middlesex (before 1843), Yorkshire (*c*. 1861), Nottingham (two, October 1890), Isle of May, Fife (November 1954), Kent (April 1955, November 1957).

Genus LOXIA Linnaeus

Holarctic and, marginally, Oriental and Neotropical genus of three species, all breeding in Europe and one in the British Isles, where the other two occur as scarce visitors.

Parrot Crossbill A
Loxia pityopsittacus Borkhausen

Northwestern Palaearctic. Breeds regularly across northern Europe from Sweden east to Finland and north Russia and south to Estonia, usually ecologically associated with Scots Pine *Pinus sylvestris*; between 67°N and 57°N. Resident or erratically migratory, and has reached as far as western and central Europe, also western Siberia.

Monotypic.

SV. Very few authentic records, but is certainly overlooked and probably occurs from September onwards in some 'invasion years' of Crossbills *L.curvirostra*. Fewer than ten reliable records during 1818–1907, between September and March, all in southeast England (Norfolk to Kent) except for two together in Gloucester. Then, apart from records in Fife in 1953 and Northumberland in 1954, none was recorded until 1962 when influxes totalling more than 50 birds were noted at Fair Isle from late September to late October, and others were recorded, October to May 1963, in Shetland, the Outer Hebrides (four), Yorkshire, Lincoln, Suffolk (20 together) and Surrey; there were also two at Fair Isle in March 1963.

Crossbill A
Loxia curvirostra Linnaeus

Holarctic, Oriental and northwest Neotropical. Breeds from Scandinavia across northern Eurasia to the Pacific, southwards locally, and in some parts irregularly, to the British Isles, Iberia, Morocco, Tunisia, southern Europe and Asia Minor, discontinuously east to the northern Himalayas and southern Indo-China, also in America from British Columbia and Newfoundland south to Nicaragua and North Carolina; between 68°N and 12°N. In Eurasia, northern populations are very erratic, engaging in immense 'invasions' following failures of cone-crops (in Europe usually ecologically associated with spruces *Picea* spp.). In western Europe recorded as a vagrant and casual breeder in many places where breeding is not regular; southern montane populations are more sedentary.

L.c.scotica Hartert is restricted to northern Scotland (and is regarded as a race of *L.pityopsittacus* by some authors).

L.c.curvirostra Linnaeus breeds western Europe (not Iberia) east to eastern Siberia, also in Transcaucasia.

RB (also an irruptive migrant). Not scarce. The endemic subspecies, *L.c.scotica*, is resident in fluctuating numbers in woods of native pine, *Pinus sylvestris*, in northern Scotland, where the breeding range extends from central Perth north to Inverness and east Ross (and perhaps to east Sutherland) and east to Banff (and perhaps to Angus, Kincardine and Aberdeen). The status of *L.c.curvirostra* in the British Isles fluctuates according to the scale of immigration from the Continent, which in 'invasion years' occurs from late June onwards. Arrivals are erratic: in some years very small numbers occur, but periodically (in the last two decades, on average every two to three years) large irruptions take place, usually from late June onwards, along the entire British east coast. In 'invasion years' these birds disperse all over Britain, spilling over into Ireland during the largest irruptions, with attempted and successful casual breeding in spring of the following year. The species has bred at one time or another in practically all counties in England and Wales, and probably most of those in Scotland and Ireland. After particularly big invasions breeding may persist for several years in some areas (at the present time notably in Dorset, Surrey, Huntingdon, Brecon, Northumberland and Dumfries), while in Hampshire breeding now appears to be regular, as it has been in Norfolk and Suffolk since about 1910 (though the population has doubtless been augmented by further irruptions).

Two-barred Crossbill   A
Loxia leucoptera Gmelin

Northern Holarctic, also northeast Neotropical. Breeds Eurasia from Scandinavia eastwards to Yakutia from the tree-line south to eastern Russia, southern Siberia and the Amur basin, and in North America from Alaska to Newfoundland south to the Prairie provinces and northern United States; between 68°N and 45°N; also in Hispaniola. Nomadic in winter within the breeding range, wandering southwards beyond it in Russia, northern China and the northern United States.

L.l.bifasciata (Brehm) breeds Eurasia.

SV. Over 50 recorded, most of them during 'invasions' of *L. curvirostra*, perhaps rather more frequently in the past than now, chiefly on the east side of Britain from Shetland southwards, but also occasionally elsewhere, including four in Ireland (1802–1927, all Ulster) and one in Wales. There have been eleven widely scattered records since 1958, including five between July and November 1966.

Genus **PYRRHULA** Brisson

Palaearctic and Oriental genus of six species, five in Palaearctic, but only one breeding in Europe and the British Isles.

Bullfinch   **A**
Pyrrhula pyrrhula (Linnaeus)

Northern and western Palaearctic. Breeds from Fenno-Scandia, British Isles and northern Iberia, east across Eurasia to Kamchatka, north to the Arctic Circle, south to Italy, the Balkans, Caucasus, northern Iran, southern Siberia and Japan; between 70°N and 35°N; also in the Azores. Essentially resident, but some eastern birds extend slightly to the south of the breeding range in winter and reach Korea and northern China.

P.p.pyrrhula (Linnaeus) breeds across northern Eurasia from Scandinavia to eastern Siberia, south to parts of central and southeast Europe.

P.p.pileata MacGillivray breeds in the British Isles.

RB. Numerous. Widely distributed, breeding in all counties in Britain and Ireland (rather locally in Scotland, especially in the northwest) except the Isle of Man, Outer Hebrides, Orkney, Shetland and probably Caithness. Essentially sedentary, with some short-distance dispersal by a few individuals within Britain, but the possibility that some may emigrate across the English Channel, especially at times of winter food shortage. Resident, endemic subspecies, *P.p.pileata*.

SV. Immigrants of the subspecies *P.p.pyrrhula* are noted in most years in very small numbers in late October and November, also occasionally in winter and irregularly in spring (late March to early May). These birds occur chiefly in the Northern Isles, also on the north Scottish mainland, but only rarely in England (mainly sight-records on the northeast coast) though there are reports from as far south as Norfolk and Berkshire.

Genus COCCOTHRAUSTES Brisson

Palaearctic monospecific genus, breeding in Europe and the British Isles.

Hawfinch   **A**
Coccothraustes coccothraustes (Linnaeus)

Palaearctic. Breeds from northwest Africa, Iberia, British Isles and southern Scandinavia east across Eurasia to the Amur basin, north to 60°N in Russia and Siberia, south to Italy, the southern Balkans, northern Iran, northern Afghanistan and Japan; between 60°N and 30°N. Partially migratory, reaching southern parts of the breeding range and beyond it to Egypt, the northwest Himalayas and eastern China.

C.c.coccothraustes (Linnaeus) breeds Europe and Siberia.

RB. Not scarce. Widely but locally distributed in England, breeding in nearly all counties, though not in Cornwall, and most of Devon; also very locally in Wales (recently in Glamorgan, Brecon, Montgomery, Merioneth, Denbigh and Flint) and southern Scotland (recently in Dumfries, Selkirk, Berwick, the Lothians, and probably Perth); in Ireland it is said to have occurred as a regular winter visitor to Dublin, Tipperary and Cork in the 19th century and a pair bred in Kildare in 1902. Now occurs in Ireland, and elsewhere outside the breeding range, as an erratic winter or passage vagrant; in Ireland and the Isles of Scilly the records are mostly in autumn (October–November), in the Northern Isles mostly in spring (late March to mid-June). The origin of these birds is obscure, but one recovered in Shetland in May 1967 had been ringed in southeast Germany in March 1962.

Family PLOCEIDAE

Genus PASSER Brisson

Palaearctic, Oriental and Ethiopian genus of 15 species; eleven in Palaearctic of which three breed in Europe and two in the British Isles, where the third has been recorded on one occasion.

House Sparrow   A
Passer domesticus (Linnaeus)

Palaearctic and, marginally, Oriental and Ethiopian. Breeds from northern Fenno-Scandia, British Isles and Iberia east through Eurasia to north Manchuria, north to northern Russia and 65°N in Siberia, south to the Sahara, Sudan, Arabia and India; between 70°N and 60°N. Essentially sedentary. Hybridizes with *P.hispaniolensis* in parts of northwest Africa, southern Italy and on some Mediterranean islands. Successfully introduced in North and South America, the Caribbean area, Australia, New Zealand, South Africa and on many oceanic islands.

P.d.domesticus (Linnaeus) breeds Europe (except from southeast France through Corsica to Italy, and in Crete) and across northern Asia.

RB. Abundant. Breeds widely in all parts of Britain and Ireland, but is rather local on parts of the western Irish seaboard and is absent from a few maritime islands there and elsewhere. Mainly sedentary, but some evidence of movements from September to November and March to April on coasts of eastern and southern England. Emigration across the English Channel has been confirmed by recoveries in Belgium (one) and northern France (two) of birds ringed on the English south coast.

Spanish Sparrow A
Passer hispaniolensis (Temminck)

Southwestern Palaearctic. Breeds Cape Verde and Canary Islands, northwest Africa, Iberia, Sardinia and from the Balkans east through Asia Minor, Iran, Afghanistan and Transcaspia to Chinese Turkestan; between 45°N and 16°N. Hybridizes freely with *P.domesticus* in parts of the Mediterranean region. Essentially sedentary, but is a partial migrant in the east, wintering south to the Nile Valley and northwest India.

P.h.hispaniolensis breeds in the western part of the species' range, east to Cyrenaica and the Balkans and perhaps Asia Minor.

SV. One: Lundy, Devon (June 1966). Race not determined, but unlikely to have been other than nominate *hispaniolensis*.

Tree Sparrow A
Passer montanus (Linnaeus)

Palaearctic and Oriental. Breeds most of Eurasia from Scandinavia, British Isles and Iberia east to the Pacific, north to the North Cape in Norway and the Arctic Circle and beyond in Siberia, south to Iberia, Sicily, Iran, the Himalayas and Indonesia, but absent from parts of the Mediterranean region and southern and northeastern Asia; between 71°N and 10°S. Partially migratory, the northern populations wintering in southern parts of the breeding range and beyond it in the Mediterranean area. Introduced in the Philippines, Australia and the central United States.

P.m.montanus (Linnaeus) breeds Europe, and across Siberia to Amurland, south to the Kirghiz Steppes and central Korea.

RB. Fairly numerous. Breeds widely in England (but only very locally or irregularly in southernmost counties, and not in Dorset, Devon and Cornwall) and southern Scotland, more locally in Wales (absent from much of the west and south) and northeast Scotland, and very locally elsewhere; since about 1960, however, the species has recolonized Shetland, Orkney, parts of western Scotland (has bred again on St. Kilda), and most maritime counties in Ireland. Some wandering or dispersal evidently occurs, otherwise the British population appears to be mainly sedentary.

WV. Immigration (and perhaps some passage migration) occurs in variable numbers late September to November, with less conspicuous return movements in March and April, mainly on the British east and

south coasts, probably largely involving winter visitors from northern
Europe. Isolated parties and individuals of unknown origin occur not
infrequently on remote western islands and headlands, especially in
May.

Family STURNIDAE

Genus STURNUS Linnaeus

Palaearctic and Oriental genus of 16 species, seven in Palaearctic, three
breeding in Europe and one in the British Isles, where one other
occurs as a scarce visitor.

Rose-coloured Starling   A
Sturnus roseus (Linnaeus)

Southern central Palaearctic. Breeds from Hungary (occasionally Italy)
east through southern Russia and Asia Minor to the Altai, north to the
Kirghiz Steppes and south to the Lebanon, Iran and Afghanistan;
between 54°N and 26°N. Winters chiefly in western India.
     Monotypic.
     SV. Probably over 200 recorded, one to six annually in recent years,
but some of these are suspected of having escaped from captivity.
Mainly July–August, fewer June, September and October, but has
been identified in all months. Records are widely scattered in Britain
and Ireland, chiefly on or near coasts, though several have been found
inland.

Starling   A
Sturnus vulgaris Linnaeus

Western and central Palaearctic. Breeds Iceland, Faeroes, British
Isles and Azores, and across continental Eurasia from Scandinavia and

France east to Lake Baikal, north beyond the Arctic Circle in Scandinavia and to 60°N in Siberia, south to Italy, Asia Minor and extreme northwest India; between 71°N and 25°N. Winters within the breeding range and beyond it to Iberia, north Africa, the Iranian region and northern India. Introduced in North America, southern Africa, Polynesia, Australia and New Zealand.

S.v.zetlandicus Hartert breeds Shetland and the Outer Hebrides.

S.v.vulgaris Linnaeus breeds Europe (not Faeroes) east to the Urals, also in the Azores.

RB. Abundant. Widespread, breeding in all areas, though only sparsely and locally in some parts of extreme western Ireland. Mainly sedentary, with a few individuals undertaking short-distance post-breeding dispersal and hard-weather movements; but few British birds reach the Continent, and there is no evidence of any substantial regular emigration. The breeding subspecies is *S.v.vulgaris* except in Shetland and the Outer Hebrides where it is replaced by the poorly defined subspecies *S.v.zetlandicus*.

WV and **PV**. Immigrants from northern and northeastern Europe arrive in large numbers over the British east and south coasts, mainly October to December, departing less conspicuously (more by night, and at greater altitudes by day) mainly between February and April. Most seen at these times are immigrants that winter in all parts of Britain and Ireland, though some movements, especially across southeast England, may include transient visitors. Immigration across the southern North Sea and from northern France sometimes commences as early as July. *S.v.vulgaris*.

Family ORIOLIDAE

Genus ORIOLUS Linnaeus

Palaearctic, Ethiopian, Oriental and Australasian genus of 24 species, three in Palaearctic, one breeding in Europe and sporadically in the British Isles, where it occurs mainly as a scarce but regular visitor.

Golden Oriole   A
Oriolus oriolus (Linnaeus)

Western and central Palaearctic and Oriental. Breeds from southern-most Sweden, the Netherlands, France and Iberia east across Eurasia to the Upper Yenisei and Turkestan, north to southeast Finland and 60°N in Russia and Siberia, south to northwest Africa, Sicily, Asia Minor, Cyprus, the Iranian region and India; between 63°N and 12°N. Winters mainly in tropical and southern Africa, and in India.

O.o.oriolus (Linnaeus) breeds range of species east to Iran and the mountains of Chinese Turkestan.

CB. Breeds sporadically, in the past most often in coastal counties of southern England (notably Kent), but since 1954 the only published confirmed breeding records are from north Lancashire (1958–59, probably also 1960–61), Shropshire (one, perhaps two, pairs in 1964) and Suffolk (1967), though breeding has probably also occurred in Sussex, Essex, Bedford, Huntingdon, Pembroke and Cardigan, while pairs have been seen in summer in several other British counties north to Kinross.

SV. Small numbers overshoot regularly on spring migration and reach southern England from late April to mid-June (some remaining into July), but the species is irregular and very scarce in autumn, August to October. Ones and twos, occasionally up to four together, have been recorded annually in recent years on the Isles of Scilly, almost annually in Cork, Kent, Suffolk and Norfolk, and fairly regularly in some other counties of England (notably Devon, Dorset, Hampshire, Sussex, Essex, Huntingdon and Lancashire) and in Pembroke, Orkney and Shetland. There are records from most counties in England and Wales, but few from Ireland and the Scottish mainland.

Family CORVIDAE

Genus GARRULUS Brisson

Palaearctic and, marginally, Oriental genus of three species, all in Palaearctic, one breeding in Europe and the British Isles.

Jay   A
Garrulus glandarius (Linnaeus)

Palaearctic and northern Oriental. Breeds British Isles, most of Europe south of 65°N, northwest Africa, Asia Minor and across southern Siberia to Japan and south through China to southern Burma and the Himalayas; between 65°N and 15°N. Northern populations are partially or erratically migratory.

G.g.rufitergum Hartert breeds Brittany and Great Britain (Scottish birds approach the nominate form).

G.g.hibernicus Witherby and Hartert breeds Ireland.

G.g.glandarius (Linnaeus) breeds northern Europe from Lapland and west Russia south to the Pyrenees, Alps and north Balkans.

RB. Fairly numerous. Widely distributed, breeding in wooded areas throughout England and Wales, and in southern Scotland in Berwick, Dumfries, Kirkcudbright and probably Wigtown; also rather locally in central Scotland (Argyll, Dunbarton, Stirling, Perth, Clackmannan, Fife, Angus, Kincardine and probably Kinross) and throughout Ireland except in the extreme west and north. Two essentially sedentary, endemic subspecies, *G.g.rufitergum* and *G.g.hibernicus* (see above).

WV. Immigrants, belonging to the subspecies *G.g.glandarius*, occur here in variable numbers and not certainly annually. These birds probably orginate from the adjacent Continent (one ringed Kent in autumn was recovered breeding in the Netherlands) and are noted chiefly in October, perhaps returning in April, in southeast England, especially Kent. Immigrant Jays are occasionally recorded in autumn elsewhere on the British east and south coasts.

Genus PICA Brisson

Palaearctic, western Nearctic, Oriental and marginally Ethiopian genus of two species, one (perhaps only a race) restricted to California, the other present throughout the rest of the range, and breeding in Europe and the British Isles.

Magpie   A
Pica pica (Linnaeus)

Holarctic, Oriental and locally Ethiopian (Arabia). Breeds from northern Fenno-Scandia, British Isles and Iberia across Europe and Asia to central Siberia, south to northwest Africa, Sicily, Asia Minor, Cyprus, Iran, the Himalayas and Indo-China, with isolated populations in extreme eastern Siberia and the Yemen; also in North America from Alaska and northwest Canada south to New Mexico; between 71°N and 15°N. Sedentary.

P.p.pica (Linnaeus) breeds Europe west of Russia from southern Scandinavia and western Germany southeast through the Balkans to the Near East and Cyprus.

RB. Numerous. Widely distributed in Britain and Ireland north to Bute and south Argyll in west Scotland, and to Aberdeen, Inverness and eastern Ross in eastern Scotland; rather local throughout eastern Scotland and apparently absent or irregular as a breeder in parts of the southeast of the country (Roxburgh, Selkirk, Peebles, Berwick, East Lothian). Sedentary.

Genus NUCIFRAGA Brisson

Palaearctic and western Nearctic genus of two species, one in Palaearctic, breeding in Europe and wandering to the British Isles.

Nutcracker   A
Nucifraga caryocatactes (Linnaeus)

Palaearctic. Breeds in the Alps and the mountains of southern Germany and southeast Europe, and from southern Fenno-Scandia and the Baltic States eastwards across northern Eurasia to Kamchatka, the Kuriles and Japan, south to central Russia, the Altai, northern Mongolia and probably Korea, also in the Himalayas, northern China and Formosa; between 67°N and 24°N. Northern populations are irregularly migratory.

N.c.caryocatactes (Linnaeus) breeds from central Scandinavia and southwest Finland south to the Alps and Balkans and east to the Urals (not in northeast Russia).

N.c.macrorhynchos C. L. Brehm breeds northeast Russia, Siberia, northern Mongolia and northern Manchuria.

SV. Until 1968 rather over 50 recorded, with very few of these in the previous two decades, and only six during 1958–67 (all in southern England). In 1968, an unprecedented influx, totalling 315 individual records, occurred in August and September, some birds remaining into October and a few through to November and December and into 1969; birds were recorded in at least 29 English counties, chiefly in Norfolk, Suffolk, Essex and Kent, but also as far south and west as the Isles of Scilly, and in Scotland (Shetland) and Wales (Monmouth, Glamorgan). Previous records have been mainly in the late autumn (especially October to December), and like those in 1968 were chiefly in southern and eastern England, with a few in Scotland and Wales, but none in Ireland. All in 1968, when identified, belonged to the slender-billed race *N.c.macrorhynchos* (an irruptive migrant), but two previously (Sussex, December 1900; Cheshire, 1860) were of the thick-billed race *N.c.caryocatactes* (which is generally sedentary).

Genus PYRRHOCORAX Tunstall

Southern Palaearctic and marginally Ethiopian genus of two species, both in Palaearctic and Europe, one of them breeding in the British Isles.

Chough A
Pyrrhocorax pyrrhocorax (Linnaeus)

Southern Palaearctic and northeast Ethiopian. Breeds British Isles, Brittany, Iberia and northwest Africa (including the Canaries) eastwards locally across southern Europe (Alps, southern Italy, Balkans, and some Mediterranean islands) and southwest Asia to the Himalayas, and western and northern China; between 56°N and 26°N; also in Abyssinia. Essentially sedentary.

P.p.pyrrhocorax (Linnaeus) breeds British Isles.

RB. Scarce. Has decreased over the last two centuries, and the present breeding population of about 700 pairs is now confined to coastal districts in Ireland (all counties from Antrim round western coasts to Cork and Waterford, except in Derry and Sligo), southwest Scotland (Argyll including some of the southern Inner Hebrides), the Isle of Man, and west Wales (Anglesey south to Pembroke) with a few pairs inland in north Wales; a few individuals are still occasionally recorded in former breeding haunts, for example in Wexford, the Outer Hebrides, Wigtown and Cumberland, but only one individual now remains (end of 1968) in Cornwall, where the species bred till 1952. The population is essentially sedentary, but birds sometimes wander to other parts of western and northern Britain where they do not breed, e.g. Somerset, Glamorgan, Orkney and Shetland.

Genus CORVUS Linnaeus

Nearly cosmopolitan (not Neotropical) genus of 28 species, ten in Palaearctic of which only four breed in Europe and the British Isles.

Jackdaw A
Corvus monedula Linnaeus

Western and central Palaearctic. Breeds from central Scandinavia, British Isles and Iberia eastwards across Europe and western Asia to Lake Baikal, northwest China and Kashmir, north to about 66°N in Russia and 61°N in Siberia, south to northwest Africa, most Mediterranean islands, Palestine, Iraq and northern Iran. Generally sedentary apart from northern populations which winter south within or just beyond the breeding range.

C.m.monedula Linnaeus breeds southern Scandinavia, most of Denmark and possibly southern Finland.

C.m.spermologus Vieillot breeds western Europe except Scandinavia, and in Morocco.

RB. Abundant. Widely distributed, breeding in all parts of Britain and Ireland, including (since 1943) Shetland. Mainly sedentary, some individuals dispersing over short distances in winter, but no evidence of emigration. *C.m.spermologus*.

WV. Immigrants (perhaps also some passage migrants) arrive chiefly during October–November, and return March–April, on the British east coast and across the eastern half of the English Channel, regularly north to Shetland (most in spring) and occasionally west to the Isles of Scilly. Ringing recoveries suggest the Low Countries and Scandinavia as the countries of origin of these birds, hence both *C.m.spermologus* and *C.m.monedula* are involved.

Rook   **A**
Corvus frugilegus Linnaeus

Palaearctic. Breeds from southern Fenno-Scandia, British Isles and central France across most of Europe (not in the extreme north and south) and middle Asia to the Pacific, north to northern Russia and 63°N in Siberia, south locally to northern Spain, Greece, northern Iran, Chinese Turkestan and the Yangtse in China; between 63°N and 27°N. Northern populations winter south within the breeding range and beyond it to northern Africa, the Persian Gulf, northwest India, southern China and Japan.

C.f.frugilegus Linnaeus breeds in western Eurasia east to the Yenisei and Tian Shan.

RB. Abundant. Widely distributed, breeding in all counties of Britain and Ireland, but only locally in extreme northwest Scotland, while in the Outer Hebrides (Lewis, colonized 1895) and Shetland (Mainland, colonized 1952) it is confined to single localities. Essentially sedentary; there is some post-breeding wandering but no definite evidence of emigration.

WV. Winter visitors (perhaps also some passage migrants) arrive mainly from late September to mid-November and return from March to April, mainly along the North Sea and eastern English Channel coasts of Britain. Ringing recoveries point to the Netherlands, Germany,

Denmark, the Baltic States and western Russia as the breeding area of
these winter visitors.

Carrion Crow, Hooded Crow   A
Corvus corone Linnaeus

Palaearctic and marginally Oriental. Breeds from the Faeroes and
British Isles across the greater part of Eurasia from the tree-line south
to the Mediterranean, Egypt, the Persian Gulf, Himalayas and south
China; between 72°N and 24°N. Northern populations are partially to
wholly migratory, wintering in southern parts of the breeding range
and beyond it to northern Africa and northwest India.

C.c.corone Linnaeus (Carrion Crow) breeds from Britain (not Ireland, nor northern Scotland) east to the Elbe and south to Iberia and the
Alps.

C.c.cornix Linnaeus (Hooded Crow) breeds Ireland, northern Scotland, Faeroes, Scandinavia, and from the Elbe and northern Italy east
to the Urals and lower Danube.

RB. Numerous. Widely distributed, breeding in every county in
Britain and Ireland. *C.c.corone* occupies that part of the British range
which lies south of a line running approximately from the Moray Firth
to the Clyde, and a small but increasing proportion of the population
on the Scottish mainland west and north of this line (a few breed as
far north as east Sutherland and Caithness). *C.c.cornix* breeds mainly
west and north of the Moray–Clyde 'line' in Scotland, including the
Western and Northern Isles, but also south to Renfrew, Perth and
Angus, throughout Ireland and in the Isle of Man. A comparatively
narrow zone of hybridization (moving gradually northwards) runs
across the central Scottish Highlands. *C.c.corone* has bred occasionally
in Ireland in Kerry, Mayo and Down, and has interbred with *C.c.cornix*
in Dublin, Down and Antrim, also in the Isle of Man (perhaps regularly
now) and at Fair Isle. *C.c.cornix* bred occasionally in the past in England.

WV. Immigrant *C.c.cornix*, from Scandinavia, Denmark and perhaps farther east, arrive on the British east coast, mainly between October and mid-November, and depart from mid-March to end April.
These birds winter in small (formerly much larger) numbers along the
British east coast, and they are now recorded only occasionally inland
in England and along south and west coasts of England and Wales.
Immigrant *C.c.corone*, presumably from adjacent parts of the Continent

(but no ringing evidence), apparently arrive mainly during October–November and depart March–April, on the coasts of southeast England. This subspecies also occurs regularly on passage in small numbers as far north as Fair Isle (where formerly rare) and fairly frequently now in southwest and southeast Ireland; the origin and destination of these birds is unknown.

Raven A
Corvus corax Linnaeus

Holarctic and northwest Neotropical. Breeds from Greenland, Iceland, Faeroes, Scandinavia, British Isles and Iberia east across Eurasia to the Pacific, from the Arctic Ocean south to northwest Africa and Canaries, the Mediterranean islands, Near East, Iran, northwest India, the Himalayas, Manchuria and Japan, also in North America south to Nicaragua and the Appalachians; between 78°N and 15°N. Mainly sedentary.

C.c.corax Linnaeus breeds British Isles, continental Europe and Mediterranean islands east to the Yenisei, Lake Baikal, central Turkestan, northern Iran and the Black Sea.

RB. Not scarce. Widely distributed from Shetland, Orkney and the Hebrides through western Scotland to the English Lake District and Isle of Man, and more locally through eastern Scotland to Perth, with a few pairs in southeast Scotland, Northumberland, Durham and northwest Yorkshire; widespread in Wales and southwest England, locally east to Shropshire, Hereford, west Gloucester, Somerset and Dorset; also in nearly all maritime counties in Ireland and in a few inland (Fermanagh, Tyrone, perhaps others). Mainly sedentary. Some dispersal occurs, but the species rarely wanders far outside the breeding range, although in recent years there have been several records in Kent in October–November.

APPENDIX 1

Alterations of sequence (from Peters) and of nomenclature (from Vaurie) adopted in the present work

Tachybaptus (p. 4)

Following Storer (1963, *Proc.* XIII *Internat. Congr.*, pp. 562–9), the Little Grebe is placed in this genus and not in *Podiceps*.

Calonectris (p. 10)

The recommendations on the nomenclature of the petrels put forward by Alexander *et al.* (*Ibis* (1965) 107: 401–5) have been accepted.

Anseriformes (pp. 29–57)

The sequence and nomenclature follow Johnsgard's recent classification (1965, *A Handbook of Waterfowl Behaviour*).

Falconiformes (pp. 58–75)

The sequence and nomenclature follow Brown & Amadon (1968, *Eagles, Hawks and Falcons of the World*).

Alle (p. 148)

The case for discarding the generic name *Plotus* for the Little Auk has been cogently argued by Amadon *et al.* (1970, *Bull. Zool. Nomencl.* 27, pp. 110–12) in a proposal to the International Commission on Zoological Nomenclature. Its replacement by *Alle*, recommended in this proposal, is here adopted in anticipation of a favourable opinion by the Commission.

Lusciniola (p. 230)

As recommended by Parker & Harrison (1963, *Bull. Brit. Orn. Club* 83, pp. 65–9), this genus is discarded as not separable from *Acrocephalus*.

Muscicapidae (p. 248)

Peters includes the Turdidae, Sylviidae, Muscicapidae and Timaliidae as subfamilies within an enlarged family, Muscicapidae. It is not considered that the merits of this arrangement are sufficiently well established, and the conventional treatment is here followed.

APPENDIX 2
Summary for 1969 and 1970
By I. J. Ferguson-Lees and J. T. R. Sharrock

It is inevitable that such a book as this becomes partly out of date before it reaches the reader. Range extensions, unusual influxes of passage migrants and rarities, even new breeding species and additions to the list, are all observed far more quickly than the records can be gathered, checked, analysed and published. As the species summaries here were generally closed at 31st December 1968 (some ringing results rather earlier), it is worth drawing attention to a selection of the more interesting occurrences in 1969 and 1970; the birds are dealt with in rough systematic order.

To take breeding records first, a pair of **Great Northern Divers** *Gavia immer* with two unfledged young was seen in Wester Ross in late June and early July 1970: although nesting had been suspected on several occasions, this was the first proven case in Britain and Ireland. No less significant, a female **Goldeneye** *Bucephala clangula* with four ducklings was observed in Inverness-shire in July 1970: again, breeding had been suspected previously in Scotland, but this was the first clear evidence anywhere in these islands apart from the supposed records in Cheshire in 1931 and 1932. On a more local scale, **Gadwall** *Anas strepera* bred in Kerry in 1969 and a pair of **Red-crested Pochards** *Netta rufina* in Gloucestershire in 1970, although the latter were undoubtedly of captive origin. The Scottish **Ospreys** *Pandion haliaetus* increased to four nesting pairs in 1969 and five in 1970, and several more pairs and individuals summered without nesting in each year. The **Golden Eagles** *Aquila chrysaetos* in the English Lake District at last laid eggs in 1969, though unsuccessfully, and then reared young in 1970. A pair of **Marsh Harriers** *Circus aeruginosus* summered in Scotland in 1969 in the same locality as in 1966. The attempt to introduce **White-tailed Eagles** *Haliaeetus albicilla* at Fair Isle failed: although three of the four were seen well into 1969, the last had disappeared by the end of August. Birds of prey in general have had a thin time in the era of organo-chlorine pesticides, but there seems to have been something of a recovery by **Peregrines** *Falco peregrinus* and **Sparrowhawks** *Accipiter nisus* since 1968 and a further census of the former was being undertaken in 1971.

Quail *Coturnix coturnix* were in remarkable numbers in 1970, probably comparable to the exceptional influx in 1964. Another reintroduction attempt, begun in 1970, was aimed at the return of **Great Bustards** *Otis tarda* to Wiltshire; this and the White-tailed Eagle are probably the only two former British breeding species for which reintroduction can be justified on the grounds that natural recolonisation is most unlikely, though January 1970 produced a Great Bustard on Fair Isle and probably two in Kent, more than the sum total of records in the previous

40 years. A species which has of course recolonised successfully, like the Osprey, is the **Black-tailed Godwit** *Limosa limosa* and the population on the Ouse Washes rose to a new peak of about 42 pairs in both 1969 and 1970; smaller numbers continued to breed in other parts of Britain. On a local scale again, more **Common Sandpipers** *Actitis hypoleucos* than usual were found breeding in southern England in 1969, for example in Surrey, and in one or other of the two years single pairs of **Oystercatchers** *Haematopus ostralegus* nested in Nottingham, Stafford, Leicester and probably Warwick, all counties well south of any previous inland breeding area; similarly, odd pairs of **Lesser Black-backed Gulls** *Larus fuscus* have taken to nesting in the Midlands, including Northampton for the first time in 1969. **Mediterranean Gulls** *L. melanocephalus* continued to summer in Hampshire in 1969 and 1970 and several males held territories, but there seemed to be an absence of females and the only proved breeding was between a hybrid Mediterranean × Black-headed Gull *L. ridibundus* and a Black-headed.

Snowy Owls *Nyctea scandiaca* reared young again in Shetland in 1969 and 1970, and other Scandinavian species continued to improve their position in Scotland. In particular, after several years of summer records in the east Highlands, **Wrynecks** *Jynx torquilla* were noted at five localities on Speyside in 1969 and three nests were found, all of which were successful: these are likely to have been of Scandinavian stock and colonisation in the north would help to compensate for the continued steady decrease of the population in south-east England. Similarly, **Redwings** *Turdus iliacus* are now well established in parts of the Highlands, while **Fieldfares** *T. pilaris* nested in 1969 on two islands in Shetland and one in Orkney, as well as in northern England. Lastly, three other recent colonists all showed signs of continuing spread: **Savi's Warblers** *Locustella luscinioides*, after several years of nesting in Kent, were suspected of breeding in Suffolk in 1969 and proved to do so in 1970; **Firecrests** *Regulus ignicapillus*, now well established in Hampshire, began to appear elsewhere in the summer; and **Serins** *Serinus serinus* nested in another southern English county in 1969.

Significant changes were not confined to breeding birds in these two years. Some passage migrants and winter visitors occurred in such numbers that, had the status accounts been written after 1970, there might have been alterations in the wording. Even more, the records of certain rarities, ranging from annual vagrants to accidentals, would have significantly affected the summary totals of the species concerned. Single **Wilson's Petrels** *Oceanites oceanicus* off Cork and Cornwall in August 1969 and October 1970 were only the second and third in the 20th century, and a **Steller's Eider** *Polysticta stelleri* on the Aberdeen coast in November 1970 was the first since 1959 and the seventh in all. Among Nearctic ducks, a **Black Duck** *Anas rubripes* in Scilly in September 1969 was the fifth, while **Ring-necked Ducks** *Aythya collaris* in Aberdeen in 1969, in Devon in 1970 and in Norfolk in both years, as well as the reappearance of others in Antrim and Oxford, brought the number of individuals recorded at least to twelve. The now regular concentration of **Bewick's Swans** *Cygnus bewickii* on the Ouse Washes rose past the thousand mark (in fact, to the remarkable figure of 1,278) for the first time in winter 1970/71. **Black Kites** *Milvus migrans* in Sussex and Orkney in April and September 1970 were only the eleventh and twelfth records, while a **Lesser Kestrel** *Falco naumanni* in Cornwall in October 1969 was only the second since 1926 (the other having been in the same county in the previous year).

Spring 1970 was remarkable for southern and south-eastern vagrants: largely as a result of an influx then, but taking into account a trickle through the year in some cases, there were in that year ten or more **Night Herons** *Nycticorax nycticorax*, at least 18 **Little Bitterns** *Ixobrychus minutus*, 25 or more **Purple Herons** *Ardea purpurea* and no less than 40 **Little Egrets** *Egretta garzetta*, all totals which would have greatly altered the figures quoted in the species summaries concerned, as well as two **Squacco Herons** *Ardeola ralloides*, the first since 1967. The same period also helped to produce a total for 1970 of no less than eight **Whiskered Terns** *Chlidonias hybrida* and about 27 **White-winged Black Terns** *C. leucopterus*. If that spring was notable for southern vagrants, autumn 1970 was hardly less remarkable for Nearctic birds, including an unprecedented 135 or more American waders of twelve species. Among these were about ten **Lesser Yellowlegs** *Tringa flavipes*, nine or more **White-rumped Sandpipers** *Calidris fuscicollis*, five or six **Baird's Sandpipers** *C. bairdii*, at least five **Wilson's Phalaropes** *Phalaropus tricolor*, as many as 25 **Buff-breasted Sandpipers** *Tryngites subruficollis* and the remarkable total of at least 65 **Pectoral Sandpipers** *Calidris melanotos*, including eight at one locality in Cornwall; the last species had had a previous maximum of 42 in one year and a recent annual average of around 24. There were also more than 40 **Sabine's Gulls** *Larus sabini* in autumn 1970. Among the rarer American waders in the two years, **Lesser Golden Plovers** *Pluvialis apricaria* in Cornwall in October 1969, in Kerry in June and September 1969 and in Cork in August 1970 brought the total to 18; **Stilt Sandpipers** *Micropalama himantopus* in Suffolk and Sutherland in July 1969 and April 1970 were the eighth and ninth; **Spotted Sandpipers** *Actitis macularia* in Scilly in October 1969 and in Cornwall in August 1970 brought the total to 16; **Least Sandpipers** *Calidris minutilla* also reached 16 with singles in Cornwall and Wicklow in June and October 1970; and two **Semipalmated Sandpipers** *C. pusillus* in 1969 and at least two in 1970 brought the total to 18 or more. In general 1969 was a poor year for American waders crossing the Atlantic (only one Buff-breasted Sandpiper, for example) and, instead, saw an unprecedented influx of **Curlew Sandpipers** *Calidris ferruginea* from Siberia. It also produced the eleventh **Sociable Plover** *Vanellus gregarius* (in Orkney in January), the eighteenth **Marsh Sandpiper** *Tringa stagnatilis* (in Shetland in May), and only the sixth **Terek Sandpiper** *Xenus cinereus* (in Sussex in May), as well as the eleventh and twelfth **Black-winged Pratincoles** *Glareola nordmanni* in Kent and Northampton in August and September.

Glaucous Gulls *Larus hyperboreus* were exceptionally numerous in Shetland in November 1969, about 100 being seen on Fetlar and more than 300 on Fair Isle. There were as many as four **Ivory Gulls** *Pagophila eburnea* in the two years, while **Ross's Gulls** *Rhodostethia rosea* in Shetland in October and on the Northumberland/Durham border in December 1970 were the seventh and eighth. From across the Atlantic, **Bonaparte's Gulls** *Larus philadelphia* in Cornwall in March-April 1969 and February–March 1970 and in Norfolk in September 1970 brought the total to 23, whereas a **Laughing Gull** *L. atricilla* which stayed in Dorset from February to October 1969 was only the sixth. A **Brünnich's Guillemot** *Uria lomvia* in Argyll in October 1969 was only the sixth in all, but the second in two years. A **Sooty Tern** *Sterna fuscata* found dead in Hampshire in August 1969 brought the total to 20. A minor westward invasion of **Pallas's Sandgrouse** *Syrrhaptes paradoxus* in 1969 resulted in one reaching Shetland in May and two

Northumberland in September, and there were several other unconfirmed reports: apart from the single record in Kent in 1964, these were the first since 1908. Similarly, a **Wallcreeper** *Tichodroma muraria* in Dorset in winter 1969/70 was the first since June 1938 and the seventh in all.

A **Great Spotted Cuckoo** *Clamator glandarius* in Kent in August 1970 was the thirteenth record in all, and a number of vagrant passerines which have been recorded here 20 times or less also had their total increased by one or two. These included the third **Olive-backed Pipit** *Anthus hodgsoni* (Dorset, May 1970), the fourteenth and fifteenth **Citrine Wagtails** *Motacilla citreola* (Shetland, September 1969 and September 1970), the second and third **River Warblers** *Locustella fluviatilis* (Shetland and Caernarvon, September 1969), the seventh **Blyth's Reed Warbler** *Acrocephalus dumetorum* (Cork, October 1969), the second **Spectacled Warbler** *Sylvia conspicillata* (Cornwall, Oxtober 1969), the sixth **Collared Flycatcher** *Muscicapa albicollis* (Norfolk, May 1969), the twentieth **Black-eared Wheatear** *Oenanthe hispanica* (Caernarvon, April 1970), the seventeenth and eighteenth **Desert Wheatears** *Oenanthe deserti* (Shetland and Lincoln, May and September 1970), the ninth and tenth **Rock Thrushes** *Monticola saxatilis* (Norfolk and Shetland, May 1969 and June 1970), the third **Blackpoll Warbler** *Dendroica striata* (Scilly, October 1970), the eleventh **Baltimore Oriole** *Icterus galbula* (Pembroke, May 1970), the third **Song Sparrow** *Melospiza melodia* (Caernarvon, May 1970), the ninth **White-throated Sparrow** *Zonotrichia albicollis* (Caithness, May–June 1970, the third American passerine at that period), and the fifth **Slate-coloured Junco** *Junco hyemalis* (Shetland, May 1969).

More significant was the fact that not less than seven **Thrush Nightingales** *Luscinia luscinia*, almost equal to the previous grand total, were recorded in spring 1970. Numbers of **Richard's Pipits** *Anthus novaeseelandiae* continued to be high with more than 50 in 1969 and 90–100 in 1970. After a poor year for rare *Phylloscopus* warblers in 1969, there was an unusual lot in 1970, including seven **Bonelli's Warblers** *P. bonelli*, eight **Arctic** *P. borealis*, five **Greenish** *P. trochiloides*, four **Pallas's** *P. proregulus* and three **Dusky** *P. fuscatus*, bringing the total for the last to 15. Two of the records of Dusky Warbler related to the same individual, ringed on the Calf of Man in May 1970 and picked up dying near Limerick in December, a remarkable story at every stage: at the outset it was the first recorded here in spring and at the end the first in December, while it had presumably survived in western Europe for nearly seven months in between. Other ringing recoveries threw new light on movements to and from Britain and Ireland and among these was a Swiss-ringed **Alpine Swift** *Apus melba* in Scilly in September 1969; incidentally, no less than twelve Alpine Swifts were recorded in 1970, chiefly as part of the unusual spring influxes.

Finally, several more species were new to the British and Irish list in these two years: some are still under consideration, but they included **Franklin's Gulls** *Larus pipixcan* in Hampshire and Sussex (February–May and July 1970), a **Desert Warbler** *Sylvia nana* in Dorset (December 1970–January 1971), a **Veery** *Catharus fuscescens* in Cornwall (October 1970), a **Scarlet Tanager** *Piranga olivacea* in Scilly (October 1970), and an **Evening Grosbeak** *Hesperiphona vespertina* on St Kilda (March 1969). These and future additions will of course be listed in the periodical reports of the Records Committee in 'The Ibis'.

APPENDIX 3
Species currently placed in Category D

Greater Flamingo, *Phoenicopterus ruber*

There have been numerous records, but most, if not all, are attributable to birds escaped from collections.

Baikal Teal, *Anas formosa*

Six occurrences in the last 50 years: Sussex (November 1927), Norfolk (December 1929), Suffolk (November 1951), Shetland (September–October 1954), Moray (February 1958), Fermanagh (January 1967). It is possible that all the records are of birds escaped from collections.

Carolina Duck, *Aix sponsa*

It is uncertain whether feral populations are yet established in southeast England and East Anglia.

Reeve's Pheasant, *Syrmaticus reevesi*

It is uncertain whether feral populations are currently established in Scotland and the Midlands.

Bobwhite Quail, *Colinus virginianus*

It is uncertain whether feral populations are yet established in East Anglia.

Blue Rock Thrush, *Monticola solitarius*

One record (Orkney, August–September 1966), possibly an escaped cage-bird.

Red-headed Bunting, *Emberiza bruniceps*

There have been numerous occurrences, but most, if not all, are attributable to escaped cage-birds (see *British Birds* 60: 344–7, 423–6, and 61: 41–3).

APPENDIX 4
Summary list of British and Irish birds

The following abbreviations and symbols are used.

Under 'Distribution'

P Palaearctic   A Australasian   Nt Neotropical
N Nearctic   O Oriental   E Ethiopian
         Oc Oceanic

Under 'RB' and 'MB'

I introduced
F or f Former breeder ('f' being in distant past, perhaps only erratically)
C or c Casual breeder ('c' meaning on only a very few occasions)
× denotes occurrence in moderate to large numbers
+ denotes occurrence in small or very small numbers

Under 'SV'

R, r or rr Race or races occur as scarce visitors, 'R' frequently, 'r' infrequently
× More than 50 recent records
+ Less than 50 records, or (in a few cases) more than 50 records but nearly all of
these more than 50 years ago

Under 'WV' and 'PV'

× and +, as under 'RB' and 'MB'

Under 'Status'

All species are in category A unless otherwise stated. Species in category B have
not occurred in the last 50 years, and those in C are introduced (see Introduction, p. xii).

	Distribution	RB	MB	WV	PV	SV	'Status'
GAVIIDAE							
Gavia stellata	P N	×	+	×	×		
Gavia arctica	P (N)	×	+?	×			
Gavia immer	N (P)			×			
Gavia adamsii	P N					+	
PODICIPEDIDAE							
Podilymbus podiceps	N Nt					+	
Tachybaptus ruficollis	P E O	×		+			
Podiceps nigricollis	P N E	×	+?	×	×		
Podiceps auritus	P N	×		×	+		
Podiceps griseigena	P N			×		(r)	
Podiceps cristatus	P O E A	×		+			
DIOMEDEIDAE							
Diomedea melanophrys	Oc					+	
PROCELLARIIDAE							
Fulmarus glacialis	Oc	×	×				
Pterodroma hasitata	Oc					+	B
Bulweria bulwerii	Oc					+	
Calonectris diomedea	Oc				×		
Puffinus gravis	Oc				×		
Puffinus griseus	Oc				×		
Puffinus puffinus	Oc		×		+		
Puffinus assimilis	Oc					×	
HYDROBATIDAE							
Oceanites oceanicus	Oc					+	
Pelagodroma marina	Oc					+	B
Hydrobates pelagicus	Oc		×		+		
Oceanodroma castro	Oc					+	
Oceanodroma leucorrhoa	Oc		×		+		
SULIDAE							
Sula bassana	Oc	×	×		+		

	Distribution	RB	MB	WV	PV	SV	'Status'
PHALACROCORACIDAE							
Phalacrocorax carbo	P N E O A	×	+	+	+		
Phalacrocorax aristotelis	P	×	+	+			
FREGATIDAE							
Fregata magnificens	Oc					+	
ARDEIDAE							
Ardea cinerea	P O R	×	+	×	+		
Ardea purpurea	P O E					×	
Ardeola ralloides	P E					+	
Bubulcus ibis	P O E N Nt					+	
Egretta alba	Cosmopolitan					+	
Egretta garzetta	P					×	
Nycticorax nycticorax	P E O N Nt					×	
Ixobrychus minutus	P E A		c?			×	
Botaurus stellaris	P E	×		×			
Botaurus lentiginosus	N					+	
CICONIIDAE							
Ciconia ciconia	P (E)		c/f			+	
Ciconia nigra	P (E)					+	
THRESKIORNITHIDAE							
Plegadis falcinellus	Cosmopolitan					+	
Platalea leucorodia	P O E		F			×	
ANATIDAE							
Cygnus olor	P	×	+	+			
Cygnus cygnus	P	C		×			
Cygnus bewickii	P			×	+		
Anser fabalis	P			×			
Anser albifrons	P N			×			
Anser erythropus	P					×	
Anser anser	P	×/I		×			
Anser caerulescens	N (P)					+	
Branta canadensis	N	I				(r)	AC
Branta leucopsis	P			×			
Branta bernicla	P N			×		(r)	

	Distribution	RB	MB	WV	PV	SV	'Status'
Branta reficollis	P					+	
Alopochen aegyptiacus	E (P)	I					C
Tadorna ferruginea	P					+	
Tadorna tadorna	P	×	×	+			
Aix galericulata	P	I					C
Anas penelope	P	×		×	+		
Anas americana	N					×	
Anas strepera	P N	×/I	×	×			
Anas crecca	P N	×	+	×	×	(R)	
Anas platyrhynchos	P N	×	+	×	+		
Anas rubripes	N					+	
Anas acuta	P N (Oc)	×	+?	×	×		
Anas querquedula	P		×		+		
Anas discors	N					+	
Anas clypeata	P N	×	×	×	×		
Netta rufina	P		c?			×	
Aythya ferina	P	×	+?	×	+		
Aythya collaris	N					+	
Aythya nyroca	P					×	
Aythya fuligula	P	×		×	+		
Aythya marila	P N		C	×	+		
Somateria mollissima	P N	×		+			
Somateria spectabilis	P N					+	
Polysticta stelleri	P N					+	
Histrionicus histrionicus	P N					+	
Clangula hyemalis	P N		c	×	+?		
Melanitta nigra	P N	×	+?	×	×		
Melanitta perspicillata	N					+	
Melanitta fusca	P N			×	+		
Bucephala albeola	N					+	
Bucephala clangula	P N		c	×	+		
Mergus cucullatus	N					+	
Mergus albellus	P			×			
Mergus serrator	P N	×		×			
Mergus merganser	P N	×		×			
Oxyura jamaicensis	N Nt	I					C

PANDIONIDAE

Pandion haliaetus	Cosmopolitan		×		×		

ACCIPITRIDAE

Pernis apivorus	P		×		+		
Milvus migrans	P O E A				+		

	Distribution	RB	MB	WV	PV	SV	'Status'
Milvus milvus	P	×					
Haliaeetus albicilla	P (N)	F				+	
Neophron percnopterus	P O E					+	B
Gyps fulvus	P O E					+	
Circus aeruginosus	P E A	×	×		×	+?	
Circus cyaneus	P N	×	+	×	×		
Circus macrourus	P					+	
Circus pygargus	P		×		+		
Accipiter gentilis	P N	C/I				×(r)	
Accipiter nisus	P	×		×	×		
Buteo buteo	P	×			+	(r)	
Buteo lagopus	P N			×	+		
Aquila clanga	P (O)					+	B
Aquila chrysaetos	P N (O E Nt)	×					
FALCONIDAE							
Falco naumanni	P					+	
Falco tinnunculus	P O E	×	×	×	×		
Falco vespertinus	P					×	
Falco columbarius	P N	×	+	×	×		
Falco subbuteo	P (O)		×		+		
Falco rusticolus	P N					+	
Falco peregrinus	Cosmopolitan	×		+	+	(r)	
TETRAONIDAE							
Tetrao urogallus	P	F/I					BC
Lyrurus tetrix	P	×					
Lagopus mutus	P N	×					
Lagopus lagopus	P N	×					
PHASIANIDAE							
Alectoris rufa	P	I					C
Perdix perdix	P	×					
Coturnix coturnix	P O E		×				
Phasianus colchicus	P O	I					C
Chrysolophus pictus	P	I					C
Chrysolophus amherstiae	P	I					C
GRUIDAE							
Grus grus	P		f			×	

	Distribution	RB	MB	WV	PV	SV	'Status'
RALLIDAE							
Rallus aquaticus	P (O)	×	+?	×	×		
Crex crex	P		×		+		
Porzana parva	P					+	
Porzana pusilla	P E A		f			+	
Porzana porzana	P		×	+	×		
Porzana carolina	N					+	
Gallinula chloropus	P O E N Nt	×		×	+?		
Porphyrula martinica	N Nt					+	
Fulica atra	P O A	×		×	+		
OTIDIDAE							
Otis tetrax	P					+	
Otis tarda	P		F			+	
Chlamydotis undulata	P (O)					+	
HAEMATOPODIDAE							
Haematopus ostralegus	P		×	×	×	×	
CHARADRIIDAE							
Vanellus gregarius	P					+	
Vanellus vanellus	P		×	×	×	×	
Pluvialis squatarola	P N			×	×		
Pluvialis apricaria	P		×	+	×	×	
Pluvialis dominica	P N					+	
Charadrius hiaticula	P N		×	+	×	×	
Charadrius dubius	P O A		×				
Charadrius alexandrinus	Cosmopolitan		F			×	
Charadrius vociferus	N Nt					+	
Charadrius asiaticus	P					+	B
Eudromias morinellus	P		×		×		
RECURVIROSTRIDAE							
Himantopus himantopus	Cosmopolitan		c			×	
Recurvirostra avosetta	P E	×	×	+	+		
SCOLOPACIDAE							
Bartramia longicauda	N					+	
Numenius borealis	N					+	B

	Distribution	RB	MB	WV	PV	SV	'Status'
Numenius phaeopus	P N		×	+	×		(r)
Numenius arquata	P	×	×	×	×		
Limosa limosa	P		×	×	×		
Limosa lapponica	P (N)			×	×		
Tringa erythropus	P			×	×		
Tringa totanus	P	×	+	×	×		
Tringa flavipes	N					×	
Tringa stagnatilis	P					+	
Tringa nebularia	P		×	+	×		
Tringa melanoleuca	N					+	
Tringa ochropus	P		c	+	×		
Tringa solitaria	N					+	
Tringa glareola	P		+		×		
Xenus cinereus	P					+	
Actitis hypoleucos	P		×	+	×		
Actitis macularia	N					×	
Arenaria interpres	P N			×	×		
Limnodromus griseus	N					+	
Limnodromus scolopaceus	P N					×	
Gallinago media	P					×	
Gallinago gallinago	P E N (O)	×	+	×	×		(r)
Scolopax rusticola	P	×	+	×	+		
Lymnocryptes minima	P			×	×		
Calidris canutus	P N			×	×		
Calidris alba	P N			×	×		
Calidris pusillus	N					+	
Calidris mauri	P N					+	
Calidris minuta	P			+	×		
Calidris temminckii	P		c		×		
Calidris minutilla	N					+	
Calidris fuscicollis	N					×	
Calidris bairdii	N (P)					+	
Calidris melanotos	P N					×	
Calidris acuminata	P					+	
Calidris maritima	P N			×	×		
Calidris alpina	P N	×	+	×	×		
Calidris ferruginea	P			+	×		
Micropalama himantopus	N					+	
Limicola falcinellus	P					+	
Tryngites subruficollis	N					×	
Philomachus pugnax	P		+	×	×		

	Distribution	RB	MB	WV	PV	SV	'Status'
PHALAROPODIDAE							
Phalaropus fulicarius	P N				×		
Phalaropus lobatus	P N			×	×		
Phalaropus tricolor	N					+	
BURHINIDAE							
Burhinus oedicnemus	P O (E)		×				
GLAREOLIDAE							
Cursorius cursor	P E					+	
Glareola pratincola	P E					+	
Glareola nordmanni	P					+	
STERCORARIIDAE							
Stercorarius skua	Oc		×	+?	×		
Stercorarius pomarinus	P N				×		
Stercorarius parasiticus	P N			×	×		
Stercorarius longicaudus	P N				×		
LARIDAE							
Pagophila eburnea	P N					+	
Larus canus	P N	×	+?	×	+		
Larus argentatus	P N	×	+	×	+?		
Larus fuscus	P	+	×		×		
Larus marinus	P N	×	+	×			
Larus glaucoides	N			×			[r]
Larus hyperboreus	P N			×			
Larus ichthyaetus	P					+	
Larus atricilla	N (Nt)					+	
Larus melanocephalus	P	c		+	+		
Larus ridibundus	P	×	×	×	+		
Larus genei	P					+	
Larus philadelphia	N					+	
Larus minutus	P (N)			×	×		
Larus sabini	P N				×		
Rhodostethia rosea	P					+	
Rissa tridactyla	P N	+	×	×	×		
Chlidonias hybrida	P					+	
Chlidonias leucopterus	P					×	
Chlidonias niger	P N		F/C		×		
Gelochelidon nilotica	P O A N Nt		c			×	

	Distribution	RB	MB	WV	PV	SV	'Status'
Hydroprogne caspia	P E O A N					×	
Sterna hirundo	P N		×		×		
Sterna paradisaea	P N		×		×		
Sterna dougallii	Cosmopolitan		×		+		
Sterna anaethetus	Oc					+	
Sterna fuscata	Oc					+	
Sterna albifrons	Cosmopolitan		×		+		
Sterna maxima	N (Nt P)					+	
Sterna sandvicensis	P N Nt		×		×		

ALCIDAE

Alle alle	P N			×			
Pinguinus impennis	(P)	f					B
Alca torda	P N	×	×	+			
Uria lomvia	P N					+	
Uria aalge	P N	×	×	+		(r)	
Cepphus grylle	P N	×					
Fratercula arctica	P N	+	×	+	+		

PTEROCLIDAE

Syrrhaptes paradoxus	P		c			+	

COLUMBIDAE

Columba livia	P	×					
Columba oenas	P	×	+	+	+		
Columba palumbus	P	×	+	+			
Streptopelia turtur	P (E)		×		+		
Streptopelia orientalis	P (O)					+	
Streptopelia decaocto	P O	×					

CUCULIDAE

Clamator glandarius	P R					+	
Cuculus canorus	P O		×		+		
Coccyzus erythrop- *thalmus*	N					+	
Coccyzus americanus	N (Nt)					+	

TYTONIDAE

Tyto alba	Cosmopolitan	×				(r)	

	Distribution	RB	MB	WV	PV	SV	'Status'
STRIGIDAE							
Otus scops	P O					+	
Bubo bubo	P O (E)					+	B
Nyctea scandiaca	P N	c				×	
Surnia ulula	P N					+	
Athene noctua	P (E)	I				+?	AC
Strix aluco	P O	×					
Asio otus	P N	×		×	+		
Asio flammeus	P N Nt (Oc)	×	+	×	×		
Aegolius funereus	P N					+	
CAPRIMULGIDAE							
Chordeiles minor	N (Nt)					+	
Caprimulgus ruficollis	P					+	B
Caprimulgus europaeus	P			×	+?		
Caprimulgus aegyptius	P					+	B
APODIDAE							
Hirundapus caudacutus	P O					+	
Apus melba	P O E					×	
Apus apus	P			×	×		
Apus affinis	E O (P)					+	
ALCEDINIDAE							
Alcedo atthis	P O A	×	+?				
MEROPIDAE							
Merops apiaster	P O E		c			×	
Merops superciliosus	P E					+	
CORACIIDAE							
Coracias garrulus	P					×	
UPUPIDAE							
Upupa epops	P O E		c		×		

	Distribution	RB	MB	WV	PV	SV	'Status'
PICIDAE							
Jynx torquilla	P		+		×		
Picus viridis	P	×					
Dendrocopos major	P (O)	×		+	+?		
Dendrocopos minor	P	×					
ALAUDIDAE							
Melanocorypha calandra	P					+	
Melanocorypha bimaculata	P					+	
Melanocorypha leucoptera	P					+	
Calandrella cinerea	P E					×	
Calandrella rufescens	P					+	
Galerida cristata	P (O E)					+	
Lullula arborea	P	×			+		
Alauda arvensis	P	×	+?	×	×		
Eremophila alpestris	P N (Nt)				×		(r)
HIRUNDINIDAE							
Riparia riparia	P N O			×	+		
Hirundo rustica	P N (O)			×	+		
Hirundo daurica	P O E					+	
Delichon urbica	P O			×	+		
MOTACILLIDAE							
Motacilla flava	P (N)			×	+		(rr)
Motacilla citreola	P					+	
Motacilla cinerea	P	×	+		+		
Motacilla alba	P O E	×	×		×		
Anthus novaeseelandiae	P O E A					×	
Anthus campestris	P					×	
Anthus trivialis	P		×		+		
Anthus hodgsoni	P					+	
Anthus gustavi	P					+	
Anthus pratensis	P	×	×	×	×		
Anthus cervinus	P					×	
Anthus spinoletta	P N	×		+	+		(r)

	Distribution	RB	MB	WV	PV	SV	'Status'
LANIIDAE							
Lanius collurio	P		×		×	(r)	
Lanius minor	P					×	
Lanius excubitor	P N E (O)			×	+	(r)	
Lanius senator	P					×	
BOMBYCILLIDAE							
Bombycilla garrulus	P N			×	×		
CINCLIDAE							
Cinclus cinclus	P	×				(R)	
TROGLODYTIDAE							
Troglodytes troglodytes	P N (O)	×		+	+		
MIMIDAE							
Toxostoma rufum	N					+	
PRUNELLIDAE							
Prunella collaris	P					+	
Prunella modularis	P	×		+	+		
TURDIDAE							
Cercotrichas galactotes	P E (O)					+	
Erithacus rubecula	P	×	+	+	×		
Luscinia luscinia	P					+	
Luscinia megarhynchos	P		×				
Luscinia svecica	P (N)		c		×		
Tarsiger cyanurus	P (O)					+	
Phoenicurus ochruros	P (O)		×	+	×		
Phoenicurus phoenicurus	P		×		×		
Saxicola rubetra	P		×		×		
Saxicola torquata	P E (O)	×	+			(r)	
Oenanthe isabellina	P (O)					+	B
Oenanthe oenanthe	P N (E)		×		×		
Oenanthe deserti	P (E)					+	
Oenanthe hispanica	P					+	
Oenanthe pleschanka	P					+	

	Distribution	RB	MB	WV	PV	SV	'Status'
Oenanthe leucura	P					+	
Monticola saxatilis	P					+	
Zoothera dauma	P O A					+	
Catharus minimus	P N					+	
Catharus ustulatus	N					+	
Turdus torquatus	P		×	+	×		
Turdus merula	P (O)	×	+	×	×		
Turdus obscurus	P					+	
Turdus ruficollis	P					+	
Turdus naumanni	P					+	
Turdus sibiricus	P					+	
Turdus pilaris	P		c	×	×		
Turdus iliacus	P		+	×	×		
Turdus philomelos	P	×	+	×	×		
Turdus viscivorus	P	×	+	+?	+?		
Turdus migratorius	N					+	

SYLVIIDAE

	Distribution	RB	MB	WV	PV	SV	'Status'
Cettia cetti	P					+	
Locustella luscinioides	P		×			+	
Locustella fluviatilis	P					+	
Locustella certhiola	P					+	
Locustella naevia	P		×		+		
Locustella lanceolata	P					+	
Acrocephalus paludicola	P					×	
Acrocephalus melanopogon	P		c			+	
Acrocephalus schoenobaenus	P		×		+		
Acrocephalus agricola	P					+	
Acrocephalus dumetorum	P					+	
Acrocephalus palustris	P		×			+	
Acrocephalus scirpaceus	P		×		+		
Acrocephalus arundinaceus	P					×	
Acrocephalus aedon	P					+	
Hippolais icterina	P		c?		×		
Hippolais polyglotta	P					×	
Hippolais pallida	P (E)					+	
Hippolais caligata	P					+	
Sylvia nisoria	P					×	
Sylvia hortensis	P					+	
Sylvia borin	P		×		×		
Sylvia atricapilla	P		×	+	+		

	Distribution	RB	MB	WV	PV	SV	'Status'
Sylvia communis	P		×		+		
Sylvia curruca	P		×		+		
Sylvia melanocephala	P					+	
Sylvia cantillans	P					×	
Sylvia conspicillata	P					+	
Sylvia undata	P	×					
Phylloscopus trochilus	P		×		×		
Phylloscopus collybita	P		×	+	+		
Phylloscopus bonelli	P					+	
Phylloscopus sibilatrix	P		×		+		
Phylloscopus fuscatus	P					+	
Phylloscopus schwarzi	P					+	
Phylloscopus inornatus	P					×	
Phylloscopus proregulus	P					+	
Phylloscopus borealis	P (N)					×	
Phylloscopus trochiloides	P					×	
Cisticola juncidis	P E O A					+	
Regulus regulus	P	×			×	×	
Regulus ignicapillus	P	+?	+	+	×		

MUSCICAPIDAE

Ficedula hypoleuca	P		×		×		
Ficedula albicollis	P					+	
Ficedula parva	P					×	
Muscicapa striata	P		×		+		

TIMALIIDAE

Panurus biarmicus	P	×		+			

AEGITHALIDAE

Aegithalos caudatus	P	×				(r)	

REMIZIDAE

Remiz pendulinus	P					+	

PARIDAE

Parus palustris	P (O)	×					
Parus montanus	P	×				(r)	
Parus ater	P (O)	×				(R)	
Parus cristatus	P	×				(r)	
Parus major	P O	×		+			
Parus caeruleus	P	×		+			

	Distribution	RB	MB	WV	PV	SV	'Status'
SITTIDAE							
Sitta europaea	P O	×					
Tichodroma muraria	P (O)					+	
CERTHIIDAE							
Certhia familiaris	P N	×				+	
EMBERIZIDAE							
Emberiza calandra	P	×		+?	+?		
Emberiza citrinella	P	×		+?	+?		
Emberiza leucocephala	P					+	
Emberiza cia	P					+	
Emberiza hortulana	P				×		
Emberiza caesia	P					+	
Emberiza cirlus	P	×					
Emberiza pusilla	P					×	
Emberiza rustica	P					×	
Emberiza aureola	P					+	
Emberiza melanocephala	P					+	
Emberiza schoeniclus	P	×		×	+		
Calcarius lapponicus	P N			+	×		
Plectrophenax nivalis	P N	+		×	×		
Zonotrichia iliaca	N					+	
Zonotrichia melodia	N					+	
Zonotrichia albicollis	N					+	
Junco hyemalis	N					+	
Pipilo erythrophthalmus	N Nt					+	
Pheucticus ludovicianus	N					+	
Piranga rubra	N					+	
PARULIDAE							
Mniotilta varia	N					+	
Parula americana	N					+	
Dendroica petechia	N Nt					+	
Dendroica coronata	N					+	
Dendroica striata	N					+	
Setophaga ruticilla	N					+	
Seiurus noveboracensis	N					+	
Geothlypis trichas	N					+	

	Distribution	RB	MB	WV	PV	SV	'Status'
VIREONIDAE							
Vireo olivaceus	N					+	
ICTERIDAE							
Icterus galbula	N					+	
Dolichonyx oryzivorus	N					+	
FRINGILLIDAE							
Fringilla coelebs	P	×		×	+		
Fringilla montifringuilla	P		c	×	+		
Serinus serinus	P	c				×	
Serinus citrinella	P					+	B
Carduelis chloris	P	×	+	×	+		
Carduelis carduelis	P	×	×				
Carduelis spinus	P	×		×	×		
Acanthis flammea	P N	×	×	×	×		
Acanthis hornemanni	P N					×	
Acanthis flavirostris	P	×	+	+?			
Acanthis cannabina	P	×	×	+	+?		
Carpodacus erythrinus	P					×	
Pinicola enucleator	P N					+	
Loxia pityopsittacus	P					+	
Loxia curvirostra	P N O Nt	×		×			
Loxia leucoptera	P N (Nt)					+	
Pyrrhula pyrrhula	P	×				(R)	
Coccothraustes coccothraustes	P	×					
PLOCEIDAE							
Passer domesticus	P (O E)	×					
Passer hispaniolensis	P					+	
Passer montanus	P O	×		×			
STURNIDAE							
Sturnus roseus	P					×	
Sturnus vulgaris	P	×	+	×	×		
ORIOLIDAE							
Oriolus oriolus	P O		c		×		

	Distribution	RB	MB	WV	PV	SV	'Status'
CORVIDAE							
Garrulus glandarius	P O	×		+			
Pica pica	P N O (E)	×					
Nucifraga caryocatactes	P					×	
Pyrrhocorax							
pyrrhocorax	P (E)	×					
Corvus monedula	P	×		×			
Corvus frugilegus	P	×		×			
Corvus corone	P (O)	×		+			
Corvus corax	P N (Nt)	×					

INDEX